IN SEARCH OF TITO'S PUNKS

intellect
Bristol, UK / Chicago, USA

GLOBAL PUNK

Series editors: Russ Bestley and Mike Dines
Produced in collaboration with the Punk Scholars Network, the Global Punk book series focuses on the development of contemporary global punk, reflecting its origins, aesthetics, identity, legacy, membership, and circulation. Critical approaches draw upon the interdisciplinary areas of (amongst others) cultural studies, art and design, sociology, musicology, and social sciences in order to develop a broad and inclusive picture of punk and punk-inspired subcultural developments around the globe. The series adopts an essentially analytical perspective, raising questions over the dissemination of punk scenes and subcultures and their form, structure and contemporary cultural significance in the daily lives of an increasing number of people around the world. To propose a manuscript, or for more information about the series, please contact the series co-editors Russ Bestley and Mike Dines (contact details available at www.intellectbooks.com).

The Punk Reader: Research Transmissions from the Local and the Global
Edited by Russ Bestley, Mike Dines, Alastair Gordon and Paula Guerra
Trans-Global Punk Scenes: The Punk Reader Vol. 2
Edited by Russ Bestley, Mike Dines, Alastair Gordon and Paula Guerra
Punk Identities, Punk Utopias: Global Punk and Media
Edited by Russ Bestley, Mike Dines, Matt Grimes and Paula Guerra
PUNK! Las Américas Edition
Edited by Olga Rodríguez-Ulloa, Rodrigo Quijano and Shane Greene
Blank Canvas: Art School Creativity From Punk to New Wave
Simon Strange
Punk Pedagogies in Practice: Disruptions and Connections
Edited by Francis Stewart and Laura Way
Punk Art History: Artworks From the European No Future Generation
Marie Arleth Skov
In Search of Tito's Punks: On the Road in a Country that No Longer Exists
Barry Phillips

ON THE ROAD IN A COUNTRY THAT NO LONGER EXISTS

IN SEARCH OF TITO'S PUNKS

BARRY PHILLIPS

First published in the UK in 2023 by Intellect, The Mill, Parnall Road, Fishponds, Bristol, BS16 3JG, UK

First published in the USA in 2023 by Intellect, The University of Chicago Press, 1427 E. 60th Street, Chicago, IL 60637, USA

Copyright © 2023 Intellect Ltd

Produced in collaboration with the Punk Scholars Network

All rights reserved. No part of this publication may be reproduced, stored in a retrieval system or transmitted, in any form or by any means, electronic, mechanical, photocopying, recording or otherwise, without written permission.

A catalogue record for this book is available from the British Library.

Art director: Russ Bestley
Copy editor: MPS, Limited
Cover designer: Russ Bestley
Indexing: Barry Phillips and Mike Dines
Production manager: Laura Christopher
Typesetting: MPS, Limited

Print Hardback ISBN 978-1-78938-731-5
ePDF ISBN 978-1-78938-732-2
ePUB ISBN 978-1-78938-733-9

Printed and bound by Shortrun

Part of the Global Punk series
ISSN 2632-8305 | ONLINE ISSN 2632-8313

To find out about all our publications, please visit our website.
There you can subscribe to our e-newsletter, browse or download our current catalogue and buy any titles that are in print.

www.intellectbooks.com

The author, Rijeka © *Tomislav 'Tompa' Zebić (2017)*

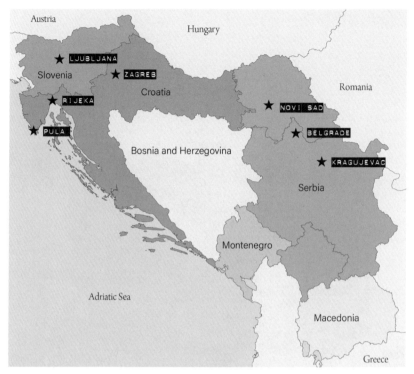

Yugoslavia: The successor states

FOREWORD

'Punk is an attitude.'
It was the first sentence in the book on punk I'd got from London – it fell apart a long time ago, and I have no idea who the author was. It was 1980. I was twelve and a half (critical distinction at that age) and about to start my first punk fanzine. But I had no idea what this word meant, not really. Still, I went on and eventually translated the whole thing, by hand, on lined sheets of paper. The fanzine was called 'Ziherica' (a safety pin).

That was the only issue. I had no readers. By the next school year, the whole bunch of long-haired, Jim Morrison-reciting boys – and one girl – emerged in skin-tight trousers and ripped shirts with safety pins, badges, and short hair.

In a country with two alphabets, three languages, four religions, five nationalities, six republics, and eight ethnic minorities, punk became a fresh new musical force that fell on the thirsty urban youth as a much-needed rain.

Fast forward a few decades, and I am tasked with writing a foreword to a book that begins with the story of how a song recorded in 1981 by a young multiracial punk rock band from a 'stagnating provincial English city' (author's words) and released on a tiny independent record label became famous in Yugoslavia.

Barry Phillips embarked on an adventure to follow the journey of that song in the hope that by doing so he might 'better understand' a country that was independent at the time of the Cold War, that was neither West nor East, that was ruled by the Communist Party but stood outside of the Iron Curtain; the country in the middle of Europe that many would barely have heard about if it had not fallen apart in bloody wars (1991–95).

However, this book offers much more to an interested reader – those familiar with Rebecca West's 1941 book *Black Lamb and Grey Falcon: A Journey through Yugoslavia* will notice some similarities in the approach. Nevertheless, unlike West, Phillips never speaks from the 'above'; he shares the frog-eye perspective of the many subjects he interviews after he prepares the stage for them and lets them take it. So they are not his roadies; each of them plays their own gig in a festival that is this book.

What sets it apart from other books of a similar ilk, among other things, is the author's way of using the histories to inform the personal 'travelogue' and not the personal travelogue to inform the histories. Perhaps it's because Phillips sees the Yugoslav punk scene as similar to the provincial punk scene in the United Kingdom and writes about it with a fondness for (and knowledge of) provincial punk. However, when you add to this his knowledge of modern European history and the meticulous historical research, as well as the interest in and understanding of the socioeconomic circumstances of the ex-Yugoslav republics-turned-states that he visits, you get much more than a travelogue – or a genre music book.

If one is, however, interested in the reception, development and history of punk in this region of the world, the book is chock-filled with interviews – not only with some key players in the scene but also with journalists and critics, as well as witnesses of the time in the place that for those few years, really held a unique position in the world – but these are never overly repetitive or dull.

Phillips skilfully constructs the chapters to let his thoughts and experiences, as well as the experiences and thoughts of locals involved in the punk scene(s), shine a light on ex-Yugoslavia and provide a more nuanced picture of the region. The book is full of excellent references to other books, movies and contemporary arts and maybe an urban legend and gossip or two (look out for the footnotes!).

I am sure it will be of interest even to those who lived then and there, let alone those who didn't – I certainly learned something about a few young, current punk voices that Phillips invites onto the stage, among the others. This amalgam approach resulted in an unexpected, in-depth perspective into the more recent changes in society. Changes that show how angry young people carry the punk torch further into the (unforeseeable?) future. 'No future' is not something they want to hear, and it is refreshing to know.

The interviews themselves speak volumes. The author kept them unfiltered, wanting them to stay as genuine as possible, which is a nice touch. His subjects were thus free to express their personal stories in their own words – from music to culture in general, politics and, inevitably, the wars.

I am aware of what a challenge it can be to write about ex-Yugoslavia and its break-up without going into an explicit deconstruction of the wars and the reasons behind them. However, Phillips managed to provide a wealth of material from which the readers will be able to draw their conclusions. In one chapter, he even visits the International Criminal Tribunal for the former Yugoslavia (ICTY) in his then home city, Den Haag, giving some insight into his thoughts and feelings on the wars, which, along with other personal little gems of insight and feeling, make the hard topics he sometimes deals with extremely readable and the author himself very personable, sympathetic and relatable.

And finally, the interviews quite clearly show how my generation, the punk generation from ex-Yugoslavia, had lost its innocence. Most of us considered ourselves punks, and then we were suddenly made aware that we were not simply punks. I remember my father telling me one day how his side of the family is Serbian, probably foreseeing that could shortly become a problem. 'Oh yeah?' I said, 'and how do you know that?' And then I added, 'maybe you are a Serb, but I am a punk'.

Alas, soon after that, we learned how to tell the difference among the Croat, Serbian and Bosniak family names. The country fell apart; the bands fell apart, some of us stayed and fought against the war, some left, and some were dragged down by it. Nevertheless, the punk spirit survived.

Fast forward to today, my eighteen-year-old nephew plays in a punk band and keeps me up with the new punk scene in Croatia. So no, punk is certainly not dead. However, at 45, it has grown-up kids and might have finally got its Ph.D., as Phillips has jokingly put it.

Rujana Jeger, novelist, columnist, cultural commentator,
canine-archaeologist, punk.
Istria, Croatia, Summer 2022

ACKNOWLEDGEMENTS

First, of course, everyone who gave up their time and energy to provide the remarkably candid and rich interviews. There is no need to name them all again here but a special mention must go to my 'Balkanese brother from another mother', Tomislav 'Tompa' Zebić, and to Daniela Forca and Dunja Črnko for all of their advice, support, hospitality and logistical help before, during and subsequent to my trip. Special mention must also go to Saša Mijatović, Ned O'Millick, Petar Janjatović, Stevan Gojkov, Sava Savić, Igor Todorović, Ljiljana Čenejac, Rujana Jeger and Aleksandar (Sale) Dragaš who all provided me with numerous invaluable contacts and supporting materials; Vinko Barić for the Timeline and so many great links; for the onerous proof-reading duties Pete 'the Big 'Un' Evans, Nick Jeans, Ante Čikara, Paul Kerr, Miloš Stošić and the man of mystery in Split; to Lar Hughes, Andy Woodcock and Valery Sonntag for their advice and skills with regards to artwork and graphics. I owe a considerable debt to Russ Bestley and Mike Dines of the Punk Scholars Network for having the faith, persistence and patience to turn the digital into the physical.

Finally, I must belatedly thank my wife, Denise Perrault, for putting up with this obsession since we met and for supporting me through it (particularly for wiring me funds when my own had run dry).

This book is dedicated to my daughters Kayleigh and Josie, and grandchildren Harris, Hugh, Orson and Emmy. It is also dedicated to the memory of my good friend Franck 'Hollywood' Boivin who metaphorically and, at times, literally kept the show on the road when it seemed destined to crash and burn.

CONTENTS

FOREWORD		vii
ACKNOWLEDGEMENTS		xi
NOTES ON PRONUNCIATION		xv
PROLOGUE	The Play-on Track: Teenage Kicks	1
ONE	Scheveningen: Paint It Black	7
TWO	The Hague to Gruška 4	11
	ALEKSANDAR DRAGAŠ: Club Limb, Zagreb	17
THREE	Zagreb: Black Lamb and Grey Falcon	24
	ZDENKO FRANJIĆ: Club 22, Prečko, Zagreb	29
FOUR	To Ljubljana: On the Brotherhood and Unity Highway	36
FIVE	A Day in Court: Vermeer in Bosnia	43
	ANTE ČIKARA: The Haven, Scheveningen and De Pijp, Amsterdam	48
SIX	Music Is the Art of Time	59
	PERO LOVŠIN: The Fish Market, Ljubljana	62
SEVEN	The Ljubljana Punk Rock Taxi Tour	66
	MARIN ROSIĆ: On the Road in Ljubljana	69
EIGHT	Return to Zagreb	77
	MATIJA VUICA AND JURE POPOVIĆ: The Bulldog, Central Zagreb	81
NINE	Zagreb (1977) ... and Tito's Coming to Town	91
	DARKO RUNDEK: Caffe Bar Albatros, Ljubljanica 4, Zagreb	95
TEN	The Hague Hilton	102
ELEVEN	Istria: Pirates and Punk Rock Heartlands	105
	RUJANA JEGER: Zagreb	115

TWELVE	Pula: Uljanik Calling	125
	SALE VERUDA: Forum Square, Pula	130
THIRTEEN	England: Back to the Forest	137
	ROBERT 'MIFF' SMITH: Coleford, Gloucestershire, England	141
FOURTEEN	To Belgrade: On the Brotherhood and Unity Highway Again	147
FIFTEEN	Internacionalnih Brigada	152
	PETAR JANJATOVIĆ: Radost Fina Kuhinjica, Belgrade	156
SIXTEEN	Lost in Belgrade Central	166
	BRANKO ROSIĆ: Belgrade café terrace	170
SEVENTEEN	Kafana Mornar: Belgrade Is Drowning	178
	POGONBGD, TRNJE AND FRIENDS: Kafana Mornar and Studio Mašina 23	178
EIGHTEEN	Novi Sad, Vojvodina: Words and Bullets	185
NINETEEN	Novi Sad: NATO Bombs and Jew Street Ghosts	190
	STEVAN GOJKOV, VLADIMIR 'RADULE' RADUSINOVIĆ AND SAVA SAVIĆ: Central Novi Sad	197
TWENTY	To Kragujevac: On the Brotherhood and Unity Highway Once More	210
	VUJA (SAŠA VUJIĆ): Kragujevac	217
TWENTY ONE	Return to Belgrade: The House of Flowers	223
SLEEVE NOTES	Standing at the Gates of the West: Hitsville Yugo	231
TIMELINE	Yugoslavian Punk from 1975 Until Break-Up (VINKO BARIĆ)	244
SELECTED DISCOGRAPHY		248
INDEX		251

NOTES ON PRONUNCIATION

These notes are not intended as a preparation for learning the language(s) but simply as an aid to hear the text more accurately. The first (and most reassuring) aspect of Croatian/Serbian/Bosnian is that it is largely 'phonetic'; the words are pronounced as they are written and there are no 'silent' letters. Having said that, some of the letters are pronounced differently in English (American or British) and some letters do not exist in English. I have selected the ones which occur most frequently in the text:

j is commonly pronounced as a 'y' as in 'yellow'.

c is commonly pronounced as the 'zz' in pizza or 'ts' as in 'cats' or 'boots'.

ć does not have a direct comparison in English but the closest would be the 't' in 'tune' or 'nature'.

č is closest to the 'ch' in 'chair' or 'hitch'.

š sounds like the 'sh' in 'show' or 'shoe'.

ž is closest to the 's' in 'treasure' or 'pleasure'.

đ has no exact counterpart but is similar to the 'd' in 'procedure' or 'schedule' where there is a suggestion of a 'g' or 'j' following the 'd'.

Finally, there are the double letters:

dž in 'Džuboks' sounds closest to the 'j' in 'journey' or 'joy' but perhaps a little harsher – as though there was a 'd' concealed somewhere within.

lj in 'Ljubljana' or 'Prljavo' is pronounced as the 'lli' in 'million'.

nj in 'Zadnji' or 'Dobrinja' is pronounced as the 'ni' in 'genius' or 'senior'.

ji in 'Krajina' is pronounced as the 'ye' in 'yell'.

ja in 'Prljavo' is pronounced as the 'ya' in 'yard'.

This book is not intended as a treatise on modern Balkan history. Sir Fitzroy Maclean, the Scottish Second World War hero, soldier, spy and the man tasked by Churchill with parachuting into Yugoslavia to locate and liaise with the Partisans, opens his biography of Tito with the words of the historian Arnold J. Toynbee, 'Our concern, however, is neither to approve nor to disapprove, but to understand.'

An academic from ex-Yugoslavia pointed out the analogy between Maclean's parachuting into the unknown Yugoslavia in 1943 and my own plunge into the tangles and murk of the modern history of the region, its culture and counter-culture – minus the inherent risk to life, Toynbee's sentiment rings equally true in the context of this book.

The title *In Search of Tito's Punks* is in no way meant to imply that all those interviewed were 'Titoists' – their own words will allow the reader to judge if that is the case. The phrase 'Tito's Punks' is used in a way familiar to the English-speaking world, but perhaps not so much beyond. It is used to identify an 'era' which is likely to be defined by an individual, a particular cultural or ideological hegemony or philosophy. It is the equivalent of 'Victorian' or 'Elizabethan' in UK terms.

Every care has been taken to reproduce, faithfully and unfiltered, the words of the interviewees, the meaning intended and, indeed, the voice. To make sure that this is the case, each transcription was referred back to the respective interviewee for their approval. The reader may, therefore, encounter unorthodox syntax, grammar and punctuation. None of this is a consequence of negligence or accident – in fact the opposite is true since it has generated significant discussion and additional work during the editorial process.

Without punk and 'Dolgcajt', the Berlin Wall would have fallen later!
Marin Rosić

Demob, 1981: Robert 'Miff' Smith, Barry Phillips, Johnny Melfah, Terry Elcock

PROLOGUE
The Play-On Track: Teenage Kicks

> I have a friend Darko Kujundžić from Sarajevo […] who now lives in Zagreb […] He was a kid, a teenager in Sarajevo, and he bought the second LP of Obojeni Program just before the war started. And he lived in Dobrinja, which was a heavily contested area. He was living on the front-line, in these high-rise blocks on the front-line. So they spent days without electricity.
>
> So what he did was, he put his headphones on, and he would play the Obojeni Program LP by spinning it with his finger on the turntable. And at a certain moment he would get to the 33⅓ rpms – to the right speed. He had mastered the technique quickly and so he would manually power his turntable hitting the 33⅓ rpm mark without a problem during the rest of the war.
>
> And he would spin that Obojeni Program record often […] he's still got the album at home in Zagreb. On the label, you can still see the mark where his finger was. He would put the finger on the same spot, and he would spin it around.
>
> Ante Čikara, Amsterdam, December 2017

Gloucester, England, 1981: multi-racial, teenage street-punk band, Demob, recorded and released what would become their best-known and most enduring song, 'No Room For You'. Three minutes and fifteen seconds of raw, chainsaw guitars, a thumping 1950s rock 'n' roll bass line and machine-gun military drumming, underscored a rasping vocal which told the story of the 1979 closure of a short-lived, punk rock venue at a disused motel on the edge of the stagnating, provincial city. Depending on your mindset, the lyrics were either a howl of rage at the injustice, a wail at the loss or a love song to an era. It began, 'Oh we don't go there anymore. It's boarded up, the doors are closed'. At the time, it achieved some critical success and sold out of the relatively modest pressing of a few thousand copies. In truth though, it would never reach much more than 'cult-status'. Still at school, I was Demob's bass player. Scroll forward to the summer of 2011; late one night I receive a Facebook Friend Request and accompanying message from a Saša Mijatović. He lives in a city called Kragujevac in central Serbia and wants to talk about 'No Room For You': 'This song is famous throughout the Balkans. Everybody knows this song […] it has been recorded by some of the most famous Yugoslavian punk bands.'

My new friend tells me the most famous version is by a band called KUD Idijoti and the Yugoslavian title is 'To nije mjesto za nas' (This is not the place for us). I search online, and sure enough there it is. The first version I find has over 150,000 views on YouTube, but there are several other versions. This is the first that I – and my former band mates – have ever heard of our 'fame' under the fringe of the Iron Curtain. It was as surreal as it was baffling and intriguing.

So it was that the journey of a song became the lens to seek a better understanding of Yugoslavia and a generation of Yugoslavs. Bonded by punk rock, and specifically this one song, I wondered about our parallel lives.

I had joined Demob in late 1980, a few months prior to the recording of 'No Room For You'. Vocalist and songwriter, Robert 'Miff' Smith, was an old friend from school. One day he called me to say the bass player had left and did I fancy joining the band? My own band, the Blitz Boys, had supported Demob on several occasions. We had released one single, the knowingly ridiculous 'Eddy's New Shoes', and had received some airplay from the legendary 'Godfather of Punk', BBC DJ, John Peel. We combined catchy guitar-riffs, light-hearted teenage-angst and high-energy as we aspired towards becoming 'the Undertones of the West Country'. Unfortunately, we lacked their lyrical dexterity, musical ability, creative genius, charisma, discipline and dedication. Nonetheless, Peel had even invited us to the BBC in London and showed us around one afternoon as we bunked school.[1] We were all school friends raised in the isolated, rural, former coal-mining villages of the Forest of Dean – a place so remote from the public consciousness as to be virtually invisible. Every few years the tabloid press, conservative politicians and Christian activists would launch a moral crusade calling for the new TV series from the 'controversial' (visionary) local playwright Dennis Potter to be banned. Other than that, the best we could hope for was an occasional 'humorous' item on the national news about a local 'character' carried home from the pub by his faithful (and sober) horse at the end of an evening's heavy drinking. We were 200 kilometres from the uber-cool, punk rock epicentres of London's Kings Road, the cliques of the 'Bromley Contingent' or the Roots and Rockers, Gangsters and Ganja, cartoon urban-landscapes of the Clash's Camden Town or the Westway. In fact, we were 30 kilometres away from the mean streets even of Gloucester, itself a backwater in rock 'n' roll terms. Or any terms.

And then there was Demob's notoriety to consider. As testosterone-fuelled teenagers from a coal-mining culture, we were no strangers to resorting to fists and boots. However, Demob's reputation as a magnet, or catalyst (depending on your

---

1. To our surprise and delight, the Blitz Boys E.P. would be re-released by New York's Sing Sing Records in 2012.

point of view), for violence was of another magnitude and had by this time begun to obscure both the band's musical ambitions and the positive things it was trying to achieve for the disenfranchised youth of the city. The most infamous outbreak reached the national UK press when the annual Gloucester Carnival was suspended after a mass brawl between local motorbike gangs and Demob's comparatively youthful 'Riot Squad'. Added to this incendiary mix, and almost guaranteed to attract unwanted violence at the end of the 1970s, was Demob's multi-racial DNA. Drummer John Melfah is black and was then a professional boxer. Guitarist Terry Elcock is also black, and never one to back down. Miff is white, and in those days a mix of inquisitiveness and impulsiveness meant he was either charming or dangerous to be with – sometimes both. Founder member and original vocalist, Andy K, was by now in prison for assault. Demob's fans were black, white, brown and mixed race. Whilst punk rock was never racist and was avowedly anti-racist, it was also overwhelmingly white in the United Kingdom before Demob. And by 1981, the United Kingdom was inarguably in the grip of serious racial tensions. The previous summer there had been race riots in St Pauls, a largely Afro-Caribbean central suburb of nearby Bristol. The summer of 1981 would see widespread disturbances in cities and towns across the United Kingdom. Some of these were nothing but vandalism and extreme mischief-making, but some undoubtedly arose out of genuine grievances amongst the black (and white) youth. Not wholly unrelated, these years also witnessed the rise of neo-fascist and racist groups such as the National Front. It was unfortunate that many of the individuals who espoused affinity with these groups besmirched the traditional skinhead culture – and attached themselves to punk rock, often through the new Oi! movement. Apparently keen to distance himself and the movement from the white-supremacist fringes, the journalist who coined the term 'Oi!' was quick to champion Demob. Somehow, the band had become the anti-racist 'conscience' of a movement whose credentials in the field were legitimately questioned. But still, how could I not say yes?

    I vaguely recall I had one warm-up gig before we joined the Angelic Upstarts tour at the very time they were making regular television appearances on *Top of the Pops* and were one of the most talked-up bands in Europe. In June – as support to 'hardcore sensations' Discharge – we took the stage in front of an audience of 1500 at Malvern Winter Gardens. This was the very same stage I had gazed upon, awestruck, watching the Jam, Elvis Costello, the Damned, AC/DC, Siouxsie & the Banshees, the Ruts, the Undertones, Stiff Little Fingers and many more. It was undeniably exciting. It was a great experience. But we had some issues with this 'new breed' of punks who, to our minds, seemed to be all studs and spit. We also played with the Exploited in Bristol and there was an almighty ruckus between the Gloucester kids and Bristol skinheads. From the stage I could see the 'martial-arts faction' of the

Gloucester kids drawing rice-flails as the crowd parted, readying to charge. Perhaps it was not just the racists and the Nazis? Perhaps the reality was becoming clearer and a little more depressing to those of us for whom punk rock had been both a deliriously unhinged, technicolour escape from the dystopian greyness and a justification for an alternative way to the priggish, Victorian, narrow-mindedness of the mid 1970s. This was the beginning of the Thatcher era.

It did not help that I was not keen on the music of many new bands. I felt that we were already becoming 'men out of time'. We were being lifted and carried on a contaminated wave. I understood the anger and the frustration which propelled these bands. I too was often angry and frustrated with our bleak and suffocating horizons. But it just was not for me. It would turn out that some of my bandmates felt exactly the same. The Coventry date with the Angelic Upstarts was cancelled by the police after they had intelligence that rival factions had entered into a local arms-race and were intending to bring shotguns. Perhaps punk was dying before our eyes? My last gig with Demob was ruined by a mind-numbingly pointless evening of wanton destruction and violence in a small South Wales town. Dismayed, I left soon after to begin a new life in Sheffield. Miff's interview for this book would later revisit all of these events in detail.

Almost exactly thirty years after that final gig with Demob I received the unexpected message from a stranger in a city I had never heard of and a country that no longer existed. Over the next five years – with Saša's unstinting support – I accumulated a network of individuals from across former Yugoslavia. I had hoped to identify a nucleus of contributors who would be agreeable to a face-to-face interview should I succeed in turning my Balkan 'homage' into a reality. I did not anticipate the scale of the response. I now had a list of potential interviewees so rich that it brought its own logistical challenge; how could I ever hope to travel to all of these places and meet with all of these people? I was now connecting with my peers from Belgrade, Ljubljana, Pula, Zagreb, Novi Sad, Kragujevac and from cities, towns and villages of which I had been previously unaware. And then from Sarajevo, Smederevo, Paraćin, Vinkovci, Split, Karlovac, Tuzla, Aranđelovac, Vienna, Berlin, Amsterdam, Toronto, Strängnäs (Sweden) and beyond they came. There were musicians, TV celebrities, esteemed journalists, filmmakers and actors, authors, cartoonists, academics, an anarchist taxi-driver, a famous fashion designer, a former shipyard worker turned second-hand record seller and a one-man publishing empire. I learned of Pankrti ('the Bastards') who were 'Yugoslavia's Sex Pistols', one of the most influential and popular bands in the history of Balkan Punk. My speculative and unsolicited e-mail to their charismatic, livewire, frontman Pero Lovšin came back with the reply, 'Nice to hear from you. Sure we can meet and talk about Tito's punks. Peter, who also made cover of "No Room For You" with the title "A še pomnite pankerji", what a song, a!!!!' I knew I had begun to plough a deep and fertile furrow. Balkan generosity of spirit, punk rock attitude and the kudos of having played on 'No Room For You' had combined to create a magical key (a deliberately ambiguous use of the word 'key'). Time and again, I was struck by how many of the old punks were 'high-achievers', articulate, cultured and successful. Each seemed to have a story. I vowed that, somehow, they would all be told. These stars may never align so kindly again.

What follows is not so much a history book as a mural of the stories collected. There are no tidy chronologies and no glib conclusions here. At its heart is the 2017 road-trip (more accurately 'bus-trip' as my companion Tomislav would comment) across Croatia, Slovenia and Serbia, although there were two brief visits (one to Serbia in 2014 and one to Croatia in 2019) on either side of that. But the narrative is not confined to the Western Balkans. Living within the shadow of the International Criminal Tribunal for Yugoslavia (the ICTY) in The Hague, I felt compelled to find out more about an institution which – apparently – continues to throw long shadows across the region.

No one of sound mind would dispute the ghastliness of the Yugoslavian Wars of 1991–99, nor that the causes were convoluted and to outsiders often incomprehensible. Mercifully for most of us, we were insulated. We viewed the horrors only through the deodorising filter of the TV screen or on the lifeless pages of a newspaper. Our daily lives remained materially untouched – even those of us on the same continent. Returning from my first (budget) package holiday to Greece, in the late 1990s, the pilot apologised that the flight would take a 'slight diversion due to the situation on the ground'. But that was fine, because now we would see the 'beautiful Dalmatian coastline below'. Meanwhile, on the ground, the lives of the contributors to this book (even those not born at the time) were irrevocably twisted. Some were enlisted, some emigrated; some had family members and friends murdered or were driven from their homes taking only what they could carry. None seem to have allowed themselves to be defined by the wars. Taking their lead, I acknowledge the conflicts only where it is manifestly valuable; mention of individuals, nation-states or specific events is kept to a bare minimum. I apologise to those who think it either unnecessary or trivial and hope that these fragments contribute to a more nuanced understanding of the issues and, perhaps, a shield against our complacency and exceptionalism.

In December 2017 I gave a presentation to a pleasingly attentive audience at the 'Fourth Punk Scholars Network Conference' in Bolton, Greater Manchester, England. As I queued for coffee with Martin Ware (Human League, Heaven 17), Gaye Black (the Adverts), Joolz Denby (New Model Army) and even Mad Macka from the Cosmic Psychos I could not help but reflect on how unlikely this would have seemed forty years ago. From snotty-minded, ideologically convinced-yet-confused, rabble-rousing, small-town, teenage-punks, drunk on lager-snakebite and dreams of being 'The Last Gang In Town', to a conference of punk academics with contributors from the United Kingdom, Australia, the United States, Poland, Czech Republic, Turkey, Portugal, France, Hungary, Austria, Romania and the Netherlands. As a senior lecturer from Birmingham City University unscrambled 'Ethnographic studies concerning ageing and exiting punk subcultures', and a young post-graduate female student led a discussion on 'punk aesthetics', I realised that punk is not dead, it just got a Ph.D.; I can hear the nihilist-punk-fundamentalist faction howling 'fucking sell-out'. Personally, I never cared for punk as a lowest common denominator. Now my own thoughts pinballed around my personal journey in search of Tito's punks. A lot of hard work stretched ahead of me to do justice to the stories I had been gifted. The journey had already been far more than I had dared hope it would be. And then it was my turn. My unashamedly 'not academic' presentation was introduced by a deservedly renowned professor of punk:

> If in 1983 you'd told the thirteen-year-old me, as I sat in my bedroom singing along with one of my all-time favourite records, 'No Room For You', that one day I'd be introducing a member of Demob at an academic conference […] I'd have told you to fuck off!

Indeed Professor. I would have said the same.
    Step lightly. Stay free. Up the punks!

ONE
Scheveningen: Paint It Black

> [I]ts coasts are stormy, and its colour is variable; in the foreground it is a scummy yellow that looks like dirty washing water, further off, a weak green, and in the distance, a faded blue that blends into the wavy line of the sky. Here and there, great clouds cast their sombre shadows obliquely over this indistinct mirror. No rocks, no cliffs break the force of the waves.
> (Vincent Van Gogh, writing to his brother Theo in 1877, quoting from *La Néerlande et la vie hollandaise* [1859] by Henri Alphonse Esquiros)

The building which housed the International Criminal Tribunal for the former Yugoslavia (ICTY) is less than 600 metres from where I write this in The Hague's coastal suburbs. It stands on Churchillplein; six storeys high at its rear on the Eisenhowerlaan side, three and four storeys high at the more public-facing side on Johan de Wittlaan. Built of, or clad in, limestone-coloured bricks and sitting behind 3-metre black metal railings it is unostentatious. Security is low-key and laid-back (although I have never attempted to illegally breach the perimeter). It is, nonetheless, an imposing building since it stretches for perhaps 100 metres or more to its fullest extent.

The ICTY formally ceased operations on the last day of 2017. Its twenty-four-year history had taken in 10,800 trial days and heard 4650 witnesses, and judgements had been delivered on 161 accused. From here the nightly news coverage carried tales of depravity beyond imagination into the living rooms of the world. And from here that many first saw the banality of some of the most reviled individuals of the late twentieth century. At its peak of activity, more than 900 staff were employed within its walls. It exudes an air of gravitas and yet, despite the reasons for its existence, it is not sinister.

Within five minutes an enthusiastic cyclist could reach the Scheveningen fishing harbours and marinas, or the 20-kilometre ribbon of beach where Vincent van Gogh painted his *View of the Sea* at Scheveningen. He regularly visited Scheveningen to sketch and paint. That August day, in 1882, as Vincent squeezed paint directly onto the canvas to accent the wave-caps, the wind blew so hard that sand stuck to his painting. Today streams of tourists from all over the Netherlands; from Germany, Italy, Belgium and France; and more recently Japan, Taiwan and China, pour onto the 1959 double-decked pier; queue at the fish and chip, or ice-cream, kiosks ('vis – patat – ijs – slush – snacks') and fill the high-end restaurants and hip beach-bars through the summer months. All this to a soundtrack of the screeching of predatory seagulls, and ubiquitous euro-techno from midday to midnight.

Indeed, the seafront here is often compared (usually in a pejorative manner) with New York City's Coney Island.

There are still significant areas of Scheveningen which betray its seafaring and fishing traditions, and its proud independence from The Hague metropolis. Stubbornly resisting the encroachment of the luxury flats and penthouse apartments which tower over them are numerous streets of uniform, three-storey, tenement-style properties, or one and two-storey cottages. In the street-level windows are model ships, ships in bottles, brass lighthouses, ceramic fish, ornamental fishing nets and the sorts of 'ethnic' bric-a-brac brought home by the seafarers of less 'connected' times. Here, compressed between the prosperous and cosmopolitan inner, north-western suburbs and the beach, in knitted-enclaves behind the beach-front hotels are street names which tell their own tale – Vissershavenstraat, Zeekant, Neptunusstraat, Haringkade and Kompasstraat. These are the living vestiges of Oude (old) Scheveningen.

Today, there is disquiet and righteous dissent in the air. Photocopied posters protesting at the gentrification of the harbour and its surrounding areas are stuck to walls, recycling bins and lampposts. New apartment blocks are being built between existing social and communal housing and the harbours, blocking both the view and the sunlight. New cafés and bars are being opened to cater for the wealthy incomers and, even-wealthier, visitors to the marinas. The posters ask what good are the facilities if the people who live here now cannot afford to use them?

The specific complex within which the ICTY sits is known as the 'International Zone' and also contains the World Forum (where Presidents Obama and Xi Jinping met in 2014), the Head Offices of Europol and the Headquarters of the Organisation for the Prohibition of Chemical Weapons (OPCW). The OPCW is housed in a free-standing, eight-storey, horseshoe tower seemingly constructed of the same kind of limestone bricks as the ICTY. During the writing of this book, the organisation would be propelled from relative obscurity into the public consciousness as, in early 2018, the 'Novichok' poisoning of Sergei and Yulia Skripal in the English cathedral city of Salisbury was followed by chemical weapons attacks in Syria. As with the ICTY, the OPCW building also lacks any sinister forbearing. The logo above the entrance is an almost child-like depiction of a partially filled, chemist's Florence Flask – familiar to generations of children around the globe from their school science labs. It looks as though it might be a pleasant place to work. In the garden at the rear of the building are poignant memorials to the victims of chemical weapons. One is dedicated to all victims of chemical weapons and is a sculpture of a woman dying from the effects of a chemical weapons attack. As her life ebbs, she transforms into doves of peace. The other is to the Kurdish civilian victims of Halabja and is a bronze sculpture which captures the real-life moment a mother died with her baby in her arms during the 1988 chemical bombardment.

It is not by chance that within a densely populated city there was space here to develop such a notable estate – nor by coincidence that this was the chosen site. The Hague's position as the 'International City of Justice' began with the eponymous Conventions of 1899 (convened by Tsar Nicholas II) and 1907 (convened by Theodore Roosevelt), but there is also a direct link between the Second World War and the location here of the International Criminal Tribunal for Yugoslavia.

From the middle of 1940, like most of the Netherlands, The Hague endured occupation by the Nazis. For much of this time, it was the very centre of Nazi military and political control of the country. Scheveningen was both a command centre and a particularly valuable strategic military asset. As such it had to be protected. In late 1941, as the Germans had turned east to face the Russian threat, they decided to build a defensive wall to protect their potentially vulnerable western flank. In early 1942, they began constructing the Atlantic Wall (Atlantikwall), from the Franco-Spanish border in the south to Norway in the north. Nearly eight million people are estimated to have worked on the Atlantikwall during the two years of its construction, the overwhelming majority of them forced labourers – although many local contractors also made significant profits.

By the middle of 1942, the time had come to make good on The Hague section of the Atlantic Wall. To that end, the Nazis completely razed a strip 300 metres wide through the city to allow for the construction of an anti-tank ditch, 30 metres wide and more than 5 kilometres long. Scheveningen was 'quarantined' from the rest of the Netherlands. The entire coastal suburb was turned into an occupied military zone (Sperrgebiet – 'forbidden to citizens') where official passes were required to enter through the twelve checkpoints. Historians put the number of houses destroyed at 30,000 and a total of 140,000 citizens displaced – evacuated beyond the city or placed with local people in other neighbourhoods.

The entire beach was a no-mans-land of tank traps, mines and bunkers. It is said that the Germans left a small stretch near the Palace Hotel free of mines in order that officers might bathe there. The Dutch Resistance and Allies knew of that weakness and audaciously exploited it to drop agents and collect escapees. Today the grim physical scars are absorbed into the landscape, attracting battlefield tour groups and day-tripping tourists alike. One of the best-preserved bunkers now stands guard over the nudist beach to the north of Scheveningen pier.

But this is still Scheveningen, its DNA still mingles with the North Sea where the palette today is shifting shades of sepia and coffee rather than Van Gogh's scummy yellow, weak green and faded blue. At times, a fungal sea-mist creeps around the ICTY and suffocates the United Nations Detention Unit where the accused are held. And in the rawest months of winter, when the beach bars have long since been packed away and loaded onto articulated trailers, the kiosks remain shuttered and unlit, and the seagulls and crows stare mournfully into empty trash cans, it is still as Jacques Brel wrote his father told him, that when the North Wind blows it feels as though the town is adrift amongst the waves:

Mon père disait	My father said
C'est l'vent du nord	It's the north wind
Qui fait craquer les digues	Which breaks the dikes
À Scheveningen	In Scheveningen
À Scheveningen…	In Scheveningen…

(Jacques Brel, *Mon Père Disait*)

TWO
The Hague to Gruška 4

DAY ONE

> 'Honey, it's nearly seven o'clock.'
> 'What? Oh shit. Oh shit!!'

Everything was planned. My alarm had been set for 5 a.m. I would leave before 6 a.m. to catch the 6:01, No. 16 tram to Den Haag Centraal station. The tram stop is immediately outside the station, so the 6:33 train to Schiphol airport would be easy. I would arrive at Schiphol at 7 a.m. with sufficient time to exchange some currency. That was all before my wife and I sat up until 3 a.m. drinking red wine and anticipating the trip ahead of me.

But now it is already 7 a.m. and I am only just out of bed. I shower, collect my bags, check I have the recording equipment and somehow make it to the 7:13, No.16 tram. At Den Haag Centraal, I check the information boards and see that the 7:33 is due to leave within a minute or two. I scan my OV Chipkaart ('travel card') at the barrier and run towards the train only to hear the beeping sound which announces the doors are closing. They close and lock as I get within 2 metres of them. I know that pressing the button will be fruitless, but I do it all the same. It is fruitless.

The option now is to get the 7:48 and change at Leiden, catch the 8:02 and arrive at Schiphol at 8:17. I do the calculations; seven minutes to get from the station to check-in desks. From there it will all depend on the size of the queues for the automated baggage check-in (usually heinous), and then security. My gut feeling is that this is not going to happen. I could try to get on a later flight but I know that it will potentially destroy what is left of my budget for the entire trip. And my budget is not flexible. This is, in all likelihood, my one chance and I have already messed it up. I feel nauseous, even before the hangover begins.

As I approach the baggage-check desks, I can already see the huge line of travellers snaking through the check-in area. There is nothing else for it but to overcome my Britishness and beg the KLM ground staff to let me jump the queue. The lady takes one look at my desperate, near tearful expression, and shows me through to the 'Priority' check-in where a human expedites the process much quicker than the adjacent machines ever could. From there I sprint to Security where the queues are about normal for this time of day at Schiphol i.e. not good. Of course, the inevitable happens and I watch, helpless, as three bags are diverted left to their grateful owners and my bag continues straight on the conveyor belt to join a line of seven bags waiting for the full security search. It is now 8:35. My bag edges along the conveyor, glacially, until it is finally at the front of the line and I step forward. I tell the Security officer that my flight leaves at 9:20. 'So it is now 8:44, it's not a problem'. I remind her that I still have to negotiate the Border Control lines. I lie and say that my tram had not turned up. Her sympathy extends as far as, 'So you didn't think you should get a tram two hours earlier and you could get here on time then?' This is very Dutch. And quite unnecessary.

The rest is a blur until I hit the deserted passenger airbridge and see the still-open door of the airplane, at which point I know I will make it. My fellow passengers are already seated and belted. I am sweating abundantly. I take my seat at the rear of the plane and have the row to myself. I see a text from Nikola, the owner of the Airbnb in Zagreb, saying that he will pick me up from the airport. He will meet me near the airport's main exit. The bitter smell of complimentary airline coffee is enough motivation for me to resist the waves of fatigue which threaten to smother me. Rarely has airline coffee tasted so good. And then I fall asleep. I wake in time for our descent and to see the metal superstructure of the Franjo Tuđman Airport, named after the Croatian President who will be eternally synonymous with Independence, the collapse of Yugoslavia and the catastrophe of the Balkan Wars.

The interior of the airport's main building is brightly-lit and tranquil. The exposed, curved, shiny, metalwork skeleton reinforces the impression of sci-fi newness. I clear Immigration and the baggage carousels with no delays and walk out to the Arrivals concourse. In front stands an indifferent band of waiting taxi-drivers and chauffeurs with name signs. I read them several times but there is no Barry and no Phillips. My phone does not find the Croatian network so I wait for ten minutes. Then it connects, so I text the number I have for Nikola. The amiable young man who has been standing next to me for the duration removes his phone from his coat pocket, looks at it and smiles at me: 'I'm so sorry, I didn't recognise you because of the beard.'

We walk out of the building and across the car park towards Nikola's car. Approaching Zagreb our pilot had said the weather was foggy, but the fog is burning away rapidly now as the mid-morning, late-summer sun rises. 'It's very warm for this time of the year', Nikola says, 'twenty-three degrees. I am sorry but my car is a mess.'

As we drive out of the airport car park, Nikola asks if I am in Zagreb on business. I explain as succinctly as I can, and in simple English. I need not have worried: 'Hladno Pivo are one of the biggest rock bands in Croatia. Maybe Number One. When they play, they get maybe 10,000 people.' This is a very encouraging turn of events. 'Punk rock was very big in the '80s and '90s in ex-Yugoslavia. Rock music is not so big in Zagreb now. There are not so many new bands.' It is a well-grounded analysis from a young man who cannot be more than his early thirties.

After twenty minutes, we pull into a car-parking space in front of a huge brutalist, concrete, 'unité d'habitation' residential development. The complex stretches unbroken for perhaps 200 metres. Eight storeys of housing sit atop the ground-level commercial units, not all of which are occupied. Three, taller, freestanding tower blocks stand a short distance along this slip road and beyond these are several more residential blocks. This is Gruška and my apartment is in the block in front of us – Gruška 4. Pushing open heavy, blue-glossed metal and glass doors, we walk into a typical tower block foyer familiar to 1960s high-rises pretty much anywhere in the 'developed' world. Heavily worn polished-concrete forms a mock-marble floor. Nikola pulls open another blue-glossed door and ushers me into a small lift. I get in and he clangs shut the door. The lift starts with a jolt. 'The apartment is between the 5th and 6th floors', Nikola says, 'like Harry Potter'.

The apartment is going to be comfortable; there is a large studio room with a sofa-bed, a separate kitchen and a small bathroom – all three off a small central lobby. Nikola gives me a quick tour and hands me a booklet of tram tickets saying, 'I thought these would be useful until you find your way around'. If I need anything or there are any problems, I should call him. Then he is gone. I go out onto the balcony to have a cigarette and collect my thoughts. The mid and far distant urban skylines are dominated by many more Gruška-style residential developments – presumably a legacy of the Tito era. Poking above these are the tops of several tower blocks and sleeping construction cranes. The slowly evaporating remains of the day's contrails deftly cross-hatch white prints on the pale blue sky.

On the kitchen table, I see that Nikola has left instant coffee, whitener, tea-bags, juice and snacks, a nice touch. I unpack my rucksack and partially unpack my suitcase, putting sufficient clothes for the next few days on a shelf in the wardrobe. I then take out my three travel guides and companions on this trip: Rebecca West's *Black Lamb and Grey Falcon: A Journey through Yugoslavia* (first published 1941), Claudio Magris' *Danube* (1986) and Geert Mak's *In Europe: Travels through the Twentieth Century* (2004). Each journeyed in what proved to be a watershed time for Yugoslav history. Together their accounts span seven decades and will be my scaffolding and reference points. For once I have not bothered with a *Rough Guide* or *Lonely Planet*. I will have little time for recreational sightseeing and have made a conscious decision to trust to serendipity and the advice of friends I have yet to meet.

At 16:30 I leave the apartment to meet with Dunja, the partner of my old bandmate from Sheffield, Patrick Walker. Pat is a master of the fretboard. Any fretboard but particularly guitars, violins, banjos, mandolins and the like. He sprinkled rock 'n' roll fairy dust liberally during our time together in the Rainsaints in the 1980s and 1990s. As such, he was in no small part responsible for us being fortunate enough to 'sign' with the legendary Belfast record label Good Vibrations. The result of which was that we spent many extremely happy weeks touring and recording in Northern Ireland. Much of that time we were in the always-anarchic company of the legendary Good Vibrations proprietor Terri Hooley – 'East Belfast's only white one-eyed Rasta'. With the 2013 release of the critically highly acclaimed *Good Vibrations: The Movie* Terri has belatedly, and deservedly, achieved a level of fame approaching 'national treasure' in Northern Ireland and way beyond. I have brought four copies of the *Good Vibrations* DVD because the film is a wonderful portrayal of the spirit of provincial punk and punks, which I hope will resonate with my new acquaintances. In May 2019, in Zagreb's beautiful and historic Upper Town, I attended the wedding ceremony of Pat and Dunja at the Zagreb Registry Office, on the same street as the 'Muzej prekinutih veza' – the Museum of Broken Relationships.

It is still a glorious day. I cross the six-lane Slavonska avenija, a major artery which links the eastern and western suburbs of south-central Zagreb, making it the longest street in the city. I head northwest along Kruge. It is clearly the beginning of the rush-hour in Zagreb. The pavements and crossings are busy with pedestrians, keeping a noticeably brisk pace. The locals are tall and there are many cyclists. The old-style blue trams are full. Commuters, students and shoppers are standing and grasping the suspended grips. It is clear from the preponderance of young people that there must be a significant university nearby.

Dunja's text says, 'Hi! Welcome to Zagreb! Meet at the corner of Savska and Tratinska, by the Nikola Tesla museum at about 5:20. Will give you a call as soon as I'm done classes'. Thirty minutes later, Dunja and I are heading towards the city centre for coffee. We walk through 'Republic of Croatia Square' which until last month was 'Tito Square'. It was then that the city's leaders folded to pressure from nationalist parties to have it renamed. The open square is framed by grand public buildings in a variety of architectural styles – museums, academies of art and music, and university faculties. Dunja halts on the pavement in front of the grandest; this is the Croatian National Theatre, a marzipan-coloured Viennese-style building characterised by a slightly over-zealous use of ornamental columns. By the time we arrive at our destination in Cvjetni trg ('Flower Market Square'), it is 5:30 p.m. Predictably, coffee becomes beer and Croatian white wine.

We sit and talk for an hour, and then another as the sun dips and the temperature drops. The office and shop workers have mostly made their way home now and the square is relatively quiet. A few people sit at the tables around us drinking beer or coffee, and a few more arrive. We talk about music of course. But, as I will find during this trip, all discussions inevitably lead to politics and despair of both the government and the opposition parties. And, just as each conversation arrives at politics, then politics leads to the other inevitabilities: corruption and nepotism, the economy, and always the epidemic of depopulation. Driven by meagre domestic employment opportunities and scant prospect of improvement, many of the best educated and motivated young people feel compelled to leave the Balkans. Again and again, I would hear that 'a coach-load of young people leaves every day and they will not return'. Since Croatia joined the European Union (EU) in July 2013, more than 20,000 have left for Ireland alone, many times that number for Germany and the rest of the world. And the number continues to increase. This in a country with a population of just four million and a birth rate so low as to place it 183rd out of 200 countries in figures collated by the UN.

Dunja says she will take me to 'Limb', the café-bar where I will be doing my first interview. It is just as well, we lose track of the time while we are talking and I now have little margin for error.

At 'Limb', I finally get to meet Tomislav 'Tompa' Zebić in person. Tomislav has been my online trip-advisor and spirit-walker for the last six months – since my trip-planning began in earnest and this became real and inescapable. There will be more about Tomislav, much more. He is to be my companion for the duration. And I have to admit that the knowledge that he will be with me gives me a good deal of comfort since there is so much of this trip which will be new territory in so many ways. I recognise Tomislav as soon as we walk into the bar – although in the flesh he looks even more Eurasian than in the photographs. He later tells me that there is Mongolian blood in his ancestry. Tomislav introduces us to his companion and partner Daniela, a slim woman with cropped blonde hair. Both are charming and smile a lot. Dunja bids us goodbye since she has work in the morning. We order coffees and wait for Aleksandar Dragaš.

I have my back to the door but Tomislav stands and says, 'Here is Sale'. I discover that most Aleksandars are known as Sale, pronounced Sal-eh. I turn around to greet a smiling, bear of a man. It is clear that his movement is a little inhibited. Much later that night he tells me, 'My Great-Grandfather was the Production Chief in a tobacco factory in Banja Luka in Bosnia [...] and I should also stop smoking. I've had cancer three times'. Sale orders a drink. Before I can even turn on the recorder, he has spoken about his love for both *Good Vibrations: The Movie* and the Joy Division/Ian Curtis biopic *Control*. At this point, I discover that gratefully received though they would be, I need not have brought the *Good Vibrations* DVDs to dispense like some patronising punk missionary; the movie is shown regularly on TV in the region and had even been broadcast the previous week.

After an hour or two Tomislav and Daniela interject to say that, since we are getting along perfectly well without needing translation services, they will head home. Sale and I continue talking until well past midnight. Sale offers me a lift back to my apartment. On the short journey home the flow of rock 'n' roll anecdotes, childhood tales and political observations continue unhindered. I have stupidly packed away the recorder. I learn my first major lessons as a citizen-journalist – always keep the recorder handy and always be prepared to leave it running. At Gruška 4, Sale tells me that the legendary Suzy Records is based on the ground floor of my apartment block. He leaves the car and we walk a few yards along the front of the building and he points out the sign: 'This is a very important place in the history of Yugoslavian punk,' he says. 'It is most appropriate for your journey.'

ALEKSANDAR DRAGAŠ: Club Limb, Zagreb

Aleksandar Dragaš. Limb, Zagreb © Tomislav 'Tompa' Zebić (2017)

Aleksandar Dragaš is one of the most renowned music critics in ex-Yugoslavia. Beginning as a teenage fanzine-maker in the early 1980s, today he writes for *Jutarnji List* (*Morning Papers*), one of the two biggest daily papers in Croatia. But he is much more than a critic. He has been an independent record impresario, responsible (with his friend Ante Čikara) for discovering and/or releasing many of the best punk, and alternative acts in the Balkans including Obojeni Program, Boye and Majke. His involvement extended to helping the likes of Bambi Molesters and Overflow to gain international acclaim. Before the Yugoslav Wars caused a decade-long hiatus, he (initially with Ante) brought then rising UK and US bands such as White Zombie, Carter USM and Mega City Four, to perform in Croatia. He was once cruelly thwarted, having agreed on a modest fee to promote a youthful Nirvana at a Zagreb club. He has been a DJ on national radio. His catalogue of notable interviewees for print media would fill several pages and his stories several books. In Italy, he once witnessed the Ramones fight about politics as Democrats Joey and Marky took on Republicans Johnny and C. J. Above all, Sale is a fan – a constant enlightened voice in the ex-Yugoslav rock scene.

* * *

I was born here in 1967. I started to listen to music in 1979 and I started to write professionally in 1985, during the last grade of high school, and at university I was mainly writing. I published my first fanzine when I was eighteen years old. That was the birthday present that I asked for from my Grandparents: 'Buy me a typewriter.' I sold ten copies! I started to write for *Polet* in 1985 as an eighteen-year-old kid. And then for some other magazines as well, and daily papers. I was in touch with *Maximumrocknroll* and *Flipside*, these American fanzines. I wrote a special for *Flipside* about the Croatian scene during the war.

I never lived from anything except music. Croatia is a small market, so to exist in the record business, or as a music critic, for thirty-three years, it's incredible. I can't complain. I still live decently from what I love to do. Basically, my hobby is my job.

We had some articles published in *New Musical Express* and *Melody Maker* hailing this scene from Yugoslavia as the best apart from the UK scene and it was true. I think only Germany had a similarly good or better punk, new wave and post-punk scene. Here you had, I would say, more than 30 or 40 great bands and the records they published would usually sell between 30,000 and 200,000 per album. For example, Azra – the most popular new wave, punk, post-punk band – would publish between 100,000 and 300,000 copies of their records. In that time, if you were a debut album artist and you sold less than 20,000 or 25,000 you were discarded because you were no good.

You had Igor Vidmar who started to release singles – he was doing concerts, doing radio shows on Radio Študent and then, very soon on the national, Slovenian, Radio Ljubljana. This is how I discovered music. I had the antennae – on the roof of my building – 7 metres high just to catch the airwaves of Radio Ljubljana to hear what they would play on the 'Sunday Show'. We had a few John Peels – Igor in Ljubljana, Ante Batinović on Radio Zagreb, in Belgrade somebody else. We also had a few journalists who wrote, the younger in youth weeklies and the older ones in *Džuboks*. In *Džuboks*, I first read about the Cramps, Crass and so on. And this was a popular music magazine; 64,000 copies monthly and you could read about Crass and Adam & the Ants.

It was a good socialist habit – not only in Yugoslavia – to have youth weeklies financed by the state and, basically, they became the channels for information about rock music. The music section was always like the pop-culture section, and they were like, 'Leave them alone, that's not important'. Usually everything concentrated on political interviews, political shows, news and not on the cultural section. And besides, this is really important – and it also started before Tito died – we had a network of state-money-supported clubs where you could play, like 'Jabuka' ('Apple'). In Zagreb, punk started in the 'Student Centre' at a picture exhibition where Pankrti played. These clubs were supported by state money because in socialism it was the idea that youth has to have cultural places and places where you could play. And then you had strong record companies that started to publish, to see what would happen. Then they saw that there was a market for those records. And then you had radio – public, state-owned radio and they played it as well.

Through the student organisation in Ljubljana, Igor Vidmar published the first single for Pankrti, 'Lublana je bulana', which means 'Ljubljana is sick'. And that was the first punk single ever published in ex-Yugoslavia. So that was the starting point for punk in Yugoslavia. It started in Ljubljana – in Slovenia – with Pankrti, with that single and with Pankrti's brief tour: three gigs, one in Ljubljana and one in Zagreb – in late '77 – and one in Belgrade in early 1978. And nobody knew what the shit is going on because nobody knew what punk was at that time – except for a few people who had been in London, or a few people who occasionally read *New Musical Express* which appeared on one news stand in Zagreb. Because in that time, of course, there was no internet and the records were released here on the basis of a licence deal with only state-owned, or socially-owned, record companies.

Basically, because of that, and a lack of information, punk didn't properly start here in '77 but in '79. And here when you talk about Punk you talk about new wave – Novi val. New wave here was not only punk but punk and post-punk, everything together. And this became strong. The highlight was between late 1979 and early 1980, and the end of 1984. So, the first punk albums from England started to appear here on licence deals in '78 and '79. I entered into the punk, new wave and ska music in late '79, as a nearly thirteen-year-old kid, because at that time they published the first album of Elvis Costello, the first album of the Specials, of Madness and the Stranglers. In that short period of time talent burst out. Maybe we were so hungry for something new because we were a little bit depressed with the older bands here – mainly hard rock like Bijelo Dugme ('White Button'),[1] Parni Valjak ('Steamroller') and Time.

There was one news stand on the main square where I used to go daily. I used to live in the suburbs on the western outskirts of town but when I started to go to

---

1. Bijelo Dugme's fusion of hard rock and Balkan folk – memorably described as 'shepherd rock' – made them synonymous with the 'old guard' of Yugoslavian rock against whom the punks could kick.

high school, in 1981, then every day I went to this news stand and asked, 'Excuse me do you have *New Musical Express*?' And sometimes you'd get lucky and sometimes you don't because maybe somebody bought it before me. We were so hungry to get more information. Luckily, that was the really big difference between Yugoslavia and other 'socialist' countries at that time; we could travel, and we had licence-deal records released here. In Czechoslovakia, or in Eastern Germany, or in Poland, Hungary, Russia, Romania and Bulgaria, they had none – or a much smaller amount of titles.

So you had a mixture of radio shows, records you could buy here, or you could buy in Graz or Vienna, or Trieste or mail order. The funny thing is how to mail order a record from Cob Records in Wales. For example, if you want to buy Joy Division – *Unknown Pleasures* was the first LP that I ordered from Cob Records – you have to put two indigo papers inside with the bill of five quid (£5) if you are lucky to get one from the bank. Because in the post they looked (Sale mimes holding an envelope up to a light) to see if you are sending money outside, which was kind of an offence. If that was OK, I send this five quid bill, ordering Joy Division, *Unknown Pleasures* and it was the longest four weeks in my life. Because four weeks I waited, and waited, and then this cardboard carton came. It was the luckiest day of my life ever. Period. And then for days and days I was listening only to *Unknown Pleasures*. I know every line, every note, every, every, every.

In the late seventies and early eighties, my impression was that Ljubljana was punk, Rijeka as well. Zagreb was new wave, Belgrade was rock 'n' roll. And Novi Sad, OK because of Obojeni Program and Boye and all that, was really post-punk and also punk. But in many cities, it was like in the UK – you know the sound of Manchester, the sound of Liverpool, the sound of Birmingham and Sheffield and so on. In those days, when you heard some band you could always immediately recognise that 'this band came from Ljubljana', or 'this should be a band from Rijeka', or a band from Zagreb, or a band from Belgrade, or a band from Novi Sad, or a band from Sarajevo or Skopje and so on.

There are two movies: one is *Good Vibrations*, and when I was watching that movie it was pretty much similar to my growing up here – except for what they had between the Protestants and Catholics! Because in that time in Yugoslavia it was peaceful, and nobody cared which nationality you were – especially not in punk. The other movie is about Ian Curtis, *Control*. When I was watching that movie, the way it was described, how Ian Curtis grew up in Manchester in the early seventies is almost the same way I grew up in the outskirts of Zagreb in the early eighties.

There was a theory which I'm not so keen about, that punk and new wave exploded here when Tito died – because then all hell breaks loose. But I'm not so sure about it because, for example, Tito officially received the first rock band from the UK in 1966: Rockin' Vickers, and you have a photo from '66 of Tito shaking hands with

Lemmy. And basically, in the late sixties, there was – published here – the first real rock album in the Croatian language with their own songs, by the group called Grupa 220. That was in '68. This was the starting point, and even before that we had lots of bands that were playing covers of Stones, Beatles and 'Gloria' from Them.

In the eighties, we had the 'Nazi Punk Affair' in Ljubljana, when nobody was a Nazi punk. A friend of mine was six months in Youth Jail because he was scratching a swastika on a table in school. But he was going to scrap it. You know, at that time you had a swastika and a cross through it like you are opposing Nazis? But they said, 'No, you are drawing a swastika, so you go to jail', although he was not Nazi at all. But he had to go to jail.

Politics didn't allow Jugoton[2] to publish the first album of the Sex Pistols, *Never Mind the Bollocks*, because they said, 'Oh it was not so good to publish this record because it could offend the Queen'. So, basically you had a socialist system that was protecting England's Queen! So, there were lots of grey areas and there were records that were published and there were records that were not published, but only the Sex Pistols were not published because of censorship.

You could really say, for example, that Laibach was the first example of trying to change the society – for Slovenia to go out of Yugoslavia, to have a democracy, or capitalism. But interestingly now, they were where? In North Korea doing a show! And now the new enemies are capitalism and the EU. And you can see why. That doesn't mean that you are against capitalism or democracy, or the European Union, but that you want to improve it. Although I'm not against the European Union per se, or against democracy per se, I'm really totally against capitalism. Because when the Berlin Wall collapsed and all this collapsed, capitalism lost natural enemy and became wild.

Recently, this summer, I did an interview with Pero Lovšin from Pankrti and I asked him, 'I know that you are not against socialism which would mean you were for capitalism, you were for democracy, but you tried to improve socialism. And many bands really tried to improve socialism, they were not opposed to socialism'. And he said, exactly the same. He said, 'No, we were not against socialism because we thought that socialism would stay forever and it just needs to be improved.'

In the last three years, 100,000 people, mainly young people, left Croatia to start living and working in Ireland, Germany, Iceland, Scandinavia, the Netherlands and the UK. I never regretted that I didn't. But I do regret the mentality and the ugly things which started during the war – because of the war. This privatisation, this turbo-Balkan-capitalism that we have had now for the last twenty-five years. This is why I

---

2. State-owned record label which released Yugoslav and, under licence, western artists. Jugoton also had an extensive chain of record shops throughout Yugoslavia.

regret that maybe I didn't leave with a few friends of mine in 1991 to start living in Amsterdam, or in London, or Dublin or whatever. I didn't leave but I really don't regret it because of my income situation, or the economy. I regret it because I am tired of this nationalism, and chauvinism, fascism, and so on. But as I see it, fascism is spreading all over Europe again. For example, in Dugave, the part of new Zagreb where I live, we have about 400 immigrants from Syria, Iraq, Iran [and] Afghanistan. I do not mind, I say, 'Welcome'. I watch them every morning when I'm walking my dog; parents walking with their kids to school and I say, 'I don't mind'. In the Czech Republic, they hate them a lot, in Hungary [and] Poland. In Croatia, maybe the majority feels the same. But me personally – and my quarter has the most immigrants in the whole of Croatia – I don't mind. Welcome. But I regret that I didn't leave because maybe my mind wouldn't be poisoned with everyday politics and nationalism. Now I am too old and too ill to live anywhere else, and the woman I have lived with for the last fifteen years does not want to leave Croatia. So, we are now in negotiation to maybe, in a few years sell my flat in Zagreb to go to live in Istria – which is the most democratic, the most left-wing and non-nationalistic part of Croatia. Because they are mixed nationalities – Croatian, Italian, Serbian [and] Slovenian. It's the most multi-cultural part of Croatia. And they still value the fact that Istria became part of Croatia because of Tito and the Partisans. And I would love to live in that kind of environment.

So, coming from where I came from, it's who I met and interviewed and hung-out with that means so much: the Cramps, REM, Henry Rollins, Iggy Pop, the Ramones, Mick Jones, Kraftwerk – mainly speaking about bicycling and music – Lou Reed, the lot of them, tons and tons of interviews. I met Billy Bragg at Reading festival in 1989 and I was introduced to him through his manager who said, 'Here is Aleksandar, a guy from Yugoslavia'. And Billy stood up, hugged me and said, 'Welcome my socialist friend'. A very political gesture.

Mick Jones of the Clash was in Zagreb with Carbon/Silicon about five or six years ago. We met a friend of mine who is also a music and movie critic, and then we went to a shop in Zagreb. It was bizarre because we strolled through the centre of the city, and for all of that stroll we had photographers from the newspapers taking pictures of the three of us as we were walking to the record shop. We bought – for his punk museum – records by the most important punk and new wave bands from Yugoslavia [at] that time. All vinyl: Pankrti, Azra, several others. And we told him that we cannot believe what is happening now, because that same guy and myself went six times in six days to the movie theatre owned by the Yugoslavian National Army to see *Rude Boy*.[3] Because that was the only way to see the Clash!! He couldn't believe it.

---

3. 1980 fictionalised 'rockumentary' following the Clash roadie Ray Gange.

Johnny Rotten in London in 2001 or 2002 got pissed off with one Italian journalist who asked him something about the Clash. He said, 'the Clash, phoney lefties, salon Communists blah blah blah'. And I got to interview him after the Press Conference and he was trying to piss me off with some questions like, 'Were you killing Serbs during the war?' And I said, 'Look buster, I'm half Serb, half Croatian'. Because he'd asked if we had red in our flag because of the killings. About twelve or thirteen years after, we met in Zagreb. He was doing a show with Public Image Ltd and we were doing the interview in the Hotel Dubrovnik in central Zagreb. He was completely different; we laughed, we took photos, we told jokes about Bono and the Pope and blah blah blah. Fantastic. REM never played 'stars' in front of me. Really, such nice people. And I must say that except for Lou Reed – Lou Reed was a completely, utter bastard – and a possible fight with Henry Rollins one time, I have had mainly nice experiences.

Paraf. Ljubljana © *Vojko Flegar (1979)*

THREE
Zagreb: Black Lamb and Grey Falcon
DAY 2

I feel as though I have had just two hours sleep. As it happens, I got back to my apartment at nearly 2 a.m. and it was after 3 a.m. before I crawled under the covers on the sofa – too tired to extend it into a bed. At 8 a.m., I was woken by what sounds like someone revving a large Italian sports motorbike in the bathroom. Tomislav calls before I have even risen and we arrange to meet at Ban Jelačić Square. From there we can go to the railway station to purchase tickets for tomorrow's trip to Ljubljana.

'Old' Zagreb has largely escaped the impulses of missiles and town-planners alike and it is possible to be confident of tracing Rebecca West's footprints from eighty years previously – so I plot my path accordingly. *Black Lamb and Grey Falcon* is a collection of stories and reflections from those trips in 1936, 1937 and the summer of 1938. Initially, I disliked almost everything about it. The text seemed gratuitous, affected even. The 'big picture' history seemed to be all about kings and princes, bishops and monuments, schisms and assassinations. The 'small picture' history little more than the monotonous bickering of the author's Serb and Croat companions. All of which is retold with remorseless detail, hence the more than eleven-hundred pages. I even disliked West. I put it aside, revisited it and put it aside again on at least three occasions. And then, something clicked. The fusillade of words cleared; a coherent narrative and a more likeable, playful, personality emerged. West had never travelled to Yugoslavia and had never met a Yugoslav before being invited for a short lecture tour in 1936. She later wrote, 'Violence was, indeed, all I knew of the Balkans; all I knew of the south Slavs'. But on that first trip, she became deeply enchanted by the country and particularly the peoples. As with all great travel, and great travellers, West felt that these experiences might deepen her understanding not just of Yugoslavia but of her own existence. She was writing less than two decades after the end of the First World War. One of the few things almost everyone knows about the Balkans is that the assassination of Archduke Ferdinand in Sarajevo was the starting pistol. Clearly with this in mind, West tells how hearing of the assassination of King Alexander of Yugoslavia, in Marseille in 1934, left her feeling it was 'inevitable that war would follow' and that in this war 'women would scarcely have any need to fear bereavement, since air raids

[…] would send us and our loved ones to the next world in the breathless unity of scrambled eggs'.

So it was that when West walked these streets, she did so knowing that the greatest massacre the world had ever seen had been triggered by events here – and suspecting that an even greater calamity, which also had roots in the region, was on the horizon. It was the journalist in her and not the tourist who craved the trip:

> there proceeds steadily from that place a stream of events which are a source of danger to me […] It was only two or three days distant, yet I had never troubled to go that short journey which might explain to me how I shall die, and why.

Whilst West travelled to Yugoslavia in the years immediately prior to the outbreak of the Second World War, by the time she finished writing the consequences she feared were all too apparent.

I had the added chronology of the intervening eighty years: the schismatic Yugoslavian experience in the Second World War, Tito's rule, the break from the Soviet Union, Tito's death and ultimately the disintegration into ruinous civil wars which set neighbour against neighbour. Each, and all, significantly shaped and continues to shape, a world we struggle to understand. The lifespan of the researching and writing of this book has been parallel to the rise of a sometimes dark and aggressive nationalism (arguably even 'fascism') across much of the 'civilised world'. The (generally peaceful) calls by Catalonia, Scotland, and elsewhere for self-determination have increased in frequency and volume; the United Kingdom left the European Union; the 'Balkan Refugee Crisis' destabilised and shamed supposed liberal-democracies; ethnic tensions resurged in Kosovo; grotesque authoritarian genies rose from supposed grass roots movements of the toxically disaffected and narcissistic, whilst Donald Trump embarked on a divisive and isolationist rampage. How often when discussing these issues today do we hear the phrase 'The Balkanisation of …'? I felt much the same way as West when she wrote, 'I had come to Yugoslavia because I knew that the past had made the present and I wanted to see how the process works'. West's observations – flawed and impulsive though they may sometimes be – seem to promise to add more to my understanding of the region than any orthodox travel-guide. Indeed, the introduction by the British author Geoff Dyer calls *Black Lamb and Grey Falcon* 'a metaphysical *Lonely Planet* that never requires updating'. The cover-notes gush the usual superlatives and on the edition I have there is also a glowing testimony from Brian Eno.

Before reading West's historical-travelogue, I had not heard of Bishop Josip Juraj Strossmayer (1815–1905), but I remembered her lengthy tribute to his character and made a mental note to visit Ivan Meštrović's statue of him. West and her husband 'found the Bishop amongst the dark bushes and drab laurels of the unilluminated morning' in the public garden outside their hotel. Today the scene is very different from that dim, early morning in the spring of 1937. It is early afternoon on a glorious late summer day. The statue stands in the park which constitutes the grounds of the Croatian Academy of Sciences and Art. The park is not one of those which sits behind fences or walls. It is a long, narrow, strip of greenery decorated with tall trees, bordered by roads and tramways overlooked by the elegant facades of nineteenth-century Austro-Hungarian style buildings.

The Academy is the oldest national academy in the region and was founded in 1866, largely as a result of the vision and efforts of Bishop Strossmayer. At the same time, Strossmayer was also responsible for establishing, or renewing – depending on your interpretation – the University of Zagreb 'to give the Croats a proper social status . . . [with] a university they could not be despised as peasants'. West saw Strossmayer as 'a passionate pro-Croat' who nonetheless 'was lamentably deficient in bigotry'; one who attempted to create friendly discourse between his Roman Catholic Church and the Russian Orthodox Church. He strove to balance his Croatian nationalism with his belief in the wider Yugoslavia and would not set Croat against Serb nor united Slavs against the Austro-Hungarians (he himself was of Styrian descent). He also took a courageous and principled stand against the anti-Semitism prevailing in a region where 'the feudal system kept the peasants bound to the land and thereby gave the Jews a virtual monopoly of trade and the professions'.

One can only imagine what Strossmayer would have made of his Yugoslav Academy of Sciences and Art being renamed the Croatian Academy of Sciences and Art from 1941 to 1945 by the Nazi puppet, Independent State of Croatia and, once again, in 1991 after the break from Yugoslavia. West described Strossmayer as 'a child of light, exempt from darkness and terror'. As West and her husband left the statue in the early morning rain, Henry remarked, 'That is one of the most beautiful lives recorded in modern history'.

The statue of Strossmayer is handsome; the verdigris Bishop is seated, his knees pushed apart as he debates with an unseen acquaintance or acquaintances. After spending time here with thoughts of Strossmeyer and West, I continue on my way to meet Tomislav. The silver-barked trees are still top-heavy with green and gold leaves, but there are now gold and sunflower-yellow leaves lying in the shaded gutters.

The woman at the station ticket office tells us that the only trains between Zagreb and Ljubljana depart at 06:50 or 18:00. Only two trains per day between two national capital cities just 140 kilometres apart seems odd, but she is adamant. We agree that 06:50 is 'practically the middle of the fucking night' and the 18:00 will arrive far too late for us. This is a setback which leaves us a little unsettled. Forced to ditch our romantic notion of using trains for our travels, we reassess the detailed logistics – conscious that this is likely to be one of the shorter journeys we will be taking; this does not bode well. Reluctantly, we head to the bus station where we buy tickets for the trip.

Tomislav has been busy making arrangements to meet Zdenko Franjić – poet, performer, publisher and one-man record industry. Zdenko must be a busy man, so when Tomislav realises that the tram we are riding is headed in the complete opposite direction to the one we need, there is an air of desperation. After calling Zdenko to explain that we will be late, Tomislav tells me that he thinks Zdenko is 'not happy'.

Since we are now at the opposite tram terminus to the one we should be at, we opt for a taxi to get to the 'Club 22' café-bar where Zdenko is waiting. We traverse Zagreb's major arterial roads and then enter a maze of short, uniform, suburban streets. Platoons of modern, low-rise four, five and six-storey apartment blocks are pushed-back from the roads by broad, tree-lined, pathways and grassed areas. On the ground-level of many blocks are small shops and café-bars. I have read of the 'expansions' of Zagreb. First, in the period between the earthquake of 1880 and the outbreak of the First World War. Then again, through the 1920s. I guess that this area was part of the third-wave which took place in the 1960s and 1970s, during which time the city increased by over a quarter of a million people – more than 50 per cent. The drive has taken perhaps twenty minutes and the taxi driver apologises for the late afternoon traffic. As we pull to a halt outside of a hessian-coloured apartment-block with chocolate-brown shutters and window-frames, I see Zdenko standing on the pavement. He is in the shadow of the weathered awning of 'Club 22', and from its open door behind him music escapes into the streets. We make our greetings and Zdenko ushers us into the darkened café bar. I need not have worried – he is extremely affable. We move to a table at the rear of the empty bar, order coffees and teas and begin the interview. Soon we are joined by two of Zdenko's friends, one of whom – a Bosnian drummer – insists on seeing my tattoos. He then shows me his 'Anarchy' Ⓐ symbol and buys everyone a drink. Within ten minutes he returns to buy me lozovača ('grape rakija'). This is the first of many, many, rakijas which will be presented to me during this trip – such is the hospitality of the Balkans.

After an hour or so, Zdenko asks if we would like to see some of the CDs and books he has published. He goes to his car parked just outside the bar and returns with a large, old-fashioned, rigid suitcase. He places it on the bench-seat next to him and carefully unlocks and lifts the lid. The case is packed full with CDs – alphabetised – and books. The artwork across the entire collection is of a quality that could stand alone in an upmarket gallery. Zdenko is clearly a man who takes huge pride in what he produces. He invites me to choose some CDs to take home with me.

When the interview is complete, we say our goodbyes, exchange contact details and promise to continue the dialogue. Zdenko still performs on the anarchist squat scene and is keen to return to Amsterdam.

Tomislav and I head towards the main thoroughfares to find a taxi. We select a likely junction and Tomislav tells me there was a 'Croatian-mafia execution here a couple of months back'. Thankfully, we do not have to wait too long for a taxi to appear. We drop Tomislav home en route to the city centre and I get the driver to take me to meet Dunja at 'Sheridan's Irish pub'; this turns out to be the same one I saw on Savska cesta the previous evening. It is now 23:15 and too late – too cold – to sit outside at a late-night bar, so we take a chance on getting a last-order at the pub. Dunja tells me she only finished work at 22:00 but that has become pretty much the norm for her now. She teaches English to students of all ages, from toddlers to adults, and is paid perilously close to the minimum wage. This is a story I will hear from others across ex-Yugoslavia.

Tomi, the barman at the pub, loves punk and rockabilly. I question whether he has ever heard of Al & the Black Cats, a young punk 'n' roll band from Lowell, Michigan? I explain that when I posted to Facebook the video of them performing 'No Room For You' in Zagreb in 2009, Saša had felt compelled to contact me. Without it, I may not have set out on this pilgrimage. Tomi laughs: 'Of course. The singer punched me in the face that night. It's on YouTube.' Tomi tells us his story of 'drinking too much and acting like a bit of a prick'. He seems like a nice guy. Later, I check YouTube – sure enough, there I find the video of Tommy getting punched. Having met Al & the Black Cats the previous year I can vouch that Italian Tony, the singer, is an easy-going sort of chap so I guess Tomi really did ask for trouble. Many months later, Tomi sent me his Al & the Black Cats t-shirt because I had complained of being unable get hold of one.

Tomi kindly serves us a couple of rounds despite the late hour. Conscious not to outstay our welcome, we thank him, tell him we will be back next week and make our way out into the night and head to our respective apartments and beds.

ZDENKO FRANJIĆ: Club 22, Prečko, Zagreb

Zdenko Franjić. Prečko, Zagreb © Tomislav 'Tompa' Zebić (2017)

Zdenko Franjić is something of a legend in the history of Yugoslavian music. Since 1988, he has been a cornerstone of the independent scene. He has also been that rare thing, given the upheavals in the region, a perennial. His record label, Slušaj Najglasnije! ('Listen Loudest'), has released approaching 1000 CDs, records and cassettes, plus books or any medium which Zdenko feels appropriate. It is difficult to identify an analogous character in the UK or US scene. For sure, there are many fiercely independent record labels, publishers and artists. But none that I know of have been quite so productive and so eclectic, whilst being 100 per cent reliant on a single individual. Zdenko is Slušaj Najglasnije! Zdenko is also a writer, poet, performer and DJ. The latter he performs under a variety of aliases, such as Wandering Zdenko or Fucking Zdenko. A Croatian national newspaper described him as 'the most famous independent publisher of southeastern Europe'.

When Zdenko leaves us alone in the bar and goes to get a suitcase packed with his wares, Tomislav tells me that during his youth, his first point of call for new music was always Zdenko's label.

* * *

In Search of Tito's Punks

I'm from here – Prečko, this part of the city. Before, in the seventies, there were no buildings just little houses. We had a club, like a Youth Club, and they would play that kind of music – the Doors and glam. We would have nights playing that music. It's commercial rock 'n' roll, and it was good.

We listened to whatever was out in England. We would find it. And when I was in the Army in '79, I was in Ljubljana and they had a great station, Radio Študent and I heard all the new punk bands there. After that, we went to Italy and there was a little town on the border, Gorizia,[1] and a guy there had all new stuff. We were going there and buying records – everyone went there.

I started as fun. I was into music. I ordered records from abroad, from England, or I went to Italy. The first records I heard were glam: Sweet, Gary Glitter, Hot Chocolate, T Rex, Bowie. Bowie we could buy here, but others we bought abroad. There's a good story about it, in '75 or '76 they licensed the album *Raw Power* by Iggy & the Stooges but it was not available in the shops. They kept it in the warehouse here until '78. So for two or three years, it was in the warehouse and one friend of mine – he was the first Croatian punker, his name is Lou Profa – had a friend who worked at the warehouse and he got it from him. Lou Profa had been singing since the sixties and he had a band – one of the first punk bands – Loš Zvuk ('Bad Sound') from Pula. And there is one recording from a rehearsal in '76 or '77 and you can hear them playing the Stooges songs because they had already heard it before it was released here.

We were listening to all those post-punk, industrial bands here in the eighties. We were going to Italy and buying those records – Joy Division, Pop Group, Residents, Clock DVA. Wow! These were the best bands for me at that time. Later they became techno and I didn't like it anymore. I was a punk, but I was also darkwave, New Romantic, Gothic, you know. But we listened to the alternative. I like those bands – you know like Joy Division, Throbbing Gristle, Clock DVA. I like the Cure also. Of the first wave of punk I like Johnny Moped best. Johnny Moped is from Croydon, yes? Is that a part of London like the one from *Only Fools and Horses*?[2]

---

1. Gorizia ('Gorica' in Slovenian) is a town on the Italian–Slovenian border, 45 kilometres north of Trieste. The two record stores there were a magnet for young Slovenian, Croatian and even Serbian, punks and played a pivotal role in the burgeoning Yugoslav punk scene. After the Second World War, the main part of Gorica was returned to Italy from Allied rule, leaving Yugoslav suburbs fragmented. Under Tito's watch Yugoslavia built Nova Gorica town, around which they could coalesce and create a viable entity. Today both towns are within the EU – and specifically the Schengen Area – and share some administrative responsibilities.
2. British TV sitcom (1981–91) set in Peckham, South East London which follows a family of market-traders and their attempts to make money – usually on the margins of legality.

Is that Cockney? I like that. I also do not sing in literal Croatian. I sing as I talk here, in 'Kajkavski', dialect. I am sure you have bands in England who sing in dialect.

When I ordered records from the US or UK, I saw that bands were doing it for themselves. I read in '88 I think – in a music paper from Belgrade – that it is possible for a private person to make a record or a cassette. So I made that compilation, *The Bombing of New York* ('Bombardiranje New Yorka') in '88–89. At that time, there were already musical studios here for recording. So I made that compilation LP here. I did it with another company which was making records and they registered it and everything. I gave them money and they pressed the records in Jugoton.[3] Today Jugoton does not have the machines for pressing. I pressed 1000 copies and sold them all. I was also doing some foreign bands like the Morlocks from the US – they were a cult band – the Humpers also and Suicide Kings. We made contact over letters. I sent my records abroad to fanzines and radio stations. I made some good connections. A lot didn't work but some, like the station 'KZSU' from California, Stanford University, did. I sent all my stuff to them. What they liked they reviewed and played it on the radio. I met the Morlocks through their friend, their manager or something like that. With the Humpers and Suicide Kings, they are from LA, and their friends were exchanging music with me by post. They sent me their cassettes and I told them I was interested in them. Nobody believes that I did it here in Yugoslavia, everybody says it's a fake story!

I was working in a bank, and, in '89, I got out of work and got money – thirteen months' severance pay. And with that money, I started. But when I started, the war started – and everything stopped. When the war started you could do nothing. Everything was closed, nothing was working. At that time I had a firm, I had registered it, but I couldn't find work and that money would not last long. Selling records was really hard. Some I sold fast – like the Morlocks. Then, I spent all my money, got divorced, started to take drugs … you know.

I don't press the CDs with other companies. I do it all myself. I like music I understand. I understand some English music but not all. I understand Croatian, Serbian, Bosnian bands because I understand the words – I think words are the most important. Music is just the cover. You have the words of one song and you can do it any style you want, it can be disco-pop, or punk or heavy metal.

I also do pirate records. That guy from Buldožer, called me 'horse thief' because I did that!

I use all kinds of ways to sell. Online I use Discogs. At my performances, I use every possible way. And I don't work at anything else, this is the only thing I do.

---

3. One of the state-owned record labels.

I need little, because I can survive. I will publish anything. Whoever comes to me, we can make a deal. If I don't like it, I will do it anyway. Because you know, we say, 'He who sings, means no harm.'[4]

On my label, I have about a thousand releases. I do digital records, CDs, comic books and books. Mostly poetry of the guys who have bands. And some bands like Majke and Bambi Molesters, Overflow and Goribor are going into 'showbusiness'– good bands – but the best bands stay with me. Becoming a business is not good, for me. I am proper underground and do-it-yourself, that kind of stuff.

> Zdenko goes out to the car and brings back a large suitcase full to the brim with hundreds of neatly stacked CDs, books and comics all of which he had published. He asks me to pick some out randomly to keep while he selects a few headline items, to keep up is a challenge. Zdenko's reputation as someone who lives for the music is justified beyond doubt at this point.

Most of these you can find online. Satan Panonski, great poet, painter.[5] He performs all kinds of things connected with music. Satan Panonski and I had a mutual friend. He [Satan Panonski] was at the lunatic hospital at the time and I wrote him a letter. He was a good actor, you know. So they would let him go to perform.

Marinada from Rijeka. They play electronic and acoustic music but great words – minimalistic. They have over twenty albums.

Machine Gun, a great band. Like punk but with a Jimi Hendrix feel. From Knin. And this band Machina is from Bosnia, great band. Bosnia has a lot of good bands. Tuzla has a great scene.

---

4. *He who sings, means no harm (Tko pjeva zlo ne misli)* is a legendary early 1970s Croatian movie. A (slightly twisted – as everything Balkan is) romantic comedy-drama set in interwar Zagreb.

5. Real name Ivica Čuljak (*b.*1960), Satan Panonski (Satan from Pannonia) was of the transgressive, theatrical-shock-poetry school of punk which involved mutilating himself onstage. Often likened to the American, G. G. Allin, the difference being that Panonski was sentenced to twelve years for stabbing someone to death at a concert in Vinkovci. He claimed it was self-defence, but the records show that he stabbed his victim fifteen or more times. Rather than serving his sentence on the notorious prison island of Goli Otok he was somehow declared insane and placed in an asylum from where he was often released for periods of time. Some say his father was well connected and was behind his preferential treatment. During the wars, he joined the Croatian Army and, surprisingly for someone who had professed that 'my nationality is punk', he seems to have become a nationalist. He died in 1992 on a street in his home-town of Vinkovci having returned from the Front. As with everything in his life, his death is a fog of rumour, conspiracy and myth. Some say he was assassinated by the 'authorities' or the Army, some that he was hit by a stray bullet but the most persuasive explanation – and that put forward by his friends in Vinkovci – is that he accidentally shot himself with his service rifle.

And this is a great band Lokalne Pizde from Celje, Slovenia. Like Pankrti, maybe even better! Lokalne Pizde, Local Cunts!

I have a lot of Croatian sixties bands, garage bands, on the label. There are a lot of bands in Pula – the Spoons, Messerschmitts, the Bugs from Koprivnica, also Celtic Souls from Vinkovci. There is a very well-known studio there. A guy was living in London and came to Croatia and built a studio. Vinkovci is a town with a big railway junction and they have a documentary film festival there.

Problemi was a great band from Pula, an early punk band. Termiti was a great band from Rijeka – that guy 'Kralj' (Predrag Kraljević), the singer he wrote great lyrics. For me, he was one of the greatest people in the punk scene. Now he doesn't do music, he works on ships. Kralj had some concerts and Satan Panonski was also performing. Afterwards we had a talk about the concert and Kralj. His grandmother and Satan Panonski's grandmother were born in the same house in Herzegovina! And they are the two figures for me who are the best in the punk scene!

There was a scene in Yugoslavia in the sixties. There were different states, different towns. In Croatia and Serbia, there are some bands that play rock 'n' roll but mix it with folk music. That gives them something different from the others, like Azra; Johnny Štulić, he is different immediately. Satan Panonski has an Eastern feel. Rijeka is a harbour and has a great musical scene. Split not so much although it is also on the sea. Pula is good. There are regional sounds here in Croatia, like Koprivnica. The towns, they have their own sound. I can say which band is from Koprivnica when I hear them.

Before the (Second) World War, there was a great scene here. It was like the scene in America. But there was also folk music – gypsy music, gypsy music is great. In Bosnia, we call it 'Sevdah' – but it is not well known.

What I want to say is that rock musicians here, punk and rock, those are the kids of people in power: generals, directors. You know? From the Party because they have money. Nobody else has money. But there were some people who worked without that – like Satan Panonski, like me. I don't want State help. On the other hand, Mp3s are good! Free music – we live in Communism! Free music, free books it's all free. I'm old and I can't understand kids – my kids don't tell me anything. It's a global thing, almost nobody is going to concerts. And what now? Is there anything new in the West? Musicians are not interested in other musicians – they should be.

That guy I told you about, Lou Profa, is from Popovača, 60 kilometres from Zagreb. He is still punk, but not just punk – he lives in a wooden house without a ceiling you know. All his possessions hang on the wall, and, in a corner, there is an old bucket. He doesn't like to work – you know cutting the grass and things – but every day he rehearses his songs. I have released about twenty of his albums.

I'm like Lou Profa, I don't want to work at those things. And what is important to me is, I want to be my own boss. It is the most important thing. So I don't do it for anybody else. You know how they say, 'If you won't work on your own dreams, someone else will work on your dreams'. And that is anarchy for me. Because we have these 'anarchists' in Zagreb and once a year they come together and they start selling their books. And I am with them, they like me as an 'anarchist', but I don't feel like an 'anarchist' because they are Left, and I don't want to be Left or Right. I want to be me.

I don't play any instruments. I have some words and I have bands, and I'm still making music with some friends. I started late. I started playing in the early eighties with one band but never recorded anything, just rehearsed. But in '95 I found the right people and made my first band Bad Guys: Loši Dečki. We recorded four albums, one on a major label, Dancing Bear. They pressed the first one and the others I did myself on Slušaj Najglasnije. At the end of that band, I started my solo project – Wandering DJ Zdena (Lutajući DJ Zdena). I would find an instrumental tune and speak my words over it. I don't know how to rap, I don't know how to sing. But to talk, scream, you know. When I made a few albums of that I found another friend who has a home studio, he's fast and listens to a lot of music and has a gift. With him I made the band Babilonci ('the Babylonians'), and we have over twenty albums. I also did gigs as DJ Zdena, when I spoke my words and the words of other people for who I published books, like Satan Panonski and Goribor. Every chance I get I am DJing. I had two guys and we made about ten albums. They would play and I would speak my words. But one went to Iceland with his wife and kid and the other is in Berlin now. So I remain alone. I change the first word of my DJ name every time: Wandering DJ Zdena, Misplaced DJ Zdena, Amazed DJ Zdena, Cracked-Up DJ Zdena. I have also Fucking DJ Zdena, and I have an album which is a compilation of my work, in English.

Next, I am doing an album as Wandering DJ Zdena. It is one song, played by all different people. The words are the same. The song is called 'Secret Double Agent Girl'. I write some in English, not translated from Croatian: 'She works for C.I.A. She works for K.G.B. She works for me. She works for free. She's my secret Double Agent Girl.' And I would like to use some instrumentals from the films, from spy movies.

I am interested in taking my work abroad. Last year, I was in Vienna. The anarchists came together and they are squatting there – great crowd. In Vienna, there is a great squat, a place for sleeping and they also have a good club. There are squats here, Metelkova in Ljubljana, in Subotica, Novi Sad, Belgrade, Niš. I have been to Malmo with Goribor, and Oslo, and I would like to go to London or Hamburg. I have been to Amsterdam a lot of times, before the war. I know some people in Paris, they are doing comics. I have never been to Montenegro, but I have been to Macedonia, Bosnia, Serbia, Slovenia, [and] Croatia. Herzegovina is a beautiful country, Croatia is also beautiful, Bosnia is also beautiful, Macedonia too and Serbia is also beautiful – Vojvodina – all beautiful countries to me. I have been to Greece but not for music, as a kid, Salonika and Athena. Me and my friend we used to buy Inter-Rail cards, so we have been all over Europe.

A lot of people go, I like to go but I like to come back. I love Zagreb, I always want to come back.

FOUR
To Ljubljana: On the Brotherhood and Unity Highway

DAY 3

Friday morning. Today is a big day. Today Tomislav and I are travelling to the Slovenian capital of Ljubljana to see the legendary Pankrti ('the Bastards'). Tonight they celebrate forty years since their first public performance, with a landmark, sold-out, hometown concert at the Arena Stožice. Ignoring my dislike for gaping indoor sports arenas as venues for gigs I secured tickets as soon as this had been announced in the late spring of 2017. Two weeks after the initial announcement, Sex Pistols original bassist Glen Matlock was named as the Special Guest – the stars had aligned. Apart from having always felt that the Sex Pistols were hugely diminished when Matlock was replaced with Sid Vicious, I was also a massive fan of Matlock's next enterprise – the mighty (if short-lived) Rich Kids, who I was lucky enough to see at their peak in 1978. I have been counting down the days. And now the day has arrived.

In the 2006 documentary *Music Is the Art of Time*, we see the central character, Marin Rosić, played by an actor as a fifteen-year-old boy, and as himself in the present day. It is his narrative from which the track-by-track story of the first Pankrti album *Dolgcajt* ('Boredom/No Fun') hangs. Describing the tedium of 1970s Ljubljana and the explosive impact of the band and the album, adult Marin's opening line is, 'Fuck! It was like somebody dropped an H-Bomb. No wonder they called the record "No Fun".'

By the time *Dolgcajt* was released in 1980, the punks of Yugoslavia knew that they would never see the Clash or the Sex Pistols in their essential, incandescent, pomp. The Pistols had become a vaudeville freak show and then split up, and the Clash had turned west to pursue their longstanding interest in the mythical rock 'n' roll Americana of Washington Bullets and Koka Kola, Broadway and Belmont Chairs, Napalm and hamburgers. But Pankrti more than filled that void because they were credible, vital and homegrown. They did not mimic or genuflect to the West by singing in English – even if Slovenian is not easily understood across the rest of the ex-Yugoslav federation.[1] The language was not a sufficient barrier – when the subject matter was Ljubljana and Sarajevo, Karlovac, red beetroot and the Iron

---

1. Serbo-Croat is a 'polycentric' language with regional variants, and different ethnicities generally have no problem understanding each other – analogous to French and French Canadian, or even English and American-English. The main exception is Albanian – although Macedonian in the south, and Slovenian in the north are also distinct entities.

Curtain, Yugoslavia's punks were united. And where the Clash could sing of Spanish Bombs and the 'shooting sites in the days of '39', Pankrti could reinterpret the Italian-left rallying cry of Bandiera Rossa, with a degree more provenance. Where the West's rock 'n' roll revolutionaries could flirt with the iconography of Che or Fidel, Pankrti had been born and raised under Tito, a figure almost as iconic to non-aligned romantics of the left. Their importance to the punk rock – and the wider cultural – scene in former Yugoslavia is enduring. Amongst 'Yugonostalgics' their music, attitude and style have perhaps taken on a mythology – and a new cultural significance – just as the Ramones, the Clash and the Sex Pistols have globally.

In *Music Is the Art of Time*, Pankrti's Bogo Pretnar describes how Gregor Tomc returned from England armed with records: 'We went to his place to listen to the records he'd bought. We wanted to hear this new music called punk.' Before that they had 'no idea what to do'. Marin Rosić tells of his mother returning from a trip to London in 1977 and bringing the Sex Pistols *Never Mind the Bollocks* album as a present – whatever happened in London was soon happening in Ljubljana. For the young, the Ljubljana of the 1970s was grey and hazed in boredom. They hung out in department-store diners and moved on to the train station bar to extend their drinking beyond 8 p.m. But this cultural suburbia – so familiar to provincial punks the world over – was on the verge of sparking into life. Punk was the fire and Pankrti the fire-starters. As Tomc says, 'No one really knew what punk was. They thought it was just another dance [...] The Party, youth, the media. Nobody knew what punk was'. They did not seek approval from the state or their elders; they knew that punk could only burn with the energy, rage, abandon and irreverence of the young. Ljubljana was not the only place where these feelings existed in Yugoslavia, but its importance was obvious. What had smouldered was now ablaze. Boris Leiner of Azra says, 'They were the detonators. But you can't detonate air'. All of this meant that Ljubljana was promising to be a high point in my pilgrimage. And Pankrti the most spiritual of guides.

I pack my small rucksack with enough clothes for two days and my passport. As I exit the apartment block it is clear that the weather is, once more, unseasonably warm. It is not yet 11 a.m. and is already perhaps 25 degrees. Tomislav meets me at the station and we have one hour until the bus is due. We while away the time chatting over coffee and cigarettes in the outdoor concourse area of the station café. Soon after midday, we descend the stairs to our assigned gate at the ground-floor embarkation point. It transpires that our bus is beginning its journey here in Zagreb, then on directly to Ljubljana, and then to Munich. With a cryptic smile, Tomislav says that this will be a 'nice journey'. He explains that these days, buses originating in the southern Balkans often have refugees on board, increasing the likelihood of problems with border guards at the crossing. The bus arrives, it is modern, clean and has lime-green and orange livery. This fleet of buses seems to offer the quickest and most direct way to traverse much of the Balkans. It also seems to be the accepted way of sending parcels throughout the region; several people hand over parcels (of varying sizes and shapes – a large letter, one that could be a printer) to one of the drivers and also appear to part with cash at the same time. Tomislav tells me that this is a normal procedure. 'Of course', he adds, 'you do need to know that there will be someone at the bus station to collect it at the other end'. Apparently, it is also a very common way of distributing small amounts of drugs to far-flung towns.

The bus is nearly full to capacity with a mixed manifest of local students, international backpackers and middle-aged weekenders. Some are loaded down with suitcases or large rucksacks, some (like us) have small rucksacks and some just a plastic carrier bag. We are soon through the Zagreb suburbs and onto a motorway which cuts through agreeable, verdant, countryside with low, forested hills never too far away. Clusters of sloping red roofs and whitewashed, or pastel shaded, houses form prosperous-looking villages and hamlets. Within half an hour (perhaps less, I really was not prepared for this), we are at the first border control. Tomislav points at the razor-wire topped fences which delineate the border: 'Look, it's crazy. Razor-wire between Croatia and Slovenia. It seems to be everywhere nowadays. People on both sides meet at night to cut the wire. It's a thing they do.' He is right, it does seem crazy.

The bus pulls up at the Croatian border hut. We wait for two or three minutes and then comes the announcement – Tomislav explains – for everyone to exit the bus for passport checks. It takes no more than ten minutes for the determinedly unsmiling border guard to check passports or ID cards and we are back on the bus and on our way again. It is a bit of a pain when many of us are used to Schengen style 'free-movement' and seems a little sad between neighbouring countries which have so much in common, but all-in-all not as heinous as I had expected. Almost immediately we stop again, and the entire process is repeated. This time we all have to troop into a border office where another, equally determinedly unsmiling (this time female) border guard once again checks every passport and ID card. Once this is done, we are held for another ten minutes before being allowed back onto the bus. OK, so we are having to check out of Croatia and check into Slovenia. Fine.

The route we are travelling is part of Tito's 'Brotherhood and Unity Highway' which stretches from the extreme north of former Yugoslavia at the Austrian border to the extreme southern border with Greece. Linking Slovenia–Croatia–Serbia and Macedonia, construction began in the aftermath of the Second World War, with the initial sections constructed by work details of the JNA (the Yugoslav

National Army) and the 'Omladinske radne akcije' (the ORA – Youth Work Action) volunteers. 'Brotherhood and Unity' was a wartime Partisan slogan which came to symbolise the Communists' commitment to inter-ethnic South Slav solidarity, and the highway became its post-war physical manifestation. Tito had not bargained for the exponential traffic increase as Yugoslavia became a popular tourist destination, and the highway became the most affordable route home for hundreds of thousands of Turkish 'gastarbeiters' working in Germany.[2] As such, prior to its upgrade in the decades preceding the Yugoslav Wars, it had earned an unenviable reputation for colossal hold-ups and multiple-vehicle pile-ups. Today, this stretch looks pretty much like any autobahn or motorway.

Tomislav and I talk often, but it is the untroubled silences which confirm he will be a fine travelling companion. The southern suburbs of Ljubljana are compact and we are soon in the heart of the city. It is beautiful, but demurely so – like a model village Vienna. We cross modest, unbending rivers banked by buildings or peaceful walkways. From small bridges we look directly downstream to a series of other bridges. There are riverside café bars and people out enjoying the late-summer, beginning-of-the-weekend, sun. Young people are the majority and this also feels like a university city. These streets are lined with trees and as the smaller branches dance and the sturdier ones lean, it is obvious that there is much more breeze here than in the Zagreb we left.

We pull into the main bus terminus at Trg Osvobodilne, an open-air bus park, adjacent to the main train station. Tomislav translates the driver's announcement: 'We have two minutes to get our luggage and he will be gone'. This done we head towards the city centre in search of food. Back at the bus station we approach what looks like a 'taxi-rank' but then grab the chance to jump into a cab which has just dropped off a passenger. This turns out to be fortunate. The young driver and Tomislav immediately strike up a conversation and there is a good deal of laughter. He is Bosnian, and his family are from Jablanica – the hometown of Daniela's mother. Later our Airbnb host will confirm that this young man charged us a very reasonable fare – and the 'rank' we had been heading towards was more a fleet of 'pirates' who preyed on the new-in-town travellers, intercepted straight off the bus or train.

Our new friend is twenty-four years old. He tells Tomislav that he works for nine hours each day, goes home to see his girlfriend, sleeps and then goes out to work again. His life is a grind, with little joy. He says he envies Tomislav being born

---

2. Literally 'guest workers' – generally applied to Turkish workers but it was also used to describe Yugoslavs who worked in western European countries. Tito had been a gastarbeiter having worked in what is today the Czech Republic, Germany and Austria.

earlier and living through much better times, before the break-up of Yugoslavia. This is the first time I hear such sentiments expressed by someone born after the death of Tito, too young to have experienced the partition and wars. We drive north from the centre of Ljubljana.

A road bridge takes us over the six-lane highway. Immediately we are in what was obviously once a small village – for the moment still separated from greater Ljubljana by the motorway, but soon to be subsumed. Down a winding semi-rural, single-width road we finally locate our destination where a tree-lined track ends at a cluster of houses. Urban, our host, is there at the gate to greet us. The house is large, three storeys tall. Urban shows us around our capacious, top-floor apartment. The rest of the house is empty and it is a five-minute walk to the village where we will find a shop selling fresh food, wine, beer and tobacco. Urban is easily likeable and seems genuinely interested in why we are in Ljubljana. After he leaves, we agree that the fates seem to be smiling at us.

We find the well-stocked shop where a cheerful assistant follows me around the cramped aisles, pointing to goods and asking, 'This?' Eventually, Tomislav intervenes to explain what we are seeking. There is a lot of laughter as we pay for our bread, wine and cheese, say goodbye and return to the apartment.

Excited and unable to settle, we set out early for Stožice. It is now dark and we can see the stadium floodlights. After following the highway for ten minutes we drop down under a road bridge. In the unevenly neon-lit, graffitied subway, Tomislav hangs back to get some shots as I walk on through patches of light and shadow. At the complex we climb some steps up to a modern sports stadium and can see down to the pitch which glows luminous emerald under the floodlights. Small groups of players are going through their pre-match stretching routines and warm-ups. This is the new home of the Slovenian national team and NK Olimpija Ljubljana, one of the country's eminent professional clubs. Tomislav speaks with a man wearing a football scarf, and he sends us in the general direction of the arena. As we get closer, there is a distinct buzz in the, now chilly, evening air. The beer and burger tents outside of the arena are doing brisk business. The football fans and the old punks mingle amiably – the two tribes are only identifiable because football fans have football scarves, and the old punks have slightly more theatrical hats.

Our VIP tickets had cost only about €5 more than the standard tickets and we had bought them in the hope that we would be allowed to bring a camera into the venue and get some decent photos. We find our box, push open the door and enter a darkened room. I turn on the light. This visibly shocks the couple already in the box who break from a passionate embrace. New to the VIP treatment I had not realised we would be sharing a box. Our box is in an upper-tier, directly facing the stage on which a rockabilly band has already got the show underway and is giving it their all. The hall – which usually caters to that Balkan obsession, basketball – is about one-third full and we head off to locate drinks.

After the rockabilly band have completed their set, the backline gear is switched and an all-female Slovenian rock-band takes the stage in a blaze of leather, denim and lavishly conditioned hair. They too are not holding back. The hall is filling and by the end of the set is at about three-quarters capacity. It is beginning to feel like an event. Now a huge screen hangs at the back of the stage and on it is projected a black and white image of Alfred Hitchcock against a red backdrop with the word 'Razprodano' superimposed. This crudely translates as 'Sold Out'. We look down at the crowd below. The main hall is full. On either side of the arena, on high gantries, TV cameras stand ready. The roadies make final preparations. The lights go down and Pankrti takes the stage. The crowd's greeting is enthusiastic but, to my UK ears, somewhat more muted than I had expected. Tomislav reads my mind: 'Slovenians', he says and mimics sitting passively with his legs pressed together and his hands firmly on his knees.

We stand in front of our glass-fronted VIP box. Pankrti turns in a set remarkable for its youthful exuberance – given that this is the fortieth anniversary of their first gig – and none is more exuberant than Peter Lovšin. He is not a physically big man, but he holds the stage with ease. The band crash through a 'best of' which draws heavily on the early years – memorably including a mass sing-along of one of my personal favourites, 'Osmi Dan' (Eighth Day). Cameras on remote-controlled cranes hover, swoop and soar over the crowd. In towering close-up, the smiling faces of the band flash across the giant screen. Tomislav and I are singing and dancing along to each song – our inhibitions lowered by cheap alcohol.

Time and songs speed by, and then Peter Lovšin announces Glen Matlock. The ex-Sex Pistol blasts through Iggy Pop's 'No Fun' and a short set of the Pistols' greatest hits. Tomislav and I sing every word at the top of our voices. Some of the more conservative of those nearby clearly disapprove whilst some others look slightly fearful. 'Slovenians are suspicious of foreigners wearing hats', laughs Tomislav. Pankrti and Glen Matlock are joined onstage by more guests. And then it is over. I have almost lost my voice.

We decide to check out the merchandise stall in the Main Hall and to investigate the possibility of convincing security that we really do have an e-mail from Peter suggesting we join the 'after-show party'. The merchandise is almost totally cleaned out. I manage to get one of the last t-shirts, which features the image of a young Brigitte Bardot. We explain to Security that we have a personal invitation from Peter, offering to show them the e-mail on my mobile phone, but they simply send us to another security check. Enough is enough. Neither of us is a party person or a ligger. We have had such an amazing night – why risk spoiling it? At the apartment, we spend some time reliving the concert, surveying Tomislav's photos and footage, and very gradually coming down from the adrenaline high before accepting that we really should call it a day. But what a day.

Pankrti. Ljubljana © Dušan Gerlica (1979)

FIVE
A Day in Court: Vermeer in Bosnia

The International Criminal Tribunal for Yugoslavia (ICTY) was established in 1993 – at least in principle. During 1994 and 1995, it settled into a physical location in The Hague. At the same time, dedicated ICTY detention facilities were created at Scheveningen prison some 3 kilometres away. Initially, there was considerable scepticism about the wisdom of attempting to begin proceedings. Bringing to justice the perpetrators, long before peace was even in view, was hugely ambitious. There are politicians and many others who still consider the ICTY to be symptomatic of some supra-national, undemocratic, new world order. To some it was only ever 'a faux-judicial arm of NATO, created to service its aims in the Balkan wars'. It is no exaggeration to say that its unpopularity spans all of the nations of former Yugoslavia where it is seen as biased against each individually and the Balkans collectively. To some, this is a measure of its objectivity and to some proof of its malevolence; to some the thankless nature of its task.

When the ICTY was established by 'United Nations Security Council Resolution 827', it was the first international war crimes tribunal created since Nuremberg and Tokyo at the end of the Second World War.

On the morning of 22 November 2017, I get up at 7 a.m., have coffee, breakfast and shower, and dress 'appropriately' for 8:30 a.m. Today, I have a place amongst the press at the 'Reading of the Judgement in the Ratko Mladić trial'. With the exception of the Appeals Verdicts to be handed down next week in the cases of Slobodan Praljak and five others, this will be the final verdict delivered by the ICTY. Its work is judged now to be complete, and it will close its doors before the end of the year. I am apprehensive. It is not so much a fear of the unknown, although I genuinely have little idea what to expect. I have never been inside the ICTY. I am not a journalist. The eyes and ears of the world's media will be there. Am I being ghoulish? Is this voyeurism dressed up as research?

It is a pleasant day for late November on the North Sea coast. A weak blue sky is smeared with white and grey-white clouds. I pass our neighbourhood rubbish-recycling point and cut down the footpath which runs alongside Europol HQ. Less than five minutes after leaving my apartment I turn left onto the public square the ICTY shares with Europol, the World Forum and the other august bodies. As soon as I turn, I can see a small crowd of perhaps 100 between myself and the ICTY. There are several TV satellite vans and dishes, some stationary police cars with constant, sequential flashing blue lights, ten or fifteen uniformed police. I approach and see that the crowd is gathered around a temporary checkpoint in front of the curved perimeter fence which guards the entrance to the ICTY. A number of journalists roam around with mics in hand, one or two are doing 'pieces to camera'. There are press photographers with kit-bags and telephoto lenses. Protestors hold up placards written in Serbian, Croatian or Bosnian. Some are unfurling a banner and stretching it out in front of them at waist height. A man is holding up a copy of *Time* magazine for the cameras as he speaks into the microphones of two journalists. The cover is the iconic image of the bare-chested, skeletal prisoner at the front of a wretched crowd of bare-chested and skeletal prisoners, all behind the barbed wire of a military prison camp. The man seems to be smiling defiantly. Or insanely. It is an image no one who saw it all those years ago will forget. It was a blinding arc, which in a flash fused the images of Belsen-Bergen or Dachau with the then-present-day Balkans. It also resulted in a high-profile libel trial as its veracity was questioned and upheld. I later find out that the man holding the magazine image is Fikret Alić, the cadaverous prisoner horribly immortalised in the 1992 photograph. Inside I check in at a desk and present my documentation and passport to be cross-referenced with the information I supplied in advance. I am given a blue and white card in a laminated pocket:

> UNITED NATIONS – NATIONS UNIES. *Prosecutor v. Ratko Mladić* – TRIAL JUDGEMENT –
> 22 November 2017. PRESS BRIEFING ROOM

I am now in the 'Press Line' at an airport-style security checkpoint. I pass through without drama and find myself in the spacious marble foyer of the ICTY. It is swarming with people. It has a buzz of anticipation. To the right are rows of long tables at which very intense and confident-looking individuals are sitting, firing up their laptops, unpacking bags or chatting. Other groups of individuals, clearly staff and important visitors, stand around in the foyer drinking coffee and talking. It does not feel like such a weighty occasion. Some people are laughing. I suppose that they have been through this many times before. They are the professionals and not the victims, or witnesses. They are not the family and friends of the accused. If it were not for the protestors outside it could be the launch of a new car. The dominant language is English.

A uniformed member of ICTY staff directs me to the Press Briefing Rooms. Each of these seats seven or eight people. I choose the room with only one other person already seated at a desk. This first journalist gets out his laptop and boots it up just as another journalist enters the room. They are both Dutch and they know each other. They begin chatting. Both have laptops and one has three cameras, one with an immense telephoto lens. I did not bring a laptop because I feared being refused entry. Now that seems really stupid. I sit down, get out my notebook and pens and try to mask my inadequacy and alienation. At least I still have my mobile phone. I log on to the ICTY network, access the ICTY site and select the live feed from the Court Room. It keeps buffering.

The previous evening I had read Lawrence Weschler's 2004 collection of Balkan-themed essays, *Vermeer in Bosnia*. It was still vivid in my mind as I sat in the ICTY just a few hours later. Sent on assignment to cover the ICTY trials, American art-critic, journalist and author Weschler asked one of the presiding judges how he could bear to absorb so much cruelty and misery. The judge's answer made perfect sense to Weschler: 'You see, as often as possible I make my way over to the Mauritshuis museum, in the center of town, so as to spend a little time with the Vermeers.' Weschler too spends his time at the beautiful little museum immediately behind the Binnenhof, the historic Parliament complex on the edge of the Hofvijver Lake. It is only after speaking with the judge that Weschler realises the hidden thread between Vermeer's work and the proceedings of the ICTY – just as it is only after reading Weschler that it clicked for me. At the time, Vermeer was painting,

> all Europe was Bosnia (or had only just recently ceased to be): awash in incredibly vicious wars of religious persecution and proto-nationalist formation, wars of an at-that-time unprecedented violence and cruelty, replete with sieges and famines and massacres and mass rapes, unspeakable tortures and wholesale devastation.

Vermeer was born into the fallout from the upheavals of Reformation and Counter Reformation. His relatively brief life spanned the Eighty Years War and the concurrent Thirty Years War, followed by three wars with England and the Rampjaar ('Disaster Year') of 1672 – so called because of the invasion, defeat and occupation of the Dutch Republic. Weschler describes how, at first, we do not see the turmoil in Vermeer's paintings. On the surface, they are depictions of serenity. But it is in the margins and backgrounds; it is what is suggested rather than what is made explicit. Lone women feature in Vermeer's paintings – even a young, pregnant woman. Often they are reading or writing letters. We imagine that these are letters to absent menfolk, away fighting. In some paintings, the soldiers return:

> When soldiers visit young girls in Vermeer's paintings, where does one think they have been off soldiering – and why, one wonders, does the country need all those civic guards? When pregnant young women are standing still, bathed in the window light, intently reading those letters, where is one invited to imagine the letters are coming from?

Vermeer was born and lived his whole life in nearby Delft. He was there in 1654 when the gunpowder supplies in the town's arsenal exploded, just a few hundred metres from the Vermeer family-inn on the market square, and his mother-in-law's property on Oude Langendijk. The colossal explosion known as the 'Delft Thunderclap' killed over 100, injured thousands and destroyed a significant part of the city. Vermeer painted his astounding *View of Delft* just seven years after, and as the art critic Andrew Graham Dixon said, 'He took a turbulent reality, and made it look like Heaven on earth'.

I spend two hours at the ICTY. And then the feed drops completely. The broadcast has now been shut down and I have no idea of the sentence. The foyer rapidly begins to fill up. There is a chatter of excitement – one-way telephone conversations to newsrooms as frontline journalists file reports, groups huddle together, block-heels echo like gunfire, flashes burst and broadcast equipment is hurriedly shifted.

I pack up my bag and leave the room. Relieved to escape, I exit through the staff entrance, past the airport-security style checks and into the waiting crowd. The first groups I see are mainly women, in their forties and fifties I guess. Undoubtedly Balkan. Some are wearing heavy make-up, and some, very little make-up. Some have well-cut, smart-looking outfits whilst others have simple, padded and hooded raincoats. To me, they all look haunted. I walk through the crowd, dodging the TV reporters doing pieces to camera, interviewing victims or witnesses, or both. Back on the main shopping street of Frederik Hendriklaan, two workmen on a cherry-picker are cheerfully stringing Christmas lights across the street. It is the strangest feeling. The sight of life going on, of the preparation for celebration, genuinely takes me aback.

At home, I switch on the TV and watch the coverage. It turns out that Mladić had extended his bathroom break for half-an-hour and then his lawyers requested a further break in proceedings because he was suffering from high blood pressure. On being refused, Mladić stood up and shouted, 'This is all lies […] I'll fuck your mother'. For the sake of objectivity, it should be added that such curses are quite common across the Balkans and usually not intended – or perceived – as the same kind of lurid and personal insult as perhaps they might be elsewhere. Mladić was then removed from the Court and the sentence of life imprisonment was delivered in his absence. At 11 a.m. GMT, *The Guardian* newspaper reported,

> The trial in The Hague, which took 530 days across more than four years, is arguably the most significant war crimes case in Europe since the Nuremberg trials, in part because of the scale of the atrocities involved. Almost 600 people gave evidence for the prosecution and defence, including survivors of the conflict.

Precisely one week after my morning at the ICTY, in hearing the Judge uphold his twenty-year sentence, seventy-two-year-old Slobodan Praljak, flanked by his co-defendants yelled, 'Praljak is not a criminal. I reject your verdict'. He then tipped his head back and opened his mouth, his hand shaking he lifted a small bottle to his lips, drank from it and said, 'I just drank poison'. Then he said, 'I am not a war criminal. I oppose this conviction'. The court officials looked stunned. Judge Carmel Agius attempted to continue the trial before it became apparent that Praljak had now fallen ill. Court officials jumped up and ran towards the dock. Agius then ordered the curtains screening the Court be closed. The entire Shakespearean act was played out in full view of the cameras. Three minutes of the most perfect, repugnant, reality TV for the twenty-first century. Praljak died hours later in a Den Haag hospital. An autopsy revealed he had taken potassium cyanide. Some had been denied their justice. Some had been gifted their martyr.

ANTE ČIKARA: The Haven, Scheveningen and De Pijp, Amsterdam

Anté Čikara. ICTY, The Hague

Ante and I met first at Dok 22 café bar amongst the indifferent gentrification of the Tweede Haven (the Second/inner harbour) in Scheveningen, a week or so after I returned from ex-Yugoslavia. Outside, the strengthening breeze gently rattled the rigging of sailing boats like wind chimes. A few weeks later we met again at the apartment Ante shares with his partner and two late-teenage sons in the (increasingly) hip De Pijp district of Central Amsterdam where they have lived from long before it became a byword for 'cool'. As I walked through the bustling, narrow streets towards Ante's home, the contrast between the forced gentrification and social cleansing of the traditional fishing communities of the harbour, and the street markets, restaurants, brown cafes and the mingling of the human tides, is evident. One is sterile, affordable only to the uncommonly wealthy. The other is organic, authentic and multifarious. The result is that it is now a hugely desirable neighbourhood, which of course presents its own challenges, but I know which I prefer.

A Day in Court: Vermeer in Bosnia

Ante was a rock-critic, independent promoter and, with his friend Sale Dragaš, was behind one of Yugoslavia's most dynamic independent record labels. A long-term resident of the Netherlands, for over twenty years he has worked at the Language Section of The Hague Tribunal (the ICTY). He still buys and sells vinyl, much of which he seems to collect/deliver on his bike. It was only during the course of the first interview that the penny dropped and I realised that this is the 'Ante' mentioned touchingly by Jim Bob from Carter USM in his tour biog, *Goodnight Jim Bob: On the Road with Carter the Unstoppable Sex Machine*. Throughout the second interview, Ante extracted items – vinyl, books, photos – from the archives in his study and recited fine detail and anecdotes about ex-Yugoslavia's most influential acts, about some less influential but still noteworthy and about some who failed even to make it to a stage.

* * *

I lived in Zagreb. I was sixteen in 1980 but I really started getting into music when I was twelve. The first thing I would listen to was hard rock, the usual stuff, Deep Purple, Uriah Heep; Uriah Heep had a couple of tours and Deep Purple played there in 1975. So being twelve in '76 I was aware of a thing called 'punk' but I'd never heard any music. I was aware that they wore these safety-pins because there were kids in my school who were covered in safety-pins just for the sake of it, but they had never heard a song of a punk band or anything. Punk was being played on Radio Zagreb but at that time I didn't know which programmes to listen to.

My first concrete action related to punk was buying the first Clash record. The first LP got released rather quickly – because it was on CBS, and CBS had a licensing deal with Suzy Records in Yugoslavia. That was the year of the gig which defined the whole scene and I was not there because I was too young – the Stranglers and 999 in June '78. It was when all of the scene actually got together because many original punks from all over Yugoslavia came to the gig.[1] That can be seen as a pivotal moment in the development of the scene. I wasn't there. I should have been, and I knew that I should have been. Missing that gig, as well as the Zagreb gigs of Dr Feelgood the same year and the Ruts in the winter of 1980, sealed my fate as a compulsive gig-goer for the rest of my life as I vowed not to repeat those mistakes ever again.

There were cool foreign rock records being released in Yugoslavia through licensing deals with the major labels. Also quite a lot of new wave stuff in retrospect – XTC, the Stranglers, the Saints, Magazine, Buzzcocks, Blondie, Public Image all had at least one record released there – but it was not nearly enough to satisfy the

---

1. In Zagreb.

appetites. So of course, the ultimate thing to get the 'real stuff' was the mail order from abroad: Cob Records in Wales. In a place called Porthmadog. We were all putting the dinars in an envelope and then waiting. My first order was *Catch a Fire* by the Wailers, *Closer* by Joy Division and *Relics* by Pink Floyd (*Relics* mainly because it was a cheap £1.95 Music For Pleasure release). I had to pay the import tax as well. When the postman rang, I opened the door, saw the brown parcel and I kissed him! I literally embraced the guy and kissed him. I was completely mad with excitement. After that, you would dream about which record you wanted to buy next. And next month you would get your dinars and wait for three weeks – sometimes even more. Once I waited for a couple of months for Echo and the Bunnymen and the Cramps to finally arrive. Oh man! And you know those Welsh addresses? G-G-Gwy-Gwynedd. GWYNEDD!! The first time I was putting all my dosh in an envelope I was thinking, 'Where the fuck is this money going to?'

    I knew somebody who was selling the photocopied catalogues of Cob Records and making money out of it! This guy would just put an ad in the rock music paper saying, 'How to get originals?' Then he would just run a photocopier amok and send all these Cob Records catalogues around – distribute them for money. Cob Records would send me all of the updates and he would come to me and say, 'Do you have the updates because I need to update mine?' Those catalogues were minuscule and that was pre-computer, so I don't know how they did it. You would almost have to have a magnifying glass to read them – to see all these lists of names of bands – it was like size five font or something. But Cob Records was the thing, everybody knew them because they had low-postage rates. A friend of mine was ordering from Gemma Records but they had a much higher postage. You could also pay with a bank transfer. You could wire the money to them from your mum or dad's bank account but I was always stuffing dinars in the envelope with Cob Records address.

    It's important to underline that punk rock and new wave in Yugoslavia was a predominately middle-class thing: you have to be absolutely certain about that. Working-class people didn't have the money to waste on imported records and those kinds of things. The thing about Tito's Yugoslavia was that the Communists succeeded in creating a relatively viable, vital, middle-class. I don't think that I knew more than two or three real punks who were working-class. Frequently, the fathers of those 'alter-kids' were military personnel. I found it always really funny that they managed to raise such liberal offspring. My dad was also retired ex-military. He was an ex-partisan who fought in the war. Yeah, one of those people – the winners of World War Two. Most of the people of my generation were living with their parents after their teens since the proper jobs were scarce and the rents high. People who travelled a lot, people who were curious and people who read a lot – they were into punk and new wave.

The predominant view, at least among my peers, was that the Yugo-style socialist system was OK, but the people who were actually implementing the system were not really good. Of course, none of us ever wanted anything to do with the people who actually joined the Party. I might be wrong, but I don't think that a single person on the Yugoslav alternative scene ever even remotely considered being a member of the Communist Party.

I started writing for *Polet* when I just turned seventeen and I spent a year reviewing gigs and records for them. After graduation from the high school, I went to the Army in late '82 to Titograd – now Podgorica – in Montenegro. It was a month after the Talking Heads gig, which was absolutely brilliant. It was the last gig on their *The Name of this Band* tour – when they had that huge band. That was in Zagreb. Fifteen thousand people, in the middle of the summer, when usually Zagreb is completely empty because everyone is on the seaside. It was a mind-blowing gig really.

When I came out of the Army, I was hibernating for a couple of years. I was trying to study electronics, which didn't happen! I spent my time basically getting drunk – successfully – and going out chasing girls – unsuccessfully. Some of the guys that I worked with in *Polet* started working for *Studentski List* – the other student newspaper in Zagreb at the time. They said, 'Come over. You can write again'. That's how I really started writing again, slowly, step-by-step. Sale Dragaš, who was a year or two younger but already had published articles in *Polet* and local fanzines, joined in as well.

As the eighties evolved, we became more serious about the music journalism. Besides writing for the 'youth press' as it was called at the time, we published more often in regular papers and magazines – not necessarily Zagreb based. Then came the proper music monthly made by an old *Džuboks* crew member from Belgrade, Momo Rajin, and some younger Belgrade-based people – most notably Dragan Ambrozić who was de facto Editor-In-Chief. The mag was called *Ritam* ('Rhythm') and many of us wrote our best work there for little or no money.

Sale, myself and a few other friends went to Reading Festival when it turned 'indie' in 1989. I simply had to see all those bands in space of three days. After I came back, I had a clear vision of what I needed to do with my life. So I started promoting foreign bands. I knew there was a market for it and I knew what you could do. And that's what I did until a week or two before I left.

Sale's dad used to work in Cuba, where he accumulated some capital because he was paid in US dollars. Everything in Cuba was cheap there, so he was stashing the dollars aside. Imagine, he made serious US capitalist dollars in Cuba representing a company from another friendly socialist country. When he came back, he recognized an entrepreneurial spirit in his son. Sale told me, 'Let's do a record together by Obojeni Program'. They are simply brilliant and they didn't have any chances of being signed by Jugoton or RTB or anyone. I have to say that it was relatively easy to accomplish since we had the cash from Sale's dad and the 'know-how' from Zdenko (Franjić) who already published *Bombardiranje New Yorka* a few months earlier. So Sale paid for the pressing of 1000 copies and I helped with promotion. Within three months we sold those 1000 copies and accumulated some money to release more records and within a year we had done about five releases. That first Obojeni Program and the first LP by Majke – a garage band from Vinkovci – are now considered legendary, so I have heard, but it needs to be said that *78* by Boye was also a great record.

There were some terrific bands at the end of the eighties in Yugoslavia. Overflow was a great hardcore band from 'up north', Koprivnica. Brilliant, brilliant, that was the best punk band that ever came out of Croatia, for my money. They were just kids at the time; they were like fourteen when Zdenko (who else?) recorded them first. I remember, I pulled them their first Zagreb gig and I just couldn't believe that fourteen-year-old kids from a small town up north could play that well. The energy was unbelievable and they were very competent players from the word go. It was just this tension they would build on their gigs at that time. Unbelievable. The first gig they played felt like it was the hundredth and one of them was still in primary school! After that gig we, and other promoters, would call them to support bands that were touring at the time – so they supported, like, Mega City Four, House of Love, Urge Overkill – they would support everybody. They also supported a band from France called Les Thugs, a great pop-punk band from the late eighties. The guy from Les Thugs was so blown away by them that he actually arranged a proper French tour in '92. But sadly, in the long run nothing worked for those kids, and I still regret not being able to do more for them. Later on they reunited; they even went to South by Southwest and to New York and whatever, but it just didn't happen – despite being superior to, for example, most of the big US punk label Epitaph's roster at the time. Yeah, easily better than most of that lot.

In 1991, I booked a short tour for Carter the Unstoppable Sex Machine. Although it was an unusually cold day for mid April, the club in Zagreb – 'Jabuka' – decided to have it in the open air because they could get more people in. We had been in the restaurant having dinner and we came back to the soundcheck and the guy said, 'You know (President) Tuđman and his lot are having a meeting up there and they are complaining about the noise!'

I said to him, 'Well have you announced the gig at the police station? Have you got a permit and everything?'

He said, 'Yeah, yeah, yeah, but they are asking us not to play'.

Tudman always boasted in interviews about his intention to create a country run by rule-of-law as opposed to the Communist dictatorship so I said, 'They can't. We have a contract. We have a permit. We live now in the 'rule-of-law' country don't we? We are a proper state now'.

At the end, they played the gig and I read somewhere that Tudman and his lot had a break while the gig was on! They continued plotting the war straight after the gig though. The late 'John the Fat Beast' came out and shouted, 'Make some noise. Make some noise to upset the President!' That's how the gig started.

The last band I booked was Miracle Workers – an American garage band. It was a few weeks after Carter USM. Miracle Workers were a true eye-opener. They had played Venice the day before and one of the guys, I think a guitar player, was late because he'd hooked up with a girl – he was then driven by that girl to the gig. The first thing he said when he met up with the rest (me included) was, 'Have you noticed how many pigs there are in this town? There's pigs on every corner. In uniform. And they are armed'. It was late May 1991, and for the first time, I thought, 'Something's definitely not OK in here. It is more than just a stubborn political crisis'. We would never have thought that the war would have started, but the voice from above came to me in the form of a long-haired Californian and said, 'Wake up!'

Going back in time, it was late 1990 when things started looking really shaky. In early 1991, there was this huge affair because – we know now – the Croatians were smuggling weapons into the country. And the MI5 of Yugoslavia knew about it. I remember the war psychosis was really bad for a couple of days to the point that I even didn't go to see a gig which I would normally never miss – Miladojka Youneed from Ljubljana were playing Lapidarium in Zagreb.[2] My mum and my sister were completely freaking out: 'You're not going out tonight! Can't you see what's happening?' Two days later I said, 'I'm not going to live through this psychosis anymore'. So, I went to the bus station, bought a ticket and boarded the first bus to Frankfurt where I had a good friend. I stayed with him for two weeks until things were temporarily settled. Early January '91, cold as fuck it was.

This is really important to point out; I'm escaping the tense situation in the country and all the other people on the bus are going to Germany to buy a

---

2. Miladojka Youneed were a Slovenian funk/punk/jazz band existing from 1985 to 1998. Lapidarium was a legendary, venue/cellar-bar in the Upper Town of Zagreb.

car! Yugoslavia had really huge taxes on imported cars to protect the industry but Croatia had recently, defiantly, lowered the import taxes and the people went to western countries to buy used cars because they were cheaper. They would go as far as Belgium to get a car! All of the other people on the bus to Frankfurt were actually going to spend their savings on a car. They never saw war coming.

My other watershed moment was when Serbia entered into the federal finances, that was the moment when I personally realised it was all over – late '90.[3] That's when I realised that Milošević and his lot didn't give a fuck anymore and that Yugoslavia was on the ropes. Still, at that moment the possibility of war happening here was furthest from my mind.

I came back from Frankfurt two weeks later in time to see Iggy Pop playing the same venue as Talking Heads nine years earlier. Again, 15,000 people on [sic] a gig. So one day you would have a real threat of a military coup and big – civil war – tensions, while the other Iggy, or Pet Shop Boys or someone else, would come and play these massive gigs like everything was normal [...] like in any other European country.

I left for good on 30 June 1991. The band I managed, Studeni Studeni, played a gig the day before. My friend, the main Studeni guy Kosta,[4] left Zagreb to go to Serbia that summer just because his parents were from there; he had family there and he stayed there – he couldn't come back. He died there in Niš, in Serbia, in June 2017. We just split, you know. There was a gig, we got drunk and then the guitar player Danijel Šuljić phoned me the next morning and said, 'Have you heard that Šentilj is closed?' It's in Slovenia and was the main border crossing with Austria. I was like, 'What the fuck?' Šentilj was always the gateway you know, you cross there and then you are in the West. Slovenia had just declared independence a day or two earlier and this time they had really started shooting at each other there. Later that day I saw the troops – the JNA – moving through my street. I lived in Zagreb near the big avenue which leads to the highway to Slovenia, and the Army convoy was moving, and the people were throwing stones at them!

You know, it was a pretty weird situation. I was just going out to play tennis and there was a column of Army vehicles moving and the people were throwing

---

3. In late December 1990, the Serbian Government under Milošević ordered Serbian controlled banks to – illegally – print $1.8bn. This was then loaned to the Serbian Government to prop up industries, pay pensions and farm subsidies. Although banking was newly decentralised in Yugoslavia at this time, each country was still expected to follow federal credit agreements as agreed.
4. Goran 'Kosta' Kostić of Novembar/Studeni and Protektori.

A Day in Court: Vermeer in Bosnia

stones at it! I said to myself, 'Woh! This is really getting out of control'. For a year it was really tense in Croatia, and you couldn't go to the parts where Serbs were a majority – they had their own rule. And there were no buses or trains going through that route – the vital route which connected Split to Zagreb. But you got used to living with that. You were thinking they were going to sort it out because the leaders were meeting constantly, every month, and they were talking and coming up with new solutions on how to end the political crisis. But when Slovenia declared independence, followed by Croatia the day later, the JNA moved in and they closed the western border. I thought, 'It's time to go'.

I had money because I did the tour with Carter a couple of months before. I had some money, not much about 1200 German Marks. I knew that could carry me for a couple of months in western Europe if I stayed with friends. Next morning I met up with two of my mates with whom I used to travel around, and they said, 'Look we only have this much money. The question is, which is the best time to go so we can prolong our stay considering the money we have?' I said, 'OK, so we are not going today. We wait'. I went home, and my mum said, 'Someone from the Municipality has been asking of your whereabouts. So you're going to Frankfurt tomorrow. I don't want you here!' I was like, 'OK, let's go!' The situation was bloody weird, and I didn't want to be part of it.

Next morning I took the first train to Budapest because that border was open. I remember sitting there on that beautiful morning, and we were waiting to pass the border. Once we crossed the border into Hungary, I started talking to the guy who was in the same train compartment and he said, 'I'm going to Vienna. This is not normal what is going on'. I said, 'I am also going to Vienna and from there I'll see whatever'. And that's how it was. I remember the guy at the Customs was saying, 'How come everybody is going to Vienna these days?' He was, sort of, tongue-in-cheek laughing at it. Half of the people on the train were just proper 'gastarbajteri' who went home on a weekend – it was just their weekend routine because it was Sunday. But there were already some like me – running away from the situation. I reckon I was among the first who escaped. Then steadily the fighting progressed in all these border towns in Croatia – Vukovar, Vinkovci and those kinds of towns. That was in July, and after July a lot of people just left.

I remember getting to the hostel in Budapest on 30 June and the people coming from inter-railing in Greece were like, 'What's going on in Yugoslavia? We want to cross to Vienna, and they've diverted us to Hungary. Why? We heard that there is a War!' And there was a television and on Hungarian TV there were pictures of fighting in Yugoslavia. At the same time in Budapest, they'd had a huge party because they'd just said, 'goodbye' to the last Russian soldier! Frank Zappa was playing a free open-air gig, so I went to that festival at one of the parks in Budapest. Zappa was just jamming with what he called his 'gypsy friends'. He was so keen on these new democracies, he came to wave goodbye to the last Russian soldier. So while the Hungarians were stepping optimistically into the new world after suffering forty years under harsh Communism, we – who had lived relatively normally – started destroying each other. Bizarre.

The next day I took a train to the border with Austria and hitchhiked to Vienna where I had some friends, because of this rock 'n' roll business. The following day I hitchhiked from Vienna to Frankfurt, and on the way, I met a couple of people who were speaking Croatian. And the guy had a small TV set that could be plugged into the car battery. So they pulled out the TV set in the middle of nowhere, at a gas station between Nürnberg and Frankfurt. They were watching the German news and I saw my neighbourhood on the news! There was a tank wanting to cross a bridge and the people were throwing Molotov cocktails at it.

I was twenty-six, I turned twenty-seven in Frankfurt a few weeks later. That's a good time to leave. The only thing I had to lose was a bunch of records. Nothing! I didn't have a proper life in terms of a family, and a job – thank heavens. But at the same time I was cannon fodder. I was very much aware that I would be drafted immediately. I wouldn't go to war, no way man.

I stayed in Frankfurt for about a month. I couldn't get a job there, because of the language barrier. So Marcus, my German mate, loaned me some money – 600 Marks or something – and I went to England because I had a letter on me that I'd received a couple of days before I left Yugoslavia from Wiz of Mega City Four.[5] In March of 1991, I did a tour with them and he said, 'If you're coming to Reading Festival this year come and stay with us. We do not live far from Reading'. So, I phoned them and said, 'Look, guys, I need to come. Can you find me a job or whatever?' So basically, they saved my arse. I stayed with them for three months. They'd just signed with a major label so they had money. Wiz had bought a house, so they were in the process of moving and recording the new stuff for the new album and single. Exciting times for them – they even made it to *Top of the Pops*.

I was there at the time and I had the time of my life because I was seeing all these gigs they were going to in London, hanging with them in studios around

---

5. Mega City Four were an English indie band who kept the flame of punk burning between 1987 and 1996. Tragically, Wiz (Darren Brown) died suddenly in 2006, aged just forty-four.

A Day in Court: Vermeer in Bosnia

Ljubljana punks: Lila, Aina and Mačka ('The Cat' – rear). Disco SV, Ljubljana © Matija Praznik (1981)

London. At the same time, it was really horrible because of the situation at home. I was also running out of money and stuff, but one of their friends had a small construction business so I started working there. I managed to save like 300 quid (£300) in three months. Meanwhile, the war was just expanding, expanding, expanding and I couldn't abuse their hospitality anymore. They were hinting politely that it was time for me to find another solution. Three of them lived together and I was sleeping on the floor in their dining room. So, yeah, I came to Amsterdam, because my very good friend, a friend of my ex-girlfriend, lived here. So I thought I could stay here and then ask for asylum.

When I came here her marriage was falling apart and they were living in a studio apartment of 40 square metres in the middle of the Red Light District. Luckily enough, on the third day, she found somebody who went to Morocco for their Christmas holidays and she offered for me to stay and guard the cats. My girlfriend came over a few days later and, from then on, we became proficient cat-minders all over Amsterdam! I've counted that we moved fourteen times, just in a year. We really couldn't find a job at all so it was [a] very improvised living. The first week in Amsterdam I met a couple of people I knew here from Zagreb who told me, 'Martha from Belgrade is throwing a party this Saturday. Come over, everybody who is in Amsterdam will come'. I'd met Martha before. I'd met her in Zagreb because she was writing for one of the Belgrade-based rock magazines. I knew she lived in Amsterdam. So I walked into the party and the late Zerkman – trumpet player from Disciplina Kičme – hugged me and said, 'Hey, what are you doing here?' And it was like, 'What are you doing here? You're here as well!' There were at least 30 or 40 people from the Belgrade and Zagreb scenes, who were already in Amsterdam for a few months, without any money, trying to survive. That was the end of 1991. A few months later, I call them the 'proper refugees', the people who really lost everything started arriving. It was in the spring of '92. Most of them were from Bosnia – they just flooded western Europe. Now you would get the whole families with people in their mid thirties and older with small kids, and they needed to start all over again.

Roughly at the same time, I scored the job in Paradiso.[6] Nothing fancy just a stagehand, but from that moment I had enough money to buy food, and since I worked in Paradiso, I could see bands regularly, for free.

From that moment on, all my needs were covered.

---

6. Paradiso is a publicly subsidised cultural centre, located in a converted church in central Amsterdam. It is one of the most prestigious live music venues in the Netherlands, and arguably mainland Europe, with a particular reputation for punk and new wave.

SIX
Music Is the Art of Time

DAY 4

When I wake, the sun is already bleaching the white walls of the bedroom. Tomislav is nowhere to be seen or heard. It is a few minutes after ten o'clock. I find Tomislav sitting quietly in a corner of the living room. He has his beanie hat pulled down over his face. 'I have a fucking migraine man. What's the plan for today then?' He has the colour of a North Sea fog and is clearly suffering. I tell him that I hope to interview Peter 'Pero' Lovšin and perhaps Marin Rosić too, but that I am not going to hassle them. I figure that the after-show party last night may have taken its toll and I do not want to taint any goodwill. Tomislav is equally philosophical, 'What will be will be mate. Let's rely on serendipity. It seems to be working OK for us so far'. Tomislav goes to his room to recover and reappears an hour or so later, much improved. We sit outside on the balcony, smoking cigarettes and enjoying the warmth of the sun. We have lunch and wait. It is only the fourth day but so much has happened; it is good to have some downtime to write up the previous day and night.

Soon after 15:30, I get an e-mail: 'Hi Barry, Do you still need me. From now on you can get me on phone 051… … …. I'm still in Lj. Peter.' Tomislav uses my mobile to call. The first call would not connect. We check area codes and international dialling codes and try again. The call connects and Tomislav begins chatting in Slovenian. It is only at this point that I realise how fortunate I am to have such a gifted linguist as my companion. Tomislav says he spoke with a woman, perhaps Peter's wife, and she has given him another number. He calls the number. After a couple of minutes of conversation, he hands back the phone:

> Peter says he can do it if we go now. He will be with some people in the city at four-thirty. He says he can do maybe an hour or so but he's tired. He said the party went on a long time and he hasn't slept yet.

Gold-dust; even an hour with Peter the day after such a momentous concert, and the post-gig celebrations will be rich reward.

We telephone for a taxi and are soon heading back to Ljubljana centre. The driver asks why we are in Ljubljana. He seems genuinely pleased that we have covered such distances to pay homage. 'Pankrti are Ljubljana legends. Slovenian legends.' We are a few minutes early, so we ask the driver to drop us at Krekov trg beneath Ljubljana Castle. Tucked away in the corner of this sleepy square is the tiny, ultra modern, funicular station from where to ride the cable car up the, vertiginous, slope to the castle at the summit.

We follow the rough directions given to us by the taxi driver; Tomislav snatching every opportunity to photograph the beautiful historic streets, still busy with late-afternoon shoppers and late-season tourists. There are tables on the sidewalks – some in the shade of parasols and some exposed to the weakening heat of the sun. On our right is a church, with faded yellow-clay and white-painted walls, and a biblical mural framed by inset religious icons. Tomislav says we are looking for a 'terrace' near the Fish Market. From within a courtyard, a man wheels an upright hand-trolley out onto the cobbled streets. It is heavily laden with large boxes. Tomislav asks him for directions. The points to a passageway across the road. As we cross, he shouts after us laughing. 'He says, don't worry it's not far', says Tomislav.

We are now in the heart of old-town Ljubljana with its cobbled market squares, narrow streets and alleyways, and pastel-washed Baroque and Austrian Art Nouveau architecture. Everywhere there are street cafés. After a couple of false alarms, we spot Peter sat with a mixed group of five or six people. They are at a table on a long pedestrianised street off a small square. Down the centre of the street is a line of trees, bare save for the last few leaves of the season. On the right-hand side is a graceful, flat-fronted, four-storey building, and facing it on the left, a single-storey building – its white walls and red tiled roof stretching way down the street. It has numerous large, wooden-arched windows and wooden-framed double doors, stepped back from the white pillars of a portico which runs the length of the building. Immediately behind is the gently curving Ljubljanica River. The low building is divided into restaurants, bars and shops. I guess this must be the old Fish Market. As we approach, Peter recognises us, stands and, in a tone as gravelly and rakish as his stage voice, says 'welcome'. He explains to his group that he has an interview to do and we move to another table in the street.

The sun is low in the sky but still above the rooftops; it provides comforting warmth to someone who three days previously was insulating against the late October, North Sea winds. My companions used to more temperate climes, clearly think otherwise and sport very stylish 'Italian' combinations of winter coats and sunglasses. Peter asks if we have eaten and if we would like to drink. He orders another carafe of Istrian white wine and it is soon followed by plates of local produce – cheese, fish, ham and bread. This sets the pattern. During the following four hours, people come and go. Peter's son joins us with two members of last night's all-female rock band. We learn they are called Hellcats. Peter insists we pose for photos. Later, Igor Vidmar, a producer, promoter, manager, journalist and political activist, appears and Peter introduces us. Igor is a truly legendary figure in ex-Yugo punk. He was one of the first people I attempted to contact at the outset of my research. I take the opportunity to ask him why he did not respond to the unsolicited e-mail from a total stranger and he laughs it off.

Later, much later, the interview comes to a natural conclusion. Peter invites us to his house to continue chatting and drinking: 'I have to get home. It is a big match tonight on TV'. Peter's love of football is well known. He is Chairman of a football club here. He avidly follows all football, but particularly the Italian Serie A. Several Pankrti songs reference football and he has even written and recorded a song for the Slovenian national team. We thank him for the offer of extending his already lavish hospitality but opt to make our way back to the apartment for an earlier and quieter evening. I am still harbouring hopes of making contact with Marin Rosić and perhaps setting up an interview for Sunday. But we have early afternoon seats booked on the coach, so the window is closing.

Tomislav and I decide to investigate the city a little more on our way to look for a taxi rank. We head further down the pedestrian walkway where we find a graceful footbridge over the river. This is 'Mesarski most', the 'Butcher's Bridge', one of the more recently opened bridges in this city of bridges. The river here is narrow, contained within culvert walls rather than banks. The bridge is broad and dotted with sculptures. On either side are handrails of steel cords which hang heavy with love-padlocks. A gentle procession of café bars and restaurants stretches down the riverside pathways on the opposite bank. Along the river's edge, a few drinkers and diners sit under smart white and brown parasols. Tomislav stops on the bridge. He gestures downstream and I can see why his photographer's eye was so taken with the view. The narrow river extends away into the city; cafés and bars throw shafts of light, and cast shadows, onto the surface; strings of lights hang along each bank, the reflections shimmering in the blackness of the almost completely becalmed water.

We cross the bridge and take a left turn in the approximate direction of the city centre. The bars here already seem to be winding down, although it is still early. Waiters and waitresses clear tables and stack away the chairs as we pick our way past groups of young people and couples promenading down the narrow, cobbled street. On a much busier thoroughfare it seems the revellers are making their way home, queuing for buses or attempting to flag down passing cars in the hope that they are cabs. It is all very low-key and civilised. We come to a large pedestrian square from which eight or nine roads radiate. In the centre is a small fair which is also shutting down. Away from the lights and the main drags we find an idling taxi rank with no queues and fifteen minutes later we are back in our apartment. We sit down for one final glass of wine. It becomes two bottles. Finally, Tomislav shakes his head, smiles and says,

PERO LOVŠIN: The Fish Market, Ljubljana

Pero Lovšin. Fish Market, Ljubljana © Tomislav 'Tompa' Zebić (2017)

> I've just spent the afternoon with Pero Lovšin. Do you know what that means to me? I have his number in my phone. These people were my heroes when I was growing up. They were the most important thing in my miserable fucking life.

In early 1977, two friends from the Kodeljevo suburb of Ljubljana – Peter 'Pero' Lovšin and Gregor Tomc – decided to form a band, with Peter as vocalist and Gregor as manager. The two would share the bulk of the songwriting responsibilities. Pankrti began rehearsing in the basement of the local music school and, on 18 October 1977, at the nearby Moste High School, played their first gig. This is generally agreed to be the first punk gig in 'communist Europe' or perhaps in any communist country.

Pankrti has been called the 'most important punk band outside of the UK and US', and 'the first punk band ever formed in a communist country'. The site of their first gig is so revered in ex-Yugoslavia that it is now marked with a memorial plaque. Their first single 'Lublana je bulana' was released in 1978. John Peel owned a copy of *Dolgcajt* (numbered 11548 in his archiving system) and featured it on his BBC radio show as early as 1980. In 1996, the band supported the Sex Pistols on their reunion tour. Other than having the documentary *Music Is the Art of Time* dedicated to their first album, they have also featured in several other important documentaries – notably the 2003 *Sretno Dijete*

('Lucky Kid') – and their music was part of the soundtrack to the ground-breaking 1997 Slovenian movie *Outsider*. The Slovenian National Museum of Modern History held a month-long photography exhibition dedicated to the band. During my first interview in ex-Yugoslavia, Sale Dragaš (who knows a thing or two about these things) told me,

> Ask Jello Biafra if you can and he will tell you that one of the best punk albums ever was, and still is, *Dolgcajt* by Pankrti. Forever in his top 10 of best punk albums of all time. And it really is. It's the perfect mixture of [the] Clash and Sex Pistols in one record.

Pero and co-songwriter Gregor Tomc, now Professor of Sociology at Ljubljana University, were renowned for incisive lyrics which combined politics with the daily life of Yugoslav youth under socialism. After sharing the bill at Pankrti's first Zagreb concert, in 1977, Branimir 'Johnny' Štulić of Azra was so moved that he changed the lyrics to his song Balkan accordingly: 'I'm shaving my beard and moustache, to look like Pankrti'. Štulić became one of the most famous and charismatic personalities in the ex-Yugoslavian alternative rock scene, later assuming almost mythical status as a reclusive-exile-mystic near Utrecht in the Netherlands. In *Sretno Dijete*, we see jumpy, grainy, hand-held, colour footage of a youthful Peter Lovšin careering around the stage of the Belgrade Student Cultural Centre whilst the narrator says, 'Exactly 25 years ago Belgrade met punk for the first time. There was an event called 3 Days of Young Slav Culture and Pankrti were on the bill. In a very short time it triggered an avalanche'.

Today, in addition to his responsibilities with Pankrti, Pero also performs as a solo artist and with Pero Lovšin and the Španski Borci ('Spanish Republican Fighters'). Pero was always, and remains, a charismatic and ebullient performer. He was born to be a frontman.

***

Yugoslavia was one of the great punk scenes, maybe because it had a great cultural history in the late sixties and seventies. We had a lot of fantastic movies; we had the Black Wave movies like the Oscar-awarded movie *Skupljači perja* (*I Even Met Happy Gypsies*). We had independent philosophers, independent universities, independent student organisations and we had a great music scene – even before punk. We had a rock scene; we had some great bands like YU Grupa, Leb i sol ('Bread and Salt'), Bijelo Dugme, Buldožer – Buldožer were fantastic. We all went to the Buldožer concerts and became good friends with them.

We had a concert, where we were invited by the student cultural organisation of Ljubljana to descend on Belgrade. At the last moment we were invited as special guest stars but our drummer didn't get to the train station, nor [did] one of the guitarists. So we took the drummer of Buldožer and the keyboard player. And we played with this line-up. Actually, the first Belgrade concert was half-Pankrti and half-Buldožer, nobody knows this!

So, the situation here was that we didn't come from nothing. We came from a good history of rebel things in culture – and also kind of political rebels too, there was also some political struggle. It was a kind of strong alternative culture.

When I started, I started as a poet. A folk artist before punk, and my texts were crazy; about masturbation, about drinking, about things like that. I was eighteen. The Pankrti members came from a University for Political Studies, Sociology and Journalism. So with some other friends from this university, we had some shows. We read poetry and cooked pasta on the stage at the same time! Drinking on the stage, having fun, and I played some guitar. So it was a little bit of a crazy situation already. On [sic] our second or third concert we accepted that we would be forbidden because we knew that we were a little bit too 'strong' in the lyrics – because at that time we drank too much! But we were not forbidden – because the police, nobody, did not know what punk was – so we were lucky. And then, we were too big for them to just cut us down.

Pankrti were hated by hardcore punks. Everybody who was good was hated by hardcore punks. Because they, for me, were simply like a Nazi way of punk. This is like the New Left or like Leninists: 'The only way which is good, is our way.' When I got a compilation of punk in the early eighties there were a lot of bands like Patti Smith, who was not a punk rocker but is a fantastic musician, or let's say the Undertones; they are perfect. I like those bands like the Members and the Skids.

In 1982, when we made the second album, *Državni ljubimci* ('State's Darlings'), it was the best-reviewed album in Yugoslavia, the best album for *Džuboks* magazine and the best album for everybody – but not in Slovenia. And student radio in Slovenia did not play it often, because it was no longer really 'punk'. But this album was the most political, with the hardest songs. We made it with Gregor (Tomc) after we left the Army and we were really pissed off with the Army because you need to be one year in the Army – without fucking! I tried to escape it, I spent one month in the psychiatric hospital in Split. The son of my psychiatrist was my friend, so she was very good for me and she said you can be in [a] psychiatric hospital for one year, but you cannot go to Ljubljana. I was in a good situation there in the hospital, but there was a lot of crazy people there. I remember one time, I had my own bed and a small closet, and I opened it and there was a big shit in it. And they said to me, 'A woman brought that for you.'

Our first time in Germany, 1982, we had five concerts – Stuttgart, Nuremberg, etc. – and we realised that the German bands were like 'nursery' bands because we were really the 'stars' of punk rock for them. We were a real attraction! We had a sold-out concert in Tubingen University with more than 800 people. In '83 we played in Rome at a big alternative festival in front of 5000 people. I thought at that time that something was happening. I don't know why we didn't have more success. That was the first time we played 'Bandiera Rossa' and it was crazy! We played in Italy again and a lot of fascists came. It was a festival for maybe 1000 people and 2000 fascist skins came. So when we played 'Bandiera Rossa' it was a little strange.

Today, our song 'Osmi Dan' is really big in the Basque country. A well-known Basque band now plays it as their encore, and it's the greatest hit of that band. A crowd of about 4000 or 5000 people [were] singing it. We realised this three or four weeks ago in Berlin when a lot of Basques came!

One of the really positive things about Yugoslavia was that we could travel all over the world at that time – much more than Americans. We could go to the Far East, we could go to African countries. We could go to Arab countries because Tito was the President of the Non-Aligned countries at that time. So, we could even go to the West. We could travel. You know, we made the song 'Behind the Iron Curtain' but it was, for us, more or less like a provocation because this was not the 'Iron Curtain'. So that's why we were a really special country. And that's why, I think, they needed to destroy us. In my opinion, Yugoslavia – and Slovenia – was destroyed because it could have been a good state. Maybe, if we went with a federated way, we could be a country with six or seven independent republics with a system which is West, or East, or maybe unaligned. The Yugoslavian way of living could be, for sure, better. But, as we see, the big rulers – like Putin or Trump – don't like unaligned states. In the world now it is not about solving the problem of how people can live better, it's about how the rich can become richer.

If we start talking politics, there is no end story. Some people were kind of anarchist and opposed to all totalitarianism in every way. I'm a little bit more liberal about it. I saw Marshal Tito's rule a little bit different. He was one of the most important leaders in the world in the twentieth century. He made some mistakes, Ok. Everybody makes some mistakes. People say, 'Oh the Communists stole so much money', but how much money did Tito steal? Nothing. He got himself somewhere he could swim, so that's like every chief. But it is not like now with the privatisation. This was not privatisation it was state-owned, by the people. Do you know Brijuni?[1] This was not the property of Tito's family. But now in Slovenia these tycoons they want to privatise everything. That was ours and they want to privatise it. Just one of these tycoons has stolen ten times more than Tito ever has.

---

1. The Brijuni Islands are a string of small islands in the Adriatic, close to the coast of Croatia. One of which, Veliki Brijun, Tito made his Summer Residence.

SEVEN
The Ljubljana Punk Rock Taxi Tour

DAY FIVE (Part One)

Triggered by fear of oversleeping and blowing the opportunity to take in more of Ljubljana before catching our return to Zagreb in the early afternoon, I wake a few minutes before the 7:29 alarm. This, despite another late night. Clearly, I am not the only one. Tomislav is already dressed and is just leaving the room. On hearing me wake, Tomislav turns back and says, 'Have you seen the weather? It's shit'. I look up at the rain-streaked windows. It is obvious that our plan to walk the 5 kilometres to the central bus station – taking in the many photo opportunities en route – will have to be abandoned. I relax, turn off the imminent alarm and pull the covers over my head. Thirty minutes later and I still cannot get back to sleep, so I admit defeat and, reluctantly, get dressed.

I make a coffee and settle down for a quiet morning. My mobile phone buzzes with an incoming text: 'Hey Barry, if you need a lift to the center I am ready, you can call me'. It is from Marin Rosić – the 'star' of the Pankrti documentary and, in the words of his Facebook profile, 'Taxiist/Anarhiist'. We pack hurriedly, tidy and exit the apartment to meet Marin on the lane at the end of the track. The rain has ceased now but the sky is a mass of bulging, grey clouds. They hang immobile, heavy and threatening. Marin pulls up, his driver-side window is down, he is smoking and shouts, 'Hey Barry, at last we meet'. Even while seated in the car, it is clear that Marin is an imposing figure in his standard-issue green bomber-jacket, beloved of skinheads the world over. He has closely cropped hair and heavy-rimmed glasses. He laughs exuberantly. His voice is deep and rasping – like a subterranean, Balkan Tom Waits. We jump into the 'taxi'. Marin asks how much time we have. We tell him of our original plan to see the punk rock sights of Ljubljana. We ask if we could pay him to take in the sights on the way to the bus station. Marin laughs again. Even more heartily. 'Of course. Of course. Let's go then. I have a plan.' This immediately makes me think of cartoons when you just know that someone is going to get into trouble. In Marin's company, it is difficult not to smile.

Marin does indeed have a plan. Over the next three hours, we are treated to his very personalised tour. We begin at the music school where Pankrti rehearsed and then it is on to the gymnasium/high school where they played their first gig, almost exactly forty years previously. Here we discover it is Election Day in Slovenia and, luckily for us, that means that these public buildings are open. On any other Sunday we would be limited to taking a few photos of exteriors. But, as luck would have it, with Marin's polite persuasiveness – aided no doubt by his daunting physique – we are allowed access to most of the buildings since they are doubling as polling stations. We stop for a quick photo opportunity with the plaque which marks that first gig. Marin tells us it is twenty years now since the plaque was placed on this spot. Our next stop is Šentvid Hall, the venue for the legendary Pankrti live album *Freedom* ('Svoboda') '82. In the suburb of Šiška, Marin points out a building which he says was once the venue for one of Eastern Europe's first gay festivals. He belly-laughs as he tells us it is now a Mormon Church. We then pull up outside another cultural centre and venue, 'Klub K-4', which has a leading role in Slovenia's punk and alternative music cultures. Marin laughs again and says that everything now seems to be about young people and nightclubs.

From there we take in various iconic venues en route to Metelkova; one-time JNA barracks and now one of Europe's longest-established, anti-establishment, counter-cultural, squat communities. Metelkova is an iconic space, and on the surface somewhat contradictory. It is a symbol of a modern post-war independent Slovenia, but one which seems to nod determinedly in the direction of a socialist past which valued cultural activities. Prior to being occupied by the JNA it had been home to the armies of fascist Italy and Nazi Germany. It is the Balkan version of the much more celebrated – despite being tainted by its association with drugs, violence and crime – Christiana Freetown in Copenhagen or ADM in Amsterdam. In the early 1990s, after the punks, artists and counter-cultural activists declared Metelkova an autonomous zone, there were tensions with local and national authorities. But in more recent years there has been consensus, albeit with existential questions over the balance between being outside of the establishment and yet reliant on its benevolence for protection from the developers and moneymen.

We stroll aimlessly through the 12,500 square metres, walled, former military base. It is almost deserted. The air this late Sunday morning is chill and damp. The rain returns, but now with a vengeance. Under geometric awnings we shelter to smoke a cigarette and hear Marin's tales of Metelkova. Beneath apocalyptic skies, the only sound other than Marin's rich rasp is the rain dripping prodigiously until it becomes a stream. Amongst the scrap-metal statues, murals and graffiti, the atmosphere just now is perhaps a little depressing. But it is at night that Metelkova comes to life as hundreds, sometimes thousands, cross the river to watch, perform, participate, debate and drink. Tomislav is talking with a man in his thirties or forties, the only resident who has approached us. He has the look of someone who knows what it is like to be exposed to the elements. He laughs, Tomislav laughs and hands him his tobacco and some cigarette papers. Marin says, 'Come on. We must go if we want to have time for a drink before you leave'.

We finish our tour, head back to the taxi and exit the complex. After a five-minute drive we stop at a roadside café bar. Protected from the rain by a large parasol, we pass an hour over coffee, beers and sandwiches. Marin is a natural host. A natural raconteur; a natural comedian. We could easily spend the rest of the day here. But reluctantly, it is time for us to make our way to the bus station. We cannot afford to miss our bus since there is still a possibility of an interview tonight in Zagreb. Marin drives us to the station and waits with us until our bus pulls in. Whilst waiting Marin hands me several CDs and DVDs. My first two attempts to pay for his time are met with a dismissive wave of the hand. My third attempt is met with that subterranean, Balkan Tom Waits: 'Do you want to leave Ljubljana alive?'

I am reasonably sure he could kill me if he really wanted to.

MARIN ROSIĆ: On the Road in Ljubljana

Marin Rosić. Ljubljana © Tomislav 'Tompa' Zebić (2017)

What is there to say about Marin Rosić? Marin is the main character, the navigator and emissary for the Pankrti documentary *Music Is the Art of Time* – like Wilko Johnson in the superb Dr Feelgood documentary *Oil City Confidential*. Marin discovered punk and, like many of us, his life was changed irrevocably. Marin Rosić is one of those who in the very best sense was born to be a punk. This means being true to yourself but having a social conscience, having a healthy disrespect for authority imposed whilst remaining true to personal ethics, being generous and irreverent whilst striving to squeeze the best out of life. And laughing. There is a lot of laughter when Marin is present. He is also a songwriter and frontman with Carina (Customs/Douane) and a fanatical collector of punk music and memorabilia. The impression I am left with is that Marin is a one-man shot of adrenaline in the Slovenian (and wider ex-Yugo) punk rock community.

For the next four hours, we are treated to a personal, punk rock taxi tour in the company of a legend.

* * *

I am of that generation, born in '64. Our parents had a flat and when they died, I inherited the flat, and I don't need a lot of money. I don't have any credit or bank cards or anything. I'm a free man!! My wife works, and I work with the taxi, but it's not such a big thing. We live normally, we don't have any money to 'invest' or such things. My mother was a home-girl and my father was a graphic engineer in a printing factory. And in the seventies and eighties, they did a great fucking job and they have a great pension. He retired in 1990, before the break-up (of Yugoslavia), and he died this year. So he took a pension from them for twenty-six years – €1080 every month![1] And he lived great. His factory was very successful, and they put a lot of money into those funds. But a lot of people who worked for forty years now have a pension of €500, and €500 is nothing. Jesus Christ! You can't live with €500.

I heard music on Radio Študent. And also Trieste, Italy. It's very close to here; it's less than 100 kilometres. And Old Gorica in the Italian part of Gorica town. These places had two brilliant record stores. In Trieste it was 'Discotheque 33' and in Gorica it was 'Old Swan' – and those two guys had all the records. If they didn't have the records they would say, 'In two or three weeks, I will order it and I will have those records'. I mean, what is 100 kilometres? You can go there by bus. I had my passport and my parents didn't know. I left for school and had two hours on the bus there and two hours back. I have one hour there, and in five hours I am back. They (parents) didn't know I had been in 'the West'. Jesus Christ! We had a source of records in our neighbourhood, only 100 kilometres away! In those two stores you could buy everything you wanted. I remember in 1980 I went to Trieste with a friend of mine and I found the first LP of the Dead Kennedys – *Fresh Fruit For Rotting Vegetables* – and they had only two copies, one for him and one for me because I found it first. And when we got back to Ljubljana we went directly to Radio Študent. And the big chief of Radio Študent stopped the programme and put this record on.

Igor Vidmar was a big, big, big man in the Yugoslavian punk scene. He was on Radio Študent in '75. Before punk of course. But he cut his hair immediately, the first day when he heard punk rock. He had – like John Peel – great radio sessions. Radio Študent had some deal with Rough Trade or Virgin, and in '78 [and] '79 we knew everything which was going on in [the] British scene.

---

1. For comparison, at this time, the UK State Pension was equivalent to €187 per week or €810 per month.

The Communist Party had the Youth Communist Party and they made this magazine *Polet*. It was a state policy. And the Youth of the Party made all of the radio stations, all of the papers. And all of the bands were playing in the shade of the Communist Party! But it was very free you know. We had a big holiday on 25 May. It's Tito's birthday – it's called the 'Day Of Youth'– and you didn't go to school. In the eighties we had concerts on 25 May and all the punk bands played these concerts. Today, only totally shit bands play on those student parties. It is unbelievable, students are totally shit today! In communist times it was the punk bands playing at those things. And today, in capitalist times, only totally pop-shit playing on those events. Because the punk bands could only make some money at concerts like this, when somebody hired you to play on the birthday party of Tito!

In '78 I first saw Pankrti in the student campus in the city centre. There were a lot of the first punk rock concerts there. In '78, '79 [and] '80, all bands played there. The first English band I saw was the Stranglers. It was '78 here in Hala Tivoli – it's big hall – with 999 as the first band. Then the second band who came here – and it's the most important concert in Yugoslavian punk – was the Ruts in early 1980. It was a great concert and I think the Croatian band Paraf played for the last time, with the original Paraf trio. they played at Hala Tivoli in January or February '80. It was a most important concert for punks in Yugoslavia because they played, also, in Zagreb and Belgrade.[2] In Belgrade I think it was the first time for people to see new music. I got *The Crack* LP before they came here. I bought it in Trieste, of course. In the summer of '80 my friend gave me the first Cockney Rejects album, *Cockney Rejects Greatest Hits Volume One*, and he said, 'Hey, now, in London this is it!'

I saw the Ramones in '79 with the UK Subs. they played here across the border in Udine, Italy; it's 150–160 kilometres from here. But the UK Subs were better to me then than the Ramones. And then in the eighties I saw the UK Subs at the student campus here in Ljubljana, in the dining hall. When we saw the UK Subs first time in '79, I said to my schoolmates, 'Fuck, this guy is so unbelievably old!' He was ten years older than the Ramones. Now the Ramones are all dead and he's still playing! But five or six years ago UK Subs were playing in Metelkova and I took my *Another Kind of Blues* LP to the concert. Backstage one old security guy asked me, 'What's this?'

I said, 'It's for Charlie to sign'.

And he said, 'Ah, old stuff'.

I said, 'I watched the UK Subs in '79'.

And he said, 'Where did you watch the UK Subs in '79?'

---

2. The Ljubljana gig was on 3 February 1980 and the Ruts also played in Rijeka.

I said, 'In Udine'.

'Wow', he said, 'when they supported the Ramones? I was there!'

That bodyguard was a friend of Charlie Harper and he was at the concert in '79 in Udine. Can you believe that? They are friends for forty years and still together. Big respect. And then Charlie Harper signed the LP and said, 'Give it to the guitarist to sign'. It was the same guitarist, Nicky Garratt! The Ramones, you know, were not a big thing here in Ljubljana. The Ramones were a big thing in Zagreb and in Pula. In Belgrade they were a totally big thing.

I was one year in the Army. After high school, if you go to college then you could go to the Army for eleven months or for one year. But if you did not go to college you would go for fifteen months. It was '82 when I went to the Army. I was sent to the Bulgarian border which was so far from here – oh fuck! I had not such a bad time there because every day you could break a lot of rules. I was very tough when I was eighteen or nineteen, and a good fighter here in Ljubljana because, us punk rockers, everybody attacked us – all the time. And my part of the city was very tough, they were aggressive if you looked different. But in my part of the city there were two or three older guys who were the chiefs there. And those guys were very 'famous', and they liked me. They told people, 'If you have some problems with him, go one-on-one', not ten people waiting for me when I came home from school. One-to-one was no problem because I was really, really, good at fighting.

And then I went to the Army and it was great, you know. I beat two, three, four older guys and everybody saw me. Some guys from Ljubljana sent me cassettes of new music – like Rudimentary Peni! I had a tape player and those poor guys from the mountains, they were people who first saw a train when they came to the Army! People from Bosnia or Kosovo, and some parts of Croatia and Serbia too. You can imagine, there's a guy who first saw the train when he came to the Army, and then he must listen to Rudimentary Peni! And when I listened to hardcore punk one guy came to me and said, 'Not this! Joy Division, can you put the Joy Division on!' The people from Ljubljana posted me fanzines, and magazines, and cassettes, with new music. And we had a lot to drink there – it was pretty free. But everything changed, maybe two or three years after I was in the Army, because in Ljubljana you have a magazine called *Mladina* which was not anti-Communist, but very anti-regime and in the Army they stopped it. We had problems then with Kosovo. And, of course, the Army was the most rigid system in Yugoslavia. Maybe the people who went to the Army in '84, '85 and '86 had more problems. But I was there in '82 [and] '83 and it was pretty free.

In the eighties – in Ljubljana – we had two important compilations: the first is *Novi Punk Val* ('New Punk Wave'), [and] the second is *Lepo Je* ('It's Nice'). *Lepo Je* is an album with five bands: one band is Sund, another is Kuzle and both are from

Idrija. Kuzle had lots of great tunes, great songs. It's unbelievable, they played in 1979 as very young kids, they are my generation – so were fourteen or fifteen years old when they started. But they made really, really good songs, great tunes, melodies with good words. So Šund and Kuzle are both from Idrija, and you also have on this compilation two bands from Ljubljana – Ljubljanski Psi and Buldogi – and the fifth band was Indust Bag from Metlika, on the Croatian border. And this band is still playing together now! We played together with them fourteen days ago.

I have a punk band and we're still playing – Carina. I'm the youngest guy in the band! The drummer and bass player played in Berlinski zid, a great punk band. For ten years they played in Laibach. One is fifty-six and one is sixty-four. So he was born in '53! But he is still looking like a desperado for Spaghetti Westerns! One bad guy who they kill in the first five minutes of the movie! We recorded an album in 2006 and then last year we recorded another album. The band was formed in 2000 and we're old punks. Now we also have two backing vocalists and we have a trombone, for fun.

Ten years ago, when Pankrti had the 'thirty years anniversary', we played before them – 7000 people Jesus Christ! We played with Chumbawamba at one big festival halfway between Ljubljana and Zagreb. We recorded our CD in the studio of the guy who played Hammond organ with Buldožer. Buldožer was my, like the Animals. My first 'wow' band. And today I have all the records, I am a really, really big fan of Buldožer, like Pankrti.

Some things from before punk I still listen to today. My favourite band from the sixties is the Animals. I don't know but maybe because when I was a little boy there was this one television show – it was in ten parts – *All You Need Is Love*. And one episode is like Country Music, or Blues and then one episode was British Rhythm and Blues – the Beatles, the Stones. But when I saw the Animals, they were playing 'We Gotta Get Out of This Place'. Jesus Christ! Great. And the Animals is, for me, the best band from Britain in the sixties. But then came punk. OK, maybe when we were kids we listened a little to glitter rock, glam rock – like Slade. I didn't like Black Sabbath and Heavy Metal, but Slade were OK, Sweet too. But the first concert I saw was Uriah Heep in Hala Tivoli. And there were chairs in there. When they started playing, people trashed all the chairs; it was '76 I think, or '77 maybe. Totally insane! Maybe the first good concert I saw was Dr Feelgood, I was a kid then! I think it was '78, I have the ticket at home.

After punk I listened to American music like Hüsker Dü and this kind of music. And then Sub Pop. I watched Nirvana when they were still a small band, in a village near Trieste – Muja (Muggia) – it's a village of 2000 people near Trieste. It's near the border, maybe 10 kilometres. I think it was in '91. I think the concert was meant to be in Ljubljana, but then we had problems here in June '91 with the war, and I think because of safety they didn't want to come to Ljubljana. I think the agency who organised this put the concert in Muja, in Italy. Maybe 500 or 600 people were there and 95 per cent were from former Yugoslavia.[3] We watched the Dead Kennedys in 1981 in Gorica, in a sports hall, and I think 90 per cent was from former Yugoslavia. I met a whole band of Goths on the bus from Rijeka – four guys and one girl – they came on and everything on the bus was black! It was the normal bus from Ljubljana to Gorica – not a special bus – and then you walked across the border. And there we met a big group of punk rockers from Bologna. I don't know why they came to Gorica, maybe the Dead Kennedys didn't have a gig in Bologna, but they were total anarchists. I think the city government in Bologna was communist during the Second World War. All the time the communists have power in Bologna. Livorno football supporters are big communists, they have Yugoslavian flags and Tito flags at the games. I saw a Stalin picture and I thought, 'Wow! This is really hardcore'. And they are always singing 'Bandiera Rossa' or 'Bella Ciao', two anti-fascist songs. Livorno is a harbour on the west side of Italy and they are really crazy communist fans – anarchist and everything else.

We drive to the Metelkova squat.

This is the squat. It was an Army complex. Millions of tourists come here. This place is my favourite place because five times a year we play here. There are three clubs here. The UK Subs played here. You can see the posters, UK Subs, TV Smith. The Cockney Rejects also played in Metelkova. Here is also the Museum of Contemporary Art and behind it is the hostel. It was a military jail and now it is a hostel – and you can sleep in a cell. In 1991, the Yugoslav Army left Slovenia, and the city and the state promised the Youth that they would make an urban centre for culture. But they started to ruin it because they wanted to sell the site to make a supermarket or something. And then, one night, the people organised and made a revolution. And we stayed here, and they could not throw us out. They tried – with police – but we made barricades. Now you have a lot of artists' studios and clubs; non-profit organisations, comic books; everything is here. We started to steal the electricity; you need only have a man with good brains. But now, everything is back on. They made some regulations with the City Council, paying electricity and water, but it is ours, you know? And it's a big complex. There are … nine clubs here. This is a result of seventies punk because all the people in the seventies and eighties who were doing the punk rock scene are now here.

We leave Metelkova and continue the tour.

---

3. See 'Sleeve Notes: Standing at the Gates of the West' (see page 231, this volume) for more on this famous concert.

Plaque marking site of first Pankrti concert, 1977 at Gimnazija Moste (Moste High School), Ljubljana © Tomislav 'Tompa' Zebić (2017)

Ljubljana had the first gay club in all of Eastern Europe. Jesus Christ! In some of the republics gays were criminals in the eighties. And then, in Ljubljana, in this disco called 'Disko FV 112/15' – which is now a Mormon Church – they made the first gay festival, in '83 or '84. The first two days were with gay philosophers and people speaking, and then they had a party. It was, I think, the first time in Eastern Europe when the gay population came into the light – legally – and nobody had a problem.

In Croatia and Serbia, it's like an epidemic of young people leaving. It's unbelievable. Slovenia is a small country you know. Small country, small problems. We had a good social system here. I think nobody was hungry here. We had few homeless people but maybe those people chose that situation. From parts of Yugoslavia which were very undeveloped, the people went to the West to work – to Germany. Maybe one million people from Yugoslavia worked in West Europe, Germany and France. We called them 'gastarbeiters', guest-workers.

We are typical ex-Yugoslavia. We adored British humour. *Only Fools and Horses* is a big thing here. They show it on television every year, a lot. Because it was our situation. In the eighties you know, every neighbourhood had its own Trotter Brothers and we understood this whole thing. How can the Germans and French understand this? No way. And *Spitting Image*! John Major? John Major looked like the boring bureaucrat. And *Monty Python's Flying Circus*! Some things in our politics here in the Balkans, in Croatia, in Serbia, in Slovenia … well Monty Python were little children compared with this! It's unbelievable. Of course, George Orwell was a big thing here too with all the punks.

I like books, comic books and records. And what else? Some alcohol and music. And all my money I put into those hobbies. I don't need t-shirts. I buy 50 black t-shirts for €100. Then I give them to a friend of mine who has a printing machine and he prints t-shirts for me, with my original designs. Nobody in the world has these t-shirts. And he charges me only one copy of the t-shirt. Some people they buy fancy t-shirts for €100. Jesus Christ! With crocodiles on or something. Fuck off!

I buy a litre of great domestic wine for a Euro and a half! 100 metres down the road from here on the right-hand side is my auto-electric service, one guy. Every day I come here and in the Frigidaire we have wine and beers because it's 'free'; six beers is €6 in the store. And my friend produces that wine. He has a vineyard near the Croatian border and he produces 1500 litres of wine. Old friends buy 200 litres and he sells the others. It is great, great, wine. No chemistry or nothing, totally free. And, at home, we drink this wine, for one and a half euros. We have great water and Coca-Cola bought some factories here because we have this water. Water is the most important thing when they build a factory. Like a beer factory. Heineken buys all of our breweries. They don't have an interest in beer, but in water.

EIGHT
Return to Zagreb

DAY FIVE (Part Two)

The bus from Ljubljana back to Zagreb is only two-thirds full. The rain is a constant for the journey. In this kind of rain all motorways are the same. The WC on the bus is out of order. Dunja had confidently predicted this. Tomislav and a number of fellow passengers ask the bus company staff if we can stop somewhere. They are all told the same thing; they will have to wait until we are in Croatia. At the border we all decant for the obligatory passport check. Again the passengers – now increasingly desperate to relieve themselves – ask the bus crew and again they are met with utter disregard. We rejoin the bus and two minutes later go through the entire passport process again. Now the rain is torrential, monsoon-like. Outside of the Croatian Customs Office we shelter under an awning, waiting for the bus to reappear. Passengers foolhardy enough to ask for the promised WCs are brusquely pointed in the direction of three blue 'portaloos' some 100 metres away. Several Chinese students and tourists take their chances and sprint through the unrelenting rain. 'Fuck that', says Tomislav angrily. His demeanour is, resolutely, that of a man who will not be told where he can take his ease.

My first acquaintance with ex-Yugoslavian bus drivers will prove to be prophetic. It is already becoming clear to me that in ex-Yugoslavia hospitality is paramount. But hospitality is for friends and guests. It does not always extend to the 'hospitality' sector – or even 'customers'. It is now apparent that ex-Yugoslavian bus companies seem to confuse customer service with National Service (conscription). Perhaps it is the years of conflict which are to blame or the legacy of conscription. Over the many months of this undertaking, I had asked Serbians, Croatians, Slovenians, Bosnians and Montenegrins to suggest the best of ex-Yugo movies. Almost every film suggested to me was a comedy; something I was not really expecting given the intrinsic darkness of the Balkan soul. Of course, on viewing these films the humour turned out to be as black as a raven. They also have common motifs: geese, mud, drunkenness, bottles and glasses being smashed, Gypsies, guns, sex and suicide – usually by hanging. A film may have any combination of these, and sometimes all. There were a handful of films which were suggested by just about everyone. One of these was *Ko to tamo peva?* (*Who Is Singing Over There?*)

Made in 1980, it is widely regarded to be one of the finest movies from the Tito, or Yugoslavian, era. Oddly, the twenty-one days of filming coincided with Tito's death and the official mourning period. All cultural and entertainment activities, including the making of *Ko to tamo peva?* were suspended and the film was delayed. Set in 1941, in the days immediately before the Axis invasion, the movie follows one bus and its motley collection of passengers – including newly weds, a First World War veteran, a Germanophile, young Gypsy musicians and a lecherous crooner – on the journey from rural Serbia to Belgrade. From the outset, the bus company owner and ticket collector, Krstić Senior is rude to passengers, attempts to defraud them and takes great pleasure in throwing them off the bus at the slightest excuse – providing they have already paid their fare. At one point, Krstić loads a number of pigs into a makeshift pig-pen at the back of the bus and lambasts the other passengers saying, 'When I sell the pigs in Belgrade, I'll earn more money than your tickets brought me'. Having travelled by bus across three of the ex-Yugoslavian nations, I totally understood why this film is so much part of the national psyche(s). Regimes and ideologies may come and go, nations may collapse and be reborn, and neighbour turn against neighbour, but in former Yugoslavia, the irascibility of bus company staff is immutable.

We arrive back in Zagreb in the middle of that Sunday afternoon. There is no rain in the city. We now have an interview confirmed for 6 p.m. with Matija Vuica and Jure Popović formerly of Trotakt Projekt, so we head back to my apartment to shower, change our clothes and refuel with coffee. The venue for the interview is to be 'Johann Franck' on Ban Jelačić trg. 'That figures', says Tomislav, 'it's one of the most chic bars in Zagreb [...] in Croatia!' Not prepared for chic, I retrieve the one shirt in my travelling wardrobe. I am self-conscious that I look a mess. Then Tomislav asks to borrow one of my t-shirts because he has no clean clothes whatsoever. We order a taxi and wait on the road outside Gruška 4. The driver is impressed that we are on our way to meet such celebrated company. Ban Jelačić square is almost deserted. From outside, 'Johann Franck' looks like it may once have been a five-star hotel or a fin-de-siècle, blue-chip bank. Inside it is all polished wood and subtle low-lighting. Above the cavernous ground level, huge stone pillars support an enormous mezzanine. It is empty, save for three or four people tucked away at corner tables.

We can see no sign of Matija and Jure. We wait downstairs at a standing table – clearly out of our comfort zones. Neither of us removes our coat or hat, nor even slips our equipment bag from our shoulder. Three underworked waiters at the bar are laughing and discussing which is going to come across and take our order. Immaculately dressed in pressed white shirts, black trousers and old-fashioned black aprons they could be straight out of an upmarket Viennese coffee house. One of them approaches; he smiles sympathetically as though understanding our unease, and takes our order. Within a minute Matija and Jure arrive, each looking every inch the self-assured celebrities. Both smile broadly and their greetings are warm and genuine. They march through the building looking for a suitable table for the interview but, having judged the smoking room too noisy, they say we should go somewhere else.

The four of us walk across the square and down a side street to another café bar. 'The Bulldog' is not as prosaic as it sounds and is quite similar to 'Johann Franck' – although perhaps without the air of exclusivity. We go upstairs and find a table on the mezzanine level where smoking is permitted. Another smartly dressed waiter approaches us but is in no hurry to take our order. I guess he recognises our famous company. Jure leaves us for ten minutes and returns with two dark-umber paper bags with white rope handles. The white logo says 'Matija Vuica fashion and design' and both are loaded with Trotakt Projekt CDs, DVDs and two of Jure's books. Matija and Jure are undoubtedly thoughtful and generous. But they are also down-to-earth in a way which suggests they have not forgotten their provincial roots. The interview lasts for more than three hours, although the time passes quickly in this engaging and candid company.

We bid our goodbyes but plan to meet up later in the week because Jure has a copy of Darko Glavan's *Punk: Potpuno Uvredljivo Negiranje Klasike* (a 'backronym' of PUNK, the rough translation being 'Punk: Completely Offensive Neglecting Classics') we can borrow. It has been a long day already, but Daniela has invited me to join her and Tomislav for a home-cooked meal since she is worried that I am not eating sufficient to maintain the demands of our planned agenda. They live in the suburb of Prečko, where we had met Zdenko the previous week. The tram skates smoothly down the centre of a broad modern highway heading west away from the centre. It is not yet 10 p.m. but there are very few people on the streets and very little traffic as we cross a major junction and pull to a halt. Tompa and Daniela's apartment is the entire upper floor of a white house beside the road, just a few metres from the tram stop at which we alighted. Tomislav apologises for the apartment being 'not very big – typical Zagreb apartment', but it is significantly bigger than my Airbnb. Daniela tells me that they are buying the apartment outright and 'in eleven years' time I can give up work, sell it, and we can move to the sea'. That night I am well fed and watered; a traditional Bosnian dish of mushrooms cooked in milk is generously accompanied by beers and Istrian white wine. Daniela, Tomislav and Daniela's cousin Kićo are easy company and it is a fine way to end the first week.

We order a cab to take me back to my apartment and Tomislav and I wait outside on the utterly deserted streets. Eventually, it arrives. The taxi driver speaks competent English and on the journey back to Gruška 4 wants to know why I am in Zagreb. I tell him I am here to write a book about ex-Yugoslav punk rock. He says,

'Do you know of KUD Idijoti?' So I tell him all about Demob and 'No Room For You'. 'You played on that? That's your record? No fucking way man. No fucking way!' I assure him that it is all true and that on Tuesday we are heading to Pula to meet Sale Veruda from KUD Idijoti. 'Fuck man. I am old punk. I know this song so well. Demob song and KUD Idijoti song. Fuck. Wait until I tell the other old punks.' I pay the fare. We shake hands over the seats and bid fraternal goodbyes and good luck. I head into the darkened apartment block. It is 2 a.m., Monday morning, Week Two.

MATIJA VUICA and JURE POPOVIĆ: The Bulldog, Central Zagreb

Matija Vuica, Jure Popović. Bulldog, Zagreb © *Tomislav 'Tompa' Zebić (2017)*

When I told Croatian friends of my plans to interview Matija and Jure they were surprised. In Croatia today, Matija and Jure are a celebrity couple – well-known and glamorous TV personalities. There was some surprise that I would be mixing in this rarefied company. But there was more to it than that. Matija and Jure had initially entered the wider public consciousness with what could be described as an art-pop band, Gracia. They had had a measure of commercial success with Gracia, but this had perhaps obscured their original enterprise – the post-punk, industrial, multimedia Trotakt Projekt. An enterprise of which many seemed only vaguely aware. Matija was frequently described to me as 'Croatia's most famous fashion designer', or 'Croatia's Vivienne Westwood'. Jure is known as a composer, musician, musicologist, author, poet and also something of a mystic. I, of course, had no backstory and was simply intrigued.

Online I found a documentary called *Trotakt Projekt R.I.P.* and was very soon enthralled. In Jure's opening sequence he walks along a dockside in their provincial hometown of Metković. A few blocks of the familiar red-roofed and white-walled houses lead lazily away from a broad river which reflects the riverside buildings against the blue sky. A green and brown flood plain stretches away to an encircling wall of mountains. The impression is of isolation. Of an outpost. On the opposite bank stand the industrial cranes, silos and warehouses which service the dockyard traffic. But in the film there is no dockside traffic. Nothing moves on the water save for a solitary seagull and the shivering reflections. Jure kicks stones into the dock. His opening lines are,

> [a]t that time the New Wave appeared. The new British scene included bands from 'smaller communities', from Sheffield, Manchester and Liverpool. My version of that was Metković, of course. Old industrial cities of England, while my reality was watching through my window those silos in Metković port. That sounds ridiculous today, but to me then, that was like an initial spur for my creative work.

Matija is filmed at the Tate Gallery in London, beside the Thames and at London Bridge station. She tells of how the young couple obsessed not only about the bands from London 'but also the bands that were springing up, outside of London, in the so-called provinces [...] as real provincials we dreamt that if they could succeed, so could we'. I was hooked.

Metković is an inland port on the River Neretva some 10 kilometres from the coast and has a population of less than 17,000. It is closer to the Albanian capital of Tirana, or Skopje in Macedonia, or even Bari in Italy, than to Zagreb which is more than 520 kilometres by road to the northeast. Hard against the border with Bosnia and Herzegovina, it lies in a complicated geopolitical location. Just 10 kilometres from Metković, Bosnia and Herzegovina has its own narrow strip of coastline – thus severing the body of Croatia from its southern exclave of south Dalmatia. To reach the historic capital of Dubrovnik – now immortalised around the world as the setting for Kings Landing in *Game of Thrones* and Cersei Lannister's 'Walk of Shame' – from Metković requires two-border crossings or a boat trip. Here was someone who knew what it was like to grow up away from the capitals or the cultural centres, not just of the world but of their own small country. Here was someone who was interested in English culture and social history. And here was someone who talked lovingly of Sheffield.

When the interview was over and the recorder shut down, Jure and Matija told me how grateful they are that a 'stranger' asked to hear their history and the many histories of punk, new wave and post-punk in Yugoslavia. Their willingness to share is not driven by unruly egos. Matija stressed that Jure is an obsessive collector and archivist, a cultural historian. 'R.I.P.' in the title of the documentary is a play on Rest In Peace, but in this case means 'Reprise of a Lost Story'.

This is part of the lost part of their story.

JURE: We were both born and raised in Metković.

MATIJA: My mother sold on the market and my dad was a baker. My mother had only two classes of Grade School and then to work. If you know how to write and to read, then you go to work. But when you think about it, we all came out really good.

JURE: My mother worked in an office, in electrical distribution, and my dad worked on maintenance in the general hospital.

JURE: Metković then was a small town that was not suitable enough for my creative aspirations even though I wanted to prove the opposite – looking for similarities with the British music of the provinces. This comparison was pure fiction – it did not have a strong point in reality. For example, if we take the relationship between Metković and Sheffield, which I then took as a musical reference, there is a huge difference in population size and the difference in industry is unimaginable. However, that fiction gave me a decisive stimulus for creative work.

JURE: Our music was completely different from other ex-Yugoslavian punk, because we started first from Krautrock and then more from British bands, for example Roxy Music – my favourite – and David Bowie. After that, in the 1980s, we listened to bands like the first Human League and Cabaret Voltaire and more electronic bands. Because when the Japanese made very cheap electronic synthesisers and other things for making music, then more bands could make music. Moog and the other American things were very, very expensive. And when I watched a BBC documentary about electronic music, I saw the same things in Depeche Mode and me. For example; Roland – the rhythm machine, 'Doctor Rhythm 55'; sequencers, the 'KORG 20' – like a 'Mini Moog' – we had the same in Croatia.

JURE: That's why the Yugoslavian electronic scene could happen at the same time as England or the US. Because instruments were cheap and available. It was different in the age before, like the Progressive Rock age, instruments for Progressive Rock were very expensive. For us with electronic instruments, it was like punk because anyone could play, you could improvise it.

MATIJA: We were like something so, so special at that time. Everything else in Metković was very small. A small city, cold boring winter, with nothing happening except our music. So, all the time we were playing his songs, and we had only five songs. And we went to Zagreb with the five songs, just like that! He explained everything he felt about small towns at that time with his songs. There is a song, 'Last Autumn In The Big City', which was about everyone who came to a big town to study. And it was our 'rap' – the first rap in Croatia. Dark, dark, very slow, very like

Joy Division. And when you listen to these songs you can discover Metković in that time. And in that time, in the early 1980s, even the people from Zagreb were like, 'Where is Metković?'

JURE: The trigger for that demo cassette was Bowie's *Berlin*. When we arrived with the demo in *Polet*, they were amazed: 'How did you come to this? Where did you get this urge to do this?' I said, 'In my imagination. I describe. I see the Cathedral with distance better than someone standing in front of her. And the ones who are praying below.' It's the same for musicians from Sheffield, Liverpool, Manchester. I took a step back and took a different perspective on things – small is better. When I listened to Kraftwerk's album *Trans Europe Express*, in my mind I was creating a vision of the Russian Steppes. But the way is harder. The way from the provinces is harder than from Zagreb or London.

JURE: In every small province, there is a small group of people who 'get it'. And back then it was without the internet.

MATIJA: Because in that time, in the early eighties, there was no Facebook, no internet, no nothing.

JURE: It was *The Face* magazine. We have all the editions of it.

MATIJA: We subscribed to *The Face* and discovered the fashion and everything about the British scene.

JURE: The logo for Trotakt Projekt, the type, is from *The Face*.

JURE: There was a magazine called *Studio* and there was a small article about the Clash or the Saints from Australia – and the Saints is for me the number one punk band, especially the first album. So I saw these pictures in the paper, without songs, without melodies and I built my own picture of what it would sound like. From the little pictures of UK bands in the studio, in the magazines we got from the UK, I would create musical images just based on those pictures with no sound. We could not hear many bands. So I imagined, 'How does this band sound?' I made a song like 'London Calling', before I heard it! The same riff. From the pictures.

MATIJA: Yes, there is a song from Trotakt Projekt which is beginning like the Clash. And the Clash at that time did not have that song released.

JURE: It was like synchronicity. I wanted to get a fusion between Nile Rogers and the alienation of Krautrock. Because I was totally obsessed with Britain and Krautrock and Chic. Because I was a DJ. And the Au Pairs of course.

MATIJA: The Au Pairs, were my favourite. Can you imagine, that in fucking Metković in that time, somebody listened to this kind of music! The Au Pairs, etc.

JURE: My big influences were always, always the Rolling Stones. Especially the film *Gimme Shelter*. And then the film with Hazel O'Conner, *Breaking Glass*. I think that was the first new wave film. But *Gimme Shelter* was the first real influence for me. T Rex was also important for me because in the poetry of Marc Bolan there were very, very mystic things. It was music for teenagers but not artificial; very sophisticated pop-music. Marc Bolan was very much like David Bowie at the beginning. Because, like David Bowie, Marc Bolan took it on himself to write it as a pop-song. I like glam rock. Glam rock is so important. Because of the visual identity.

MATIJA: But what about Suzi Quatro? Because in all this T Rex, etc., etc. there is the great Suzi Quatro!!

JURE: In 1981, the Gang of Four performed the Biennale concert, I was there. It was the biggest concert on that tour – 4000 people. And in Europe, in that time they were playing in front of a few hundred people. And we went by train to see the Human League in Ljubljana in '82.

MATIJA: Yes, and after the gig I slept at the train station.

JURE: We slept on the benches.

MATIJA: And then he went away to Split (to college), but I was in Metković.

JURE: I was in parallel in Split and Metković.

MATIJA: I was just in Metković. One time when he was coming back from Metković, he came with the songs. And I was his brand-new girlfriend at that time. And because he came with these songs and I was his girlfriend, he said, 'Can you sing these songs?' And he called some other musicians from Metković, they were very, very, young. Much younger than we were. They were seventeen years old, Jure and me twenty-three. So, he made four or five songs and we were playing gigs in like some kind of, not garage, but something like that. And at the same time here in Zagreb was this great project YURM.[1] And we sent a cassette up because we had nothing more than a cassette, recorded with a cassette player on the floor. They were playing and I was singing. Of course, we had no studio. And we sent this cassette to Zagreb, to *Polet*. By this time I was studying here in Zagreb. I came back and *Polet* are

---

1. Annual Yugoslavian National Rock Music Awards organised by the Communist Party Youth magazine *Polet*.

calling me, they are looking for me: 'Who is this band?' It was like, 'What? What is this that's happening?' And it just happened like that.

MATIJA: I have to tell you how we came to Zagreb for the first YURM competition. Of course, we came on the train with all these instruments, sitting on the floor and with a Leslie amplifier and speakers. In that time, from Metković to Zagreb would take about ten to twelve hours! With the train stopping everywhere. With all those instruments! And I was sitting on this Leslie.

JURE: In the toilets.

MATIJA: And then walking from the train. The Leslie has trailing wheels and we didn't have the money for taxis, no van, no taxi, nothing. And the next year, they called us again, as guests for YURM. And everything was super, but no LP. There was no LP, they decided it was not commercial.

JURE: We had three cover stories in *Polet*. And were the winners of YURM two times.

MATIJA: We were playing all over ex-Yugoslavia. Travelling with our instruments on the train. No money but a lot of fun.

JURE: After YURM, there was touring and demos and demos and demos and demos, again, again, again. New demos; four, five, times.

JURE: And later we played the Biennale in Zagreb, with the Anti-Nowhere League! It was the Anti-Nowhere League, Hallucination Company – which was Falco's band – and Laibach. And us! Trotakt Projekt! Regarding the Biennale in Zagreb, I am very proud of that because it really was only for avant-garde music. It was only for two years they had rock-bands like Anti-Nowhere League. I managed to position fucking 'Metković' on the big posters. 'Trotakt Projekt, Metković, Hallucination Company, Wien and Anti-Nowhere League, London'. Can you imagine these three? Metković, Wien, London? Yes, finally we have it!

MATIJA: So, this is an anecdote about that gig; this was the first big money we ever earned from our playing, 1983. It was big. At that time, big! It was din3000 (Yugoslavian dinars), which was like today, €3000 Euros.

JURE: A full-bag!

MATIJA: It was like, 'Finally, money!' And we went, all the band on the train to Split, to make the first album. We were going to make our first album in the studio in Split. And we now, finally, have money for the studio. We went to the train and the money was in this 'pocket' from my father. A very old, vintage wallet. We put the money inside and it was the full sleeping car for the three of us. We were travelling by night. The man who was selling the drinks came into the sleeping car and asked, 'What do you want to drink?' I took out this wallet and he saw that money. I paid him for the drinks, and we went to sleep. We woke up at Split, and there was no money. We were without any money. And then our drummer had to work a lot – a lot – just so that we can pay for the studio. In Croatia, we have a saying, 'Easy come. Easy go'. We went looking for that man but of course he had disappeared, because it was great money at that time. Our first money.

MATIJA: In that time, there were only two or three bands with women singers. It was Paraf, with Vim Cola, it was Xenia, Vesna Vrandečić and me. And from the very beginning, it was like, 'What is she doing in the band?' There were a lot of women singers but not 'in the band'. They were like, girl backing singers. We were so popular in that time, we had every cover of the student magazines, everything. They were coming to see, 'Who is that girl?' I was so different from how I am now. I didn't care what was happening in front of me; I was so cool. Only thinking I don't know what! No smile, no nothing. I am not that person now. You see me, I am so completely different! But because of the songs, because of what I brought from Metković, because of having nothing … In those days, in ex-Yugo, the boys and the girls tried to be equal, but they weren't.

JURE: Only in Rijeka were the male and female punks equal. It's very important to say that Rijeka was a very big punk city. And the sailors were very important, they brought LPs with new music.[2]

MATIJA: There were women singers, pop singers, jazz singers, etc. but there were not girls' 'rock' bands. It was so strange. For me, it was also not easy because my mother and my father were expecting me to finish university, to find a job, to settle down, to get married, to have children – and it was that atmosphere around the girls. Every girl. So when I started to play it was like, 'It's not a woman's place'. It's coming from a different view on the world. Different families, different backgrounds, different views on the world. And then punk happened. But there were some conservative families here. We had to break with that.

JURE: And it's a very different religion. Croatian Catholicism is very different to British Protestantism.

---

2. In the documentary Jure says that he wanted to be a sailor because then he would travel to places where he could go to gigs and buy records to bring back to Metković.

MATIJA: You know why I can be a woman singer in a men's band? Even in Metković? Because I was different in Metković, different to other girls. I dressed different. I had a mini skirt and everyone else had a midi skirt. But I was excellent in school, this is the only reason I can do everything I did – why I can do everything I liked to do. Because I was excellent in school. I was 'Tito's Pioneer'. I had Tito's scholarship. It really surprised everybody because I was not in the Party. But my family was poor and, in some situations, excellent children can get this scholarship. And that was me. But I was different to other girls. That's the reason I could be in that band at that time. Nobody else from Metković was like that.

JURE: And since then, until now, there has never been another band from Metković.

JURE: But there is a philosophical question – it doesn't matter where you are born – about Tito, religion and other things. It was the 'outlet vent' that Tito allowed us – through pop and rock music. But the main people on the scene were children of military officers.

MATIJA: So in that situation, when you came from Metković, you were nobody here in Zagreb.

MATIJA: What was very important for us in that time was that we were a multi-media brand. Because in that time we had our photos, we had strips, projections, for action. But it was too early for that here. And we also had our own fashion. Our first concert I sewed everything for the boys – the trousers and the shirts and everything; metallic colours, it was my first beginning in fashion.

JURE: Everyone thought the photos were like Anton Corbijn and Joy Division and Manchester. But Joy Division was not the inspiration, it was Krautrock and Bowie's *Berlin* phase.

MATIJA: At that time, our record label Jugoton did not want to publish our songs because they were too 'alternative', not commercial. Very dark. So, we did all of this project ourselves. On our own label.

JURE: I insisted we would be a band from the provinces. And I referred to the bands from Sheffield. It was for me, something like that scene. But I knew that Metković, my hometown, was very small.

MATIJA: And then Jure decided to make two commercial singles: 'Now I will show you I can do that, but I don't want to do that.' And he made two songs and they were two hits in all ex-Yu. And they sold, these two singles. And, even then, they didn't give us an LP.

JURE: I made a mistake, I was very angry and mad, in Yugoslavia it was usual to copy songs from Britain and America. So I did it – and said I did it – and no-one liked it. Everyone did it. But it was my crime.

MATIJA: Then you went to the Army and that was a great problem because the boys were not the same age. The first one went in 1983 – the piano player – and then I took that place. When I was young, I had a piano teacher, so I was learning again. I was playing piano, playing chords and singing. That's why I always had to be so cool, because I had to keep concentrating. That was the second period, with me as piano player. And then Jure went to the Army, and the next one went to the Army and that was a hole in the work.

JURE: And after that, we started to be zombies! Because of the Army. It killed you in the brain. It was twelve months in the Army, it was never-ending. In this time, it was silence. I wrote only one song, called 'I Don't Care'. And we decided to finish Trotakt Projekt, period. It was three years lost in the Army. Because of the difference of the ages of all of us.

MATIJA: When he came back, he decided to have just the pyramid of the band – him, bass guitar and me. Because we knew, the other members of the band wanted to stay in Metković and we wanted to be in Zagreb. So Jure, me and the youngest – he was very young, sixteen years old – were living as three people together in that period.

JURE: We used a combination of guest players. It was the end of the eighties and it was the moment when we decided to have our own LP.

MATIJA: So Jure founded our own label, 'Magick Music'. It was the first private label in this area, of this kind of group. And with this label we published our first LP.

JURE: One year before the war.

MATIJA: The LP is out. A great LP. It is a blue cover and I am like Marilyn Monroe. And we changed the name of the group to Gracia because it was very difficult for everyone to say 'Trotakt' and everyone was, 'Why Trotakt?' and, 'What is Trotakt?' And with this LP everything is coming so good and they were inviting us, 'Come to Sarajevo, you are great. You are in first place on our top list.' But then the war is starting. Really, the war is starting. At the moment when we were at the top, war is coming. We were in Metković, because we knew war was coming and we went 'home'. It was summer and we went home. Jure, I thought he was an idiot but now I don't think so, he enlisted in the Army – like, 'Here I am, take me'. And from Sarajevo, they called us on the phone and said, 'Can you come here? You are great stars here.'

And we told them, 'No, there is a barricade around Metković we can't go anywhere'. Bad luck, again. Can you imagine that?

JURE: History recognises some, whilst the others …

MATIJA: *In Search of Tito's Punks* is a great title – I think we are exactly that. Punk is not only the way of playing guitar. It is a kind of thinking of society, of politics, and everything. So, in England, there is a different people and mentality. And their musicians express their feelings by playing strong guitars and jumping around. Our punk, that we are holding inside at that time, was inside us. And our songs – inside us. It is Zen punk! It's really Zen punk! Because we expressed – at that time – our feelings, not like you do, but a completely different way. Tito's Zen Punks!

JURE: Our souls are different to Saxon or German or …

NINE
Zagreb (1977) … and Tito's Coming to Town

DAY 6

Today is going to be a quiet day. I spend the morning checking the audio recordings from the first five days and writing up some observations while they are still fresh in my mind. This done, in preparation for today's interview, I decide to watch again the first ex-Yugo punk documentary I had seen. *Sretno Dijete* ('Fortunate Child') is an autobiographical, 2002 journey across ex-Yugoslavia, Europe and the United States in which the noted political-journalist and filmmaker Igor Mirković recalls the teenage Igor's induction into the emerging punk scene. The film begins with vivid footage of crowds celebrating Tito's 1977 visit to Zagreb. The opening images roll over a soundtrack of the song 'Sretno Dijete' by Prljavo Kazalište ('Dirty Theatre'). 'I grew up with colour war (partisan) movies. And frequent fights at school'. 'With folk songs full of pain. I'm a really happy child'.

Filmed from a moving vehicle, the newsreel shows billowing red flags and cheering masses lining the streets; some in national dress, some dressed as partisans, some on stilts, all waving the red, white and blue of Yugoslavia. Mirković's understated narrative continues,

> 1977 is an important year in the life of my generation. Punk spreads over the world, new music, new rebellion. The Queen in London celebrates her Silver Jubilee while some Sex Pistols obscenely grin at her. We also have a jubilee. Comrade Tito celebrates 40 years of Party leadership. He's coming to my town, but it wouldn't be wise to grin at him.

The footage pans back to follow Tito, wearing a sharp black suit and black gloves, waving to the crowds from a gleaming black, open-top limousine at the centre of a cavalcade. There, in the background of the tracking shots, I recognise the Croatian National Theatre where Dunja and I had paused on my first day here.

It was in *Sretno Dijete* where I first heard of the importance of *Polet*, the official paper of the 'Socialistic Youth League', to the punk scene. Talking heads tell how, prior to the 'Novi val' (new wave), *Polet* had targeted 'young Party mutants in tweed trousers'. But in 1978, it changed overnight as a group of 'rockers' appeared on its cover alongside a headline which read, 'Something's Going On'. The first of this new breed of rockers was the unknown band Prljavo Kazalište from Zagreb – whose members were just seventeen and eighteen years old. At that time, the unsophisticated teenage musicians did not know that bands like Azra, Pankrti and Paraf existed, but when *Polet* associated them it, arguably, fused a 'movement'. In the movie, *Polet* staff discuss how it was imperative that the magazine sold in sufficient numbers. The same was true for the output of the state-run record labels too. As in the United Kingdom or the United States, idealism often had its place in Yugoslavian punk. But, just as in those countries, without commercial success it would not have its platform. Perhaps the differences between our cultures may not actually have been so stark after all. Many old British punks will think immediately of Jethro Tull or Genesis when Jasenko Houra of Prljavo Kazalište says,

> The Rock Scene was actually divided. Everybody was walking around in some fur coats. Bijelo Dugme and Parni Valjak wore fur coats and high boots. Their lyrics were always about sheep or something. Always about country boys. So we never caught on to their music.

Sretno Dijete also scratches the surface of the enigmatic Johnny Štulić of Azra. Štulić was disillusioned with so much about the break-up of Yugoslavia and, claiming to have been robbed of a small fortune by the record industry, these days only occasionally breaks his reclusive cover in Utrecht to release recordings of medieval folk songs. Mirković travels to the Netherlands in an attempt to interview Johnny but, perhaps now reliant on the contradictory fame of the recluse, Štulić does not respond.

The film then maps the death of Tito onto the burgeoning new wave scene. The mother of Mirković reads the fourteen-year-old Igor's farewell to Tito:

> Zagreb said goodbye to comrade Tito yesterday, the day before. Days go by. Days go by and he is still with us. Even though Tomislav's Square was crowded it echoed with some strange omnipresent silence, silence that penetrates the heart. The blue train whistled and then departed.

Mirković describes tying and untying a red scarf in front of the mirror as he tried to emulate the singer who had had the biggest hit of that year, Darko Rundek of Haustor. This afternoon I am due to interview 'Rundek' as he is better known here. I check the clock; there is time to watch this chapter of the film before leaving for the interview. In a snow-covered park, under cold grey skies by an icy lake, a heavily made-up Rundek fronts early Haustor in a 1981 promo video. This dark – but playful – art school theatricality, making use of costumes and props, was the essence of Haustor's musical DNA. Mirković travels to Paris where Rundek is filmed cycling down busy Parisian boulevards and hanging out in the – archetypally central Parisian – neighbourhood where he and his wife have a home.

The movie identifies the 1980 staging of the 'Omladina Festival' (Youth Festival) in Subotica, Serbia as the moment when bonds emerged between the Zagreb and Belgrade new wave bands. Established in 1961, Omladina was a national, annual competition which included non-competition performances and an evening of patriotic songs. The first punk bands appeared in 1979 when Pekinška Patka ('Peking Duck') and Prljavo Kazalište performed in the non-competition section. In 1980, Omladina completed its transformation from a popular-music competition for young composers to a competition for, and festival of, rock bands. Haustor appeared alongside Šarlo Akrobata ('Charlie Acrobat' – a name sometimes used in pre-Second World War in Yugoslavia for Charlie Chaplin), Idoli, Električni Orgazam and Film. Although the new wave bands were still in a minority at Omladina 1980, they swept the board with Film taking first prize. Serendipity was at play that year; Omladina was always scheduled for May, but in May of 1980 most of Yugoslavia was mourning the death of Comrade Tito. As a result, the event was postponed until October. Mirković is one of those who attribute this chance-delay to giving momentum to the scene. He says that several of these bands who met, performed, bonded and would subsequently collaborate were still embryonic in May. But in those breakneck and combustible times, the few extra months allowed them sufficient space to develop. Rundek, characteristically, puts it rather more enigmatically: 'These guys and us, we emerged as some kind of heroes. I remember when I ate half a windowpane with mayonnaise. I'd have never done it before. You had to perform miracles'.

Dunja has arranged the interview with Rundek and leaves a voicemail telling me to be at, 'Albatros café bar at Ljubljanica 4, at 5:30 p.m'. She says mockingly that it is near to the tram terminus we had mistakenly been to the previous Thursday. And then she texts me Rundek's mobile number.

Tomislav and I meet at the bus station. Jure Popović, who we had interviewed the previous evening, calls Tomislav to make good his offer to loan us Darko Glavan's book. When Tomislav tells Jure that we are on our way to Ljubljanica to interview Rundek, Jure says for us to wait where we are and he will give us a lift. We soon discover that today's late afternoon traffic is gridlocked. We crawl up to traffic lights and wait. I text Rundek to let him know we are at risk of running late. His reply is instant, 'Me too, so easy'. We edge forward, we stop. Jure is telling me about Saša Stojanović and Brian Rašić, two Serbs who moved to London at the height of punk there. Stojanović was a journalist and Rašić a photographer. The two of them combined to provide *Džuboks* magazine with a series of *Letters From London*. Jure says, 'It was the main source of information [...] I have kept all of those letters'.

Since the traffic is now congealing, Jure suggests we will be quicker getting out here and walking. We thank him and say our goodbyes, promising to stay in touch. Soon we see the small bridge across the stream as Dunja described. There are shops and cafés on both sides of the street. We see Albatros on the right, we enter, acknowledge the barman clearing tables and take a seat at the window. There are only a handful of people there, and none is Rundek. We order coffee. Rundek arrives ten minutes after we do. He is instantly recognisable – tall and slim; a life-lived charisma, weather-beaten handsome with grey-blonde hair, wearing a dark-brown, battered leather jacket. He is clearly tired and apologises in advance. He orders a coffee and lights a cigarette. He speaks quietly and deliberately and has a fine sonorous speaking voice. Even his jokes are imbued with a certain gravitas. He smokes frequently and orders more coffee.

After the interview is over Tomislav goes home to pack for tomorrow's trip to Pula to 'eat properly and get some sleep', since we have an early start. I head back to my apartment to pack. Then I see I have a message from Dunja suggesting we meet for a quick drink. She wants to know how the interview went. She is a big Rundek fan and clearly does not intend to wait until I return from Pula. On the way back to my apartment I text Dunja to say that I cannot make it a late night because 'I leave for Pula tomorrow at some ungodly hour and I still have to pack'.

DARKO RUNDEK: Caffe Bar Albatros, Ljubljanica 4, Zagreb

Darko Rundek. Ljubljanica 4, Zagreb © Tomislav 'Tompa' Zebić (2017)

Darko Rundek, better known simply as 'Rundek' was, and is, a figure with no immediately obvious analogy in UK or US punk rock. But in some ways, he typifies 'something' of the ex-Yugoslavian punk scene. Rundek is a composer, musician, actor, poet, and radio and theatre director. He divides his time between Paris, Zagreb and the coast. He had one of the biggest hit albums in Croatian history with the 1997 release *Apokalipso* – at first listen a mix of Balkan, Caribbean and African influences – which collected numerous national awards. Many of his videos on YouTube have in excess of three and four million views. In Ljubljana, two days before we meet Rundek, we saw that the walls were plastered with posters advertising an upcoming date for the Rundek Cargo Trio.

* * *

I was born in Zagreb but for the first six years of my life I lived in a little town north of Zagreb called Jertovec; it is a little town constructed for the people working in the power station. And it was interesting because during this first six years of my life living there, the people working in this power plant came from different places in Yugoslavia – mostly Croatian but also there were some people from Serbia, maybe some Macedonians. Young engineers, you know, it was their first job. They started their families in this little town in Zagorje. And when the time came for me to start school, my parents decided to move to Zagreb because it would be easier for me to do my scholarship in Zagreb. So, the rest of my life that's my hometown, Zagreb.

I started playing guitar on the coast during summer. My parents had a summer house on an island – Veli Lošinj – and there was a big camp there, a beautiful camp with big pine trees, with people from all around the world. We are talking about the beginning of the seventies when I was, kind of, an adolescent. At that time, it was like a hippy kind of company coming there. In the evenings we would drink some wine [and] smoke a joint. Playing what you would play with a guitar on a hot summer evening – Bob Dylan, Simon & Garfunkel [and] Cat Stevens. There were some really good players and I started to learn guitar so that I could also do a few songs. It was nice because girls like people who can play guitars. In fact, my official learning at school was one year of guitar school in some 'Workers Cultural Society', something really basic.

But there was a Czech teacher and he was recruiting people for their tambura orchestra – it's like a mandolin, with double strings. In local folk music there are these kinds of string orchestras, mandolin orchestras, which have all the range from the double bass to the soprano instrument, all that you would have in a string orchestra. So they were recruiting youngsters for their orchestra and they had an accelerated course for guitars. It was very useful. Later my son was learning how to play guitar in some official school, and what I would play at the end of the first year, he would play at the end of the fourth year. So, it really was a very, very effective accelerated way to learn. And I had quite a hard guitar to play, you know metal strings and very high action. It was painful to play, especially with this classical repertoire that I was supposed to learn. I found out that I could produce a similar emotional, and beautiful, effect with some simplifying of this classical music. So that was the start of my composition – how to write something in music which would have a similar effect but would be easier to play. I was fifteen or sixteen years old.

In Yugoslavia at that period, at the end of the sixties and early seventies, like today there were many Germans, many Dutch people, Austrians; even some English people would come – some Americans too. Today we have to explain, on and on, that we lived in quite an open country. Just a year later, when I was seventeen or eighteen, I hitchhiked to Amsterdam, to Copenhagen, just like that. I left my place and stuck my finger out; it was easy to travel.

This Yugoslav new wave coincided with things in other countries. It was something parallel, we didn't try to imitate some international hits or something like that. But the feeling of open and creative possibility was there. Yugoslavia was one of the leading countries of the Non-Aligned Movement and in this movement, somehow, we felt we were part of a society where we had some leading position. Also, Tito was old, he was dying, and I think that even in that period there was a certain kind of 'mini' cultural revolution. I remember there was this 'centre for the cultural activities of the youth' which was one of the organs of the cultural politics of the Communist Party here. These guys were really supporting rock music, visual arts, multimedia performances, 'happenings', quite modern forms of art.

This kind of exploring and creative movement wasn't only in the music. There was *Polet*, and *Studentski list*, the student magazine. Graphically it was really interesting. All the photos were black framed with no cropping, so there was a documentary feel. I finished high school and everybody was going to university after. And it was free, so everybody could study. I wanted to study film because I wanted to make films. But I was too lazy to prepare materials for this kind of exam to enter the Film School. So I had, as a back-up solution, a place at the Faculty of Philosophy in Zagreb and I started to study Comparative Literature and Russian Language. I really liked the Russian language and I was really very much inspired by the avant-garde movement of the twenties in Russia. I would decorate myself with a military cap and I would put on it some badges of Mayakovksy's posters and all that stuff.

And at this faculty, at the 'cave' we would jam nearly every evening. There were girls, mostly coming from Dalmatia, whose parents had money from tourism so they were quite wealthy. We would all go up to the hall of the Faculty, ask the girls for some money, and in ten minutes we would pick up enough for a few litres of cheap wine. We would just jam, and they would come and join us. I think that this cave of the Faculty was one of the places where this critical mass of artists was exchanging, not only materials but appearances (performances). We took ourselves for heroes, so some people finished bad because they took themselves too seriously as heroes. They started to take too much heroin and be even more heroes, and it killed them.

Two years later, in the late seventies, I moved to the Academia for Dramatic Arts to study Film and Theatre, and later just Theatre. My interest was between music and theatre. Maybe I wouldn't have gone so much towards theatre if there had not been a very good theatre festival in Zagreb. It took place twice a year, in the springtime and the autumn, and it would bring students of experimental theatre from all around the world. And I could feel at this time that this field of expression was even more vibrant than music for me. It pushed me into that direction. And then, gradually, this theatre movement kind of slowed down and music started to boom. So, even whilst studying theatre, we started the group called Haustor. In this group, the two main authors were Srđan Sacher and me. He was interested in ethnology and anthropology, so he would bring mostly African music – he was really very inspiring. I was looking for the scene as a possibility to do something more theatrical, more cabaret-like. So, it was these two influences that came together. From one side some black, punk, cabaret which I was inspired to do – I put on some white mask, I had a lot of make-up and some strange costumes – and some of these different, ethnic, musical influences which we took as inspiration. So, from those two influences we built our style. I think it was so much in the spirit of the time – Talking Heads were so much inspired by Fela Kuti for example. We tried to play with some black guys who were studying here. But the fact that you are black African doesn't mean that you are a good percussionist. It was one of the things that we found was not true.

The 1981 Biennale was interesting because Biennale was a festival of modern classical music, something quite high-culture which usually wouldn't let rock music in. But these separated cultural zones – the zone of modern classical music which was high culture, and rock which was low, more popular culture – started to penetrate each other. So they invited the Gang of Four, and we played as support; Haustor and Šarlo Akrobata. Haustor and Šarlo were bands which had something strongly authentic which could make a meeting between Gang of Four and us, to exchange and to compare. I respected Šarlo Akrobata a lot, I think it was really great what they did. Also, Idoli, they had a beautiful album *Odbrana i poslednji dani (The Defense and the Last Days)* which is marvellous. Gang of Four were not bad, quite powerful.

In school, in everyday life too, we had such a range of traditional music from Macedonian rhythms, to Istrian melodies which are really weird. There were so many different regional traditions in Yugoslav folk music which probably inspire people to look for something interesting, not so simple. Something which makes some pleasure of discovering music. Here the Orient was more present than in the West. We had the chance to work in that period when there were a lot of different but interesting things happening. But we didn't want to become a part of any movement. If what we did was sounding too much like something else we would throw it away. We tried to find our style, our way, our sound – not to be part of some general style or sound.

We had a little problem with a song called 'Radnička klasa odlazi u raj' – which means 'The Working Class Is Going to Heaven'. We had an important clash with the politics of the *Studentski list* magazine. In 1978 I was part of the production of *Studentski list* and as it was '78 we wanted to have one issue which focused on the '68 great political movements. The people from the Communist Party in Zagreb didn't like that. We were told that it was not good to release this. So we finished the issue and it went to the printing press and the guys in grey came there and just took it away. Like the Sex Pistols, exactly the same thing. The working class and the Queen are the same level of sacred social symbol!

Haustor released four albums. We tried to do the fifth one in 1990, but it was already the beginning of preparing for the war and it was a really shitty time. We tried to play music, but you simply didn't feel like playing music. The hatred was all around, and too much violence. You could feel mass hysteria and mass fear. The first people had been killed and when somebody is killed for some political reasons then it starts; revenge and the snowball of violence. This moment of '89, '90, it's really hard to understand from the point of view of somebody who is not from some ruling position – as a part of the people. In my opinion, it was part of the breaking up of the Iron Curtain – part of the restructuring of powers on a global scale which somehow erupted here for some reason. What is special, all [of] Europe was at war all of the time. And then came this period of calm when countries can't imagine themselves going to war anymore. And in ten years, or even sooner, they would be there. It was so easy, people who were non-violent and living lives which were not so bad. It's unimaginable how quickly it can turn into something else.

What seemed to be special in the Balkans was that it's a place where eastern and western culture and civilisation meet. We have modern civilisation and we have traditional civilisation – and between modern and traditional is a friction point. It's probably why it was more violent here. Behind this 'modern way of life' in every village, they would still know exactly who is part of which tribe. What we are witnessing now is how to describe what Yugoslavia was by the people who are writing new history based on these new national states. Kids with parents who grew up in Yugoslavia are learning about Yugoslavia as something completely different to what it actually was.

We tried to record the fifth album and after a few months in the studio we said, 'It doesn't sound really right'. So we just threw it into the bin and said, 'OK, that's the end. We are not going to publish it'. I went to France. My wife had just given birth to our first kid in '91 in France. You couldn't stop this crazy war. It was so huge. So the only thing to do was to step aside. I was already doing quite a lot of theatre music and film music, and when I went to France I was lucky – my wife is a theatre director and she had some projects of hers [for] which I composed music and played live. Then there was a French company which produced theatre in English, and they were a really self-sufficient, but poor, theatre company with one hundred shows a year. I was travelling around in one van with the stuff and four actors – and I was [a] technician and driver. We would play in schools, universities, theatres … Paris for a few weeks. It was a beautiful period, I really enjoyed it. In fact, it was the first time I went to Australia; we spent a few months there. We had a show in London too. During the war, we were in Paris mostly.

After the war was over, I didn't plan to continue as a singer and songwriter but still there were some songs dropping out of the theatre work. And 'Apokalipso' came out as a song and I could hear it was a big hit. And there were these two guys in Zagreb – war was over and people had a taste of big events, good music, good atmosphere without this war shit. So they established some festivals and produced a kind of rock award. They convinced me that it was time to come back to the stage. I really had the best studio I would like to have, any musicians I would like to play on the record would come with a lot of joy. So, it was twenty-five musicians who came to this album called *Apokalipso* and it was a big success. It was a good starting point for a solo career after being part of Haustor. And after that, the band which formed in the studio started to tour. We were touring for four years before producing the album called *U širokom svijetu* ('In the Wide World') which was maybe '99 or 2000.

Then, as I was still living in France, I kind of felt that it would be better if I had a band there instead of coming here to rehearsals and then going on the road. I was missing someone in common to work with on the music. Already I was an expatriate person, so I didn't feel only part of this world here. I felt part of some new nation of people who were not nationally defined anymore – people of the world. So, I joined a French violinist, a Portuguese trombone player, a Bosnian drummer and keyboard player, and a French double-bass player and we produced the album *Ruke* ('Hands') which came out in 2001. We then started touring, mostly in Yugoslavia, but also internationally. We had a showcase at WOMEX and we played in Portugal, Spain, London a few times, Paris, Vienna, Stockholm and Italy; in nearly all European countries. And then the second album, *Mhm A-Ha Oh Yeah Da-Da* came out in 2006. We played in Scandinavia a few months ago; we regularly play in Vienna, Prague also, [and] Paris.

It was Rundek Cargo Orkestar which did *Ruke* and the second album. Then it started to be too big, too complicated for touring with eight on stage; video, lights, blah blah. It's too much machinery, that's not really necessary. I was ready for something more tough, like a trio. You can't hide in a trio. So, Rundek Cargo Trio started in 2009 with Isabel – she is really an exceptional musician – and Dutso who is also multi-talented. He plays [the] piano and many instruments in bizarre combinations. So, we are a trio but there is much more sound than you would expect from a trio because of Dutso playing so many instruments, and Isabel playing the violin but with a lot of effects. So we've really had fun and we released two albums. The first was *Plavi avion* ('Blue Aeroplane') in 2010, and the second *Mostovi* ('Bridges') in 2015. Isabel was playing with Peter Brook[1] for a few years and with Nina Simone when she was younger. She also produced music for theatre and she played in the theatre. And Dutso is also a natural-born actor and showman. So with this trio, it is a real pleasure to do music for dramatic purposes. And, last year we were awarded the Gold Arena for Music at Pula Film Festival for a film called *Generation '68*.

There was a period when I started to act quite a lot. I had a leading role in a Slovenian film, a Montenegrin film [and] one Croatian film and it was beautiful – the film set was always for me something magic. I said I would like to be on a set for a few weeks and live this kind of life on the film set. That's why I started to act on film. It was quite good, except that we drank too much. It's even worse than being in a band; we were shooting a film in the summertime and the director didn't want to have any shots with the sunlight in. So we would wait, in the Alps for example, for one week and we would start to shoot a scene where there was a cloud and it was '*Stop!*' And we would wait again in the bus full of costumes and make-up – drinking whisky. I finished a film and I was ten kilos more than before. So it was quite a short period of acting. I did quite a lot of music for theatre and for film and I enjoyed it very much. I already had my diploma of theatre director. I think the experience of studying theatre is quite fun but we didn't learn a lot. I still know more than some film composers though. Even though I am not classical I know how to use sound for dramatic purposes.

Where to go after that? For me somehow the story is finishing there and it's time for another story. So after two albums with the trio, the new project is on; it's called *Apocalypso Now*, and it started as a celebration of twenty years since *Apokalipso* was published. After the trio, there are again eight on stage. It's a combination of four musicians who I played with before and four young musicians from Zagreb. In Zagreb, there is a really nice, improvised music scene and there are some bands which are really exploring some new stuff. So I've formed a band of four older collaborators and four youngsters from the new scene. When I say 'youngsters' I don't mean anything pejorative they are really very mature in mind, and beautiful people, and now we are touring. We started in Belgrade, in front of 10,000 people, the first show. And the majority of those youngsters had never played in front of more than 500 people or 300. They were so brave, they are 'present' and they know that something exceptional is happening, they know it will never happen again but they are enjoying it with full concentration. At this age you are so much more open, everything is circulating quicker.

---

1. The British theatre director.

TEN
The Hague Hilton

At the northern end of Pompstationsweg, before it becomes a cycle path traversing the vast expanse of windblown, undulating and scrub-covered dunes is Scheveningen Prison. Within this complex is the United Nations Detention Unit (UNDU) where all who stand trial at the International Criminal Tribunal for Yugoslavia (ICTY) are held until verdicts are delivered and, if a guilty verdict is reached, sentences are handed down. Also held here – although isolated from the Balkan inmates – are the detainees of the International Criminal Court (ICC): these have included the Liberian politician and warlord Charles Taylor (known as 'Pappie' to his child soldiers), the Ivorian politician and warlord Laurent Gbagbo and the Congolese politician and warlord Thomas Lubanga Dyilo. All three were accused of having committed or 'abetted' War Crimes and Crimes Against Humanity – rapes, murders, 'other inhuman acts' and more besides. This is where many of the 'World's Most Wanted War Criminals' and terrorists have resided – or may yet reside. If ever arrested this is where President Assad of Syria, Joseph Kony of Uganda's Lord's Resistance Army or perhaps Myanmar's leaders will be held.

The prison complex sits on the corner of Pompstationsweg and Van Alkemadelaan. 'Pompstationsweg 32' is the mundane-sounding address of one of the most infamous prison complexes in the world. Adjacent are neat houses with green and white striped sun canopies shading the windows, to the front are terraces and patios decorated with shrubs, bushes and flowers. A dozen trees are dotted around a well-tended strip of grass in the foreground. On a summer day like today, it is colourful and far from unpleasant – an urban village green. Children play here. Pompstationsweg itself is lined with trees and on the side opposite the prison are larger detached houses. It is a picture of Dutch middle-class suburbia.

The view to the Van Alkemadelaan side is much more recognisable as a prison facility. Here a high wall of dark-red, pointed brickwork, runs virtually uninterrupted for 150 metres. Seven or eight wires are stretched for the entire length of the wall – presumably an electric fence. Standing tall behind this are floodlights facing inwards, punctuated occasionally with CCTV cameras. This is the place the locals call the 'Hague Hilton'. At the peak of ICTY activity, residents were familiar with the sight of speeding limousines and 4 × 4s, blue lights flashing, intersecting roads temporarily blocked and all traffic coming to a brief halt as prisoners were transferred here in relatively low-key police convoys.

When fully operational, the unit extended over five floors with cells leading off the main corridor. There were communal and private meeting rooms and it had the capacity to hold a maximum of 84 detainees, although by the time the ICTY closed it was reduced to a little over 50.

The number of detainees held at any one time had peaked at 64 (in 2005) whilst a total of 178 had been detained. Detentions varied from days to eleven years. By the summer of 2017, a total of seven hundred and eight years of detention had been served here. Of the 161 detainees who faced accusations of having committed offences during the Yugoslav Wars of the 1990s, just one was a woman. The lowest average age of the prison population had been thirty-five years but by the time the ICTY was winding down its prosecutions the average age had risen to nearly sixty-seven years. With this came different health issues. In the early days many had war wounds, but in the later days skeletal and cardio-vascular problems dominated concerns. These later detainees were, primarily, prominent public officials with high levels of education – well above those of the prison officers and staff (unlike in a 'normal' prison). This meant that there were very few of the behavioural issues seen in other prisons. There was no violence and no smuggling, trading or use of drugs. One of the challenges staff faced was hunger-strikers. These ranged from one, high-profile 'motivated and experienced hunger-striker' to some less motivated individuals who actually gained weight.

But here is the thing, in the ICTY wing, 'Detainees are not separated according to their ethnicity, nationality, religion or class'. Nationalists and supremacists from different sides lived daily, unsegregated, alongside one another. One inmate told of a particularly notorious individual, excoriated in the media and the outside world, arriving in the 'Hague Hilton' having not taken account of the cooler North Sea climes. His former nemesis, accused of equally heinous crimes on the opposing side of the conflicts, loaned him a jumper for his stay. Men who led their people into those 'hellish orgies of persecution', took English or IT classes together, cooked together, played board games together and loaned each other knitwear. One former Yugoslav General later wrote, 'The war separated us, and The Hague has put us together again'.

If found not guilty the detainees were freed. Some even returned to the Balkans to lead their country. If found guilty the detainees were sentenced. But they do not serve their sentences in Scheveningen. Their sentences are being served in Germany, Sweden, Finland and the few countries who offered to take part in the reconciliation process and signed up to the relevant UN Treaty.

A one-legged, sixty-two-year-old detainee, found guilty of aiding and abetting one of the most horrific crimes of the conflicts, was transferred to Yorkshire, England, to serve his thirty-five-year sentence. Whilst there, three of his fellow inmates – muscular young men in their twenties – entered his cell and slashed his throat and body. Noting that all three devoutly practised their religion, the judge described the attack as an 'act of revenge … for the purpose of advancing a religious or racial cause'. Each of the attackers was in prison as a convicted murderer. One was also a serial rapist who sexually abused and then murdered a young mother in front of her ten-month-old baby. Another was part of a gang which had kidnapped, gang-raped, tortured and then murdered a schoolgirl and attempted to murder her friend by shooting her in the head. He had arrived in Britain as an illegal immigrant from Kosovo aged thirteen or fourteen years. He was due to have been deported when he reached the age of eighteen years old – two weeks before the murder. Their one-legged victim survived the attack and was subsequently transferred to another UK prison, and then another. At each he was attacked again. He was later awarded £50,000 in compensation because the UK Ministry of Justice had not met their 'duty of care'. Transferred away from the UK – initially back to the Netherlands – he now resides in Poland, where he remains to serve out his sentence.

ELEVEN
Istria: Pirates and Punk Rock Heartlands

DAY SEVEN

Oh shit! Oh shit! Oh shit! Not again.

I put down the mobile and check the time – 9:19. I then realise it was the ringtone which had woken me and not the alarm. I pick up the phone again just as Tomislav cheerily says, 'Good morning brother', and asks if I am on my way yet. He has arrived early at the bus station. Last night, in spite of resolutely telling Dunja that I was heading back to my digs to pack, I once again fell victim to Balkan hospitality. With no time to reflect on my weakness, I get dressed and ready to leave as fast as is humanly possible in the circumstances and pack my bag.

I run down the partially tiled, concrete-slab stairs. Out into the street. The sun is already making its presence felt despite the relatively early hour and the time of the year. I do not dare check the time. I have very little belief that there is a realistic chance I could make it the 1.5 kilometres to the bus station before the departure time of 9:45. And had not the young woman at the ticket office told us we had to be there fifteen minutes early?

My mobile rings. It is Tomislav. He confirms my suspicions, there is no chance of making it onto this bus. But there is a later bus with spare seats which – contrary to what we had been told the previous day – will get us to Pula at a reasonable hour.

So it is that we leave Zagreb some two hours later than initially planned but still in good heart. The bus is barely one-quarter full and we occupy the rear bench seats. The sky is a particularly vivid blue and the clouds sparse and isolated. After perhaps half an hour we are on the outskirts of Karlovac. Several of the buildings lining the city-centre-bound roads have the unmissable and unmistakable pockmarking of artillery and small arms fire from the war. Karlovac is the childhood hometown of Ned O'Millick – aka Nenad Milić – so I was forewarned of this scarring. Over the course of our late-night Skype calls, Ned has proved a priceless and unstinting source of advice and contacts. Whilst he has rarely spoken of his personal adversity during the convulsions of the 1990s, I have heard enough to surmise he has navigated through turbulent waters most of us would struggle to imagine. And that like so many others, the reverberations continue, to this day, to shape his life.

Ned remains a refugee; his family sought sanctuary in Germany during the wars, after which he moved to Istria where poor prospects drove him back to

Germany. He is now living in Munich, teaching in a kindergarten and making music. Ned is a force of nature, big-hearted, passionate and talented. He is the singer-songwriter and driving force behind Tito's bojs ('Tito's Boys') and the man who masterminded the LP *Za tebe: A Tribute to KUD Idijoti* which features many of ex-Yugoslavia's finest punk acts such as Pankrti, Goblini, Psihomodo Pop, Atheist Rap, Novembar and Hladno Pivo, whose chosen homage is 'To nije mjesto za nas'.

The visible legacy of conflict is hardly surprising, given that Karlovac was on the frontline with the self-proclaimed secessionist 'Serbian Republic of Krajina'. What surprises me is just how close it is to Zagreb. The Slovenian border is even closer, just 10 kilometres from here, whilst the town of Velika Kladuša in Bosnia and Herzegovina is only 50 kilometres to the south. Perhaps Karlovac – founded in the late sixteenth century as an Austro-Hungarian frontier-post fortress against the Ottoman threat to their south – is a prisoner of destiny. A proud, resilient and prosperous city, it was repeatedly besieged over four centuries but never yielded. However, it was to prove no match for asset-stripping, corruption and incompetence when, according to the then town mayor, it was 'plundered by tycoons', and 'turned into a ghetto of hungry workers', in the disaster-capitalist feeding frenzy of the post-war years.

Today, in keeping with much of Croatia, Karlovac struggles to pull itself clear from the sludge of high unemployment and low wages – and the consequent depopulation. It remains home to the historic Karlovac Brewery which produces the hugely popular Karlovačko beer, although the company is now a subsidiary of the Heineken behemoth. In a more sinister nod to the recent past, the other major employer is a firearms manufacturer. In fact, if you are ever staring down the barrel of a pistol drawn by a Chicago police officer – or for that matter a Missouri housewife – and you are particularly attentive, there is a reasonable chance you will notice 'Made in Croatia' stamped above the grip since 90 per cent of the company's XD series (X-Treme-Duty) handguns are legally exported to the United States. Still, as we pass through Karlovac we catch glimpses of its once renowned Habsburg-era architecture. With its historic six-pointed star street-plan and four rivers, the city is once again showing signs of forging a future away from the double-edged curse of 'dark tourism'. The stop in Karlovac bus station is brief and just two new passengers to join.

From Karlovac we climb modestly but interminably, through limestone cuttings and road tunnels. Dark green conifers dominate the landscape, splattered with deciduous autumnal reds, oranges and yellows, and leafless skeletons. We continue to climb, leaving the foothills behind until both sides of the road drop away from the raised highway and the foreground is arid and stony. In the middle and far distances are waves of forested low hills. Ahead we glimpse the peaks and passes which presumably infer our route. Now and again, a red-roofed white house, or a smallholding, stands beside the road. Occasionally, in the mid-distance, there are entire villages and towns of white and red mosaics. We stop again after an hour. This time, on the outskirts of a town. There is a small café and convenience kiosk. The sign outside advertises 'No. 1 Ice Cream In Ukraine'. Despite the late summer heat, we resist.

As we reach the plateau, the vegetation becomes more verdant – less conifers but more coarse grasses and stunted deciduous trees. And then the outlook becomes noticeably more rocky and jagged. The trees become shrubs, and the shrubs become bushes, of the 'Maquis' scrub kind familiar to anyone who has travelled in Greece, Spain or the untameable upland tracts of Southern France. We cannot yet see the sea, our view interrupted by the hills below, but it is obvious that it is somewhere on our left-hand side. A smoky-blue haze hangs where I imagine the horizon to be. We leave the main highway, crest a peak and begin a twisting descent. This road follows a jagged canyon, dropping down towards what we can now see in front of us is the deepest-blue Adriatic Sea.

Above us on our right-hand side are modern tower blocks, eight or nine clustered on top of a rock. Rising from the valley below until it looms over us is an industrial chimney. Then to our left, we pass a large pharmaceutical factory. Down in the gorge to our right is a river; warehouses and apartment buildings cluster hard along its banks on the narrow, valley floor – partially obscured by the leaves of the overgrown roadside trees clinging to the steep, rocky inclines. At the bottom of the hill, we go under the iron railway bridge which straddles the valley. The river is now on our left. This then is Rijeka. One of ex-Yugoslavia's undisputed 'punk rock heartlands'. Hometown of Paraf, Termiti and Kaos – amongst many others – and the site of the first proper punk gig in Croatia, and arguably (depending on your demarcation between 'garage' and 'punk'), the first punk rock gigs anywhere in Eastern Europe. At first sight, it is impossible not to notice the contrast with more familiar 'punk rock heartlands' – London, New York, Berlin or Belfast. The sky and the sea are zaffre-blue.

From the windows of the bus, Rijeka itself looks immensely appealing. Immediately I regret that we will not be able to spend time here. The architecture looks to be Venetian and Austro-Hungarian sprinkled with a little Turkish/Ottoman. Moustachioed jacket-wearing, pork-pie-hatted men play cards and gesticulate over espressos on the pavement terraces outside faded-lemon, or nougat-pink, café bars. At sea level, the views open out considerably as fewer buildings block our line of sight. I can see that this is still a working city and not a tourist resort or post-industrial theme park. The cranes which stand between the coastal road and the water testify to its continuing reliance on the sea – on shipbuilding and shipping. Rijeka has long been the biggest port in this area. Today, though, the city's two major shipyards – 'Viktor Lenac' and '3. maj' – are both in debt and struggling, with the predictable knock-on effect throughout the local economy.

As we pass through Titov trg, I point out the sign to Tomislav. He nods and tells me that Rijeka is traditionally the 'most red' area in Croatia – apart, that is, from a tumultuous period from 1919 to 1920 when it was seized by the diminutive, ultra-nationalist 'Father of Fascism' and self-proclaimed 'Superman', Gabriele D'Annunzio and his followers who thus declared it the world's first 'fascist free-state'. An Italian bombardment on Christmas Eve of 1920 drove D'Annunzio and his forces from the city. But his legacy of straight-armed salutes, black-shirted goons, call-and-response rabble-rousing political slogans and racial supremacy have proved a harder stain to remove. Rebecca West did not attempt to hide her contempt for D'Annunzio who she had once observed in Florence as he grandstanded to adoring fascist crowds. Sadly, so little progress has been made that her words resonate as clearly today as they did eighty years ago:

> All this is embittering history for a woman to contemplate. I will believe that the battle of feminism is over, and that the female has reached a position of equality with the male, when I hear that a country has allowed itself to be turned upside-down and led to the brink of war by its passion for a totally bald woman writer [...] Here in Fiume (Rijeka) the bald author had been allowed to ruin a city: the bald authoress would never be allowed to build one.

We stop at the Rijeka central bus terminus, just a few metres from the Adriatic. We alight the bus and step out into what is now a temperature comfortably in the twenty degree Celcius. From a café on the fringe of the bus terminus, we buy double-espressos. I can see loading jetties and beyond them a harbour wall. We board the bus once again and take our seats. Several new passengers have joined but the bus remains more than half-empty. Departing the terminus we turn left along streets busy with shoppers and office workers. The buildings are slightly more prosaic versions of those we passed on the way in. Faded and peeling ornate buildings are dwarfed under a wall of towering harbour-side silos. On both sides, our view is obscured by offices, shops and silver-barked trees, but it is clear that we are travelling parallel to the coast on our near left.

Having descended to sea level, we resume our steady climb and gradually the buildings to our left peter out. The land falls away so that now I am looking out over the rooftops of hotels and houses below, and towards the sparkling azure sea. It is a glorious afternoon and there really is not a single cloud in view. Through breaks in the trees bordering the road, I catch sight of the sun striking a colossal, glittering-white flash across a sheet of becalmed water. Ahead, the green-black silhouette of the mainland stretches away into the blue sea, at which point it meets the green-black outline of an island rising from the surface of the water. It is travel-brochure perfect. We make our way out onto the headland. Now to our left, at a right angle, we look back across the sweeping coastline of the bay, all the way back to Rijeka. It is the most vivid canvass of deep blues, dark greens, blacks, greys and phosphorescent white.

From here, it is easy to see why Rijeka is called the 'Gateway to the Islands'. To the west and southwest are the islands of Krk, Cres, Rab and Lošinj – where, at campfire parties in the early 1970s, a teenage Darko Rundek played guitar to impress the hippy girls 'from all around the world'. Rightly or wrongly (although not wholly without historical basis), the entire Balkan region is synonymous with banditry. The Balkan bandits even have their own name – 'hajduks' – deriving from the Magyar for 'cattle-drover'. As with other regions where banditry was familiar, these were not perceived by the majority population as unprincipled 'robbers'. In *Bandits*, the great historian Eric Hobsbawm wrote, 'The Balkan cattle – or pig – dealers may well have doubled as bandit leaders, just as merchant captains in pre-industrial days might well dabble in a little piracy'. Banditry implied something more noble; a refusal to meekly accept the ingrained repression, inequality and injustice. Bandits were often fighting to break free from serfdom. For these reasons, local folklore is rich with tales and songs of bandit heroism and even chivalry; just as the English-speaking world has Robin Hood, Jesse James and Ned Kelly. That is not, of course, to say that bandits were not robbers. So it is, in this corner of Istria which is so bound to the sea, banditry would take the form of piracy.

It was from the port of Senj on the mainland behind these islands, that the admirably disorderly Uskoks[1] operated their piracy. The Uskoks were refugees from the hinterland around Senj – fleeing Turkish aggression and oppression, and keen to exact revenge. Their piratic activities wrecked treaties and provoked wars between major naval powers. And all the while they targeted the ships of Jewish and Muslim merchants whilst playing on their Christian background to cultivate the support of powerful local figures including the Bishop of Senj.

Of course, these activities could not go unpunished. The Venetians once sent a ship laden with poisoned wine to sea and allowed it to be captured by the Uskoks.

---

1. The name Uskok can be traced to the word for 'the ones who jumped in' – infiltrating Ottoman-held territories.

It is not known how the Uskoks avoided poisoning, but they did. It was a temporary reprieve and soon the Venetians and others were capturing and beheading the pestilent pirates. Finally, they went too far, inciting hostilities between the Austro-Hungarian and Spanish empires on the one hand and the Dutch, Venetians and English on the other. This time their forts were razed, their ships wrecked and the survivors banished back to the rural hinterland.

The road rises away from the coast as we head inland. On both sides of the road, pumice-grey stones and fern-green scrub trees splashed with grape-red foliage, stretch away as far as the eye can see. At a roadside bus stop in a drowsy hamlet we halt, and an old lady departs the bus, loaded with her shopping from Rijeka. We stop briefly in another small village but no one exits or enters the bus. Washing hangs on a line stretched taut between two window balconies. On a Post Office wall a street name sign reads, 'Ulica Nikole Tesle'. Visitors to former Yugoslavia soon become familiar with the Tesla legend. At Karlovac, Tomislav told me that Tesla had lived nearby, and joked that the Serbs and Croats both claim Tesla as their own. There are Tesla museums, Tesla schools, Tesla streets, Tesla statues, even Tesla restaurants and bars strewn across the major cities. Tesla was an ethnic Serb who was born and raised in Croatia, is claimed by both as a symbol of national prestige and is said to have been proud of his Croatian homeland and his Serbian heritage.

Eventually, we come to another settlement. Twenty or more pastel-washed low-rise tenement apartments line the green spaces adjacent to the road. Up on the hillside, the picturesque historic old town is visible. On a sunny day like today, it is a colourful scene. But it has the feel of a mining town and I can imagine that in these isolated uplands, in the depths of winter, Labin could feel forsaken. 'You are right', says Tomislav:

> This is the famous town of Labin. It had a darkness and a sadness. There was a lot of addiction here. But it is very famous for artists. The Labin Art Express was formed here in the war years. Kind of underground movement like a New York, Warhol kind of thing. In 1921 the coal miners here rose-up and established the revolutionary state of Labin. They say it is the first anti-fascist revolt anywhere in the world.

We pass through acre upon acre of agricultural land, rich with vines and olives, and then drop down through the outskirts of Pula. Neat, brightly coloured, low-rise apartment blocks encircle a roundabout. On top of one is a McDonald's billboard. A right turn delivers us into a large coach and car park dotted with tall trees.

We have arrived at Pula bus station ahead of schedule. Sale has kindly called to say that he will pick us up and take us to our apartment. His stage name is Sale Veruda (his given name is Saša Milovanović); he takes the 'Veruda' from the district of Pula where he has lived for many years. It is also where our apartment for tonight is located. On the café-bar terrace, we take wicker and chrome seats at faux marble tables in the shade of parasols. The external walls of the café-bar and ticket office are hung with information boards detailing numerous routes, rival operators' notices and timetables. The bus station is soaked in sunshine, broken by the shadows of fir trees and overlooked by more tidy low-rise blocks. A car pulls into a shaded parking space and Sale gets out. Wiry and athletic, with long wavy hair and John Lennon glasses, he is wearing jeans, sneakers and a dark t-shirt and jacket. With him, he has two small children who we soon find out are Maja, aged seven, and Frank, aged five. Sale joins us for a coffee and the children have espresso cups of something topped off with generous swirls of frothy cream.

We linger over the drinks before leaving the café-bar and getting into Sale's car. The children sit in the back with Tomislav and immediately strike up a conversation, despite this being the first time they have met. Sale asks if we are hungry and offers to drop us in the town centre to get a meal and supplies. He tells us to take our time and just call him when we are done; he will collect us and take us to our apartment. We ask for recommendations of places to eat – ones which meet the needs of the awkward vegetarian. We are a little out of the tourist season, many restaurants are in the suburbs away from the centre, and we are too late for daytime restaurants and too early for evening restaurants. Our choices will most likely be limited. Sale pulls the car over by an outdoor market where some of the stallholders are beginning to pack away unsold goods into white-panel vans. He and Tomislav have a conversation which involves a good deal of gesticulation and pointing. Tomislav leans forward and says, 'Sale says we can get some fruit and some wine at the market. And then, if it is not beneath your honour, we should eat at this restaurant here'. He points to an unpretentious, sizeable, but perfectly fine-looking café opposite the market. Tomislav can see that I am a little confused.

> This place serves what we in Croatia we call 'gablec'.[2] It's very popular – kind of a 'workers restaurant'. So this one would be where the workers from Uljanik shipyard come to eat. They sell cheap, nutritious, traditional food with mostly local ingredients. I told him you will be fine with it.

Leaving our bags in the car, we cross the square and head into the restaurant. Immediately inside is a canteen-style service area with three food counters and

---

2. 'Gablec' – also known as 'marenda' – is the name given to a traditional, simple but hearty, 'working-man's meal', usually served around midday and typically consisting of a selection from bean-stew with meat, stuffed-peppers, tripe/offal and thick soups. In socialist times the canteens of state-owned industries would serve 'gablec' as a source of supplementing the workers calorie intake. Today, some restaurants still adhere to the standards set by the Yugoslav state.

a cash-till. There are just two customers sat at separate tables. A woman waits behind the counters to serve us. We make our selections, place them on our trays, take some bread and move to the till. A group of workers in overalls who followed us in, and the two already here, are quite openly staring at us. They look bemused rather than hostile. 'They can't believe that someone from overseas and an out-of-towner with a smart jacket would be eating here', says Tomislav grinning. We have both selected a dish of potatoes and kale, 'manestra' which seems like a local version of 'minestrone' and Tomislav has 'faširanci' which looks like some kind of meatball, patty or fritter. Finally, the woman comes to the till and we settle our bill. It comes to around €8 for both of us – for five dishes, bread, one beer and one coffee.

We depart the restaurant. Outside, night has rapidly overcome dusk. Most of the stalls have packed up or are packing up. There is a steady flow of pedestrian traffic through the market square as workers return home at the end of the day. Tomislav purchases a litre of fresh pomegranate juice in an unlabelled glass bottle and a carrier bag of mandarin oranges. He says they are from Metković and that the hometown of Matija and Jure is famous throughout ex-Yugoslavia for the quality and variety of its oranges. I wander through the lines of empty stalls and arrive at a market square. It is a little busier here. From a stall I buy two bottles of Istrian wine and then go back for a third as a small gift for Sale. We cut back through the market and wait beside the road at the point where Sale had dropped us a couple of hours earlier. He duly picks us up and drives us the fifteen-minute journey to our apartment. Before dropping us off, he asks if our meal was OK and if we have everything we need. We assure him that life is certainly good for us at the moment and we are perfectly happy to spend the evening relaxing here before exploring a little more of Pula tomorrow. We make our arrangements for the morning and say our goodbyes.

Our accommodation for the night is a whitewashed, upper-floor, studio apartment. The complex has an end-of-season feel. It appears to be otherwise uninhabited, thus granting us sole use of the small communal smoking terrace. Sadly, our view of the nearby sea is blocked by neighbouring holiday-lets, also apparently deserted. We throw down our bags and open the wine. Devoid of the summer tourists the residential streets are quiet.

Tonight will be my last opportunity to unwrap Tomislav's own backstory. On our second day together in Zagreb, he suggested we go for a drink prior to meeting with Zdenko Franjić. Even though Tomislav is an extremely infrequent drinker, I thought nothing of it. But as we sat outside a café bar close to a busy main road he told me that he had some 'bad news' and he had to tell me immediately.

Istria: Pirates and Punk Rock Heartlands

'You know I was an addict right? And you know I am on Methadone treatment? Well, because I'm on Methadone I can't come to Serbia with you'. I was momentarily devastated. He was my guide, my translator, my shield against the unknown. What would I do without him? Tomislav's utter despondency was so obvious that I immediately felt ashamed of my selfishness. With the help of his sympathetic doctor, he had legally secured enough prescribed Methadone to allow him to accompany me within Croatia and Slovenia. But then they hit the impenetrable barriers of travelling to Serbia, a non-European Union country. This had been his 'dream'. It was more than an expedition for Tomislav, it was to be 'a pilgrimage'. He had been clean for a long time but suffered bouts of depression. The promise of our punk-rock road-trip and the potential to meet so many of his 'fucking heroes' had filled his thoughts for weeks. It had kept him sane. I could see he was crestfallen. Melancholic. I also realised my own culpability for holding out such a tantalising prospect without making sufficient provision should such a crisis befall.

And here we are now in Pula, our last night together in Croatia. Tomorrow we will return to Zagreb. I will pack my bags in preparation for an early departure the following morning. After just a week together, it was not so much Tomislav's linguistic skills and local knowledge I was going to miss, it was his company and his friendship. I ask if I may set the recorder going as we chat. He knows, of course, that I am hoping he might lower his guard.

That evening Tomislav does indeed talk. For three hours Tomislav talks. Each story is an exhalation. Some are obviously connected. Some seem utterly random. It is only when enough pieces are scattered before me that the bigger picture takes shape.

> A friend of mine and his late wife were driving back to Zagreb from Zadar on the coast. The war had just ended, it was '96 or something like that. When you drive from Zadar it's a really fucked up road. And he just ran straight ahead when he should have turned. Bang! Crashed. And the car landed on the roof. His wife was bloodied, she was unconscious. His dog was thrown from the car and died. He was also cut and shit but the first thing he thought, after he had checked his wife and seen that – although she was bleeding – she was alive, was 'Where the fuck is my dog?' So he got out of the wreck and started searching for the fucking dog.
>
> Of course, by this time someone had called the cops and after fifteen minutes or so they had arrived. But the cops stood 50

113

metres away and didn't go to help him. They stood across the road from the field the car had landed in. They shouted, 'Please get out of there!' He just shouted back, 'I'm looking for my dog.' They shouted back, 'You're in a mine-field. Please get out of there. We can't come to get you. Please get out of the fucking mine-field!' Then he saw his dog and it was dead. So he had to walk across the minefield and get out onto the road. Watching every step he took. For twenty minutes he was looking for his dog in an active minefield! Which is still active today. You know man, some things were different here. Some things are still different here.

War did stop, but the butchering of people by any means, not so much. Instead of tanks, banks came in, and the free market, and the EU – and that was that. We became a 'small country for a big holiday!'[3] Still, as one can see today, from that all of that tourism income, which is most of what we now have, almost no one lives better. That is significant because the last four or five years were apparently all record income years. Every year is now a record income year, yet somehow there is less and less money.

People go away from Croatia every day, in pretty big numbers. I could write a thousand examples of it but there is no point. Today we are like Ireland was before. The only thing that probably comforts people is the fact that Ireland is now one of the main providers of jobs to Croats! And, maybe, Ireland is now what we once had in Yugoslavia. That's a bone that many Croats can't chew – Yugoslavia. But again I digress.

I am still here. I still feel like a second class citizen. I still feel like a punk.

---

3. *A Small Country for a Great Vacation* is one of Croatian tourism's enduring slogans. Croatia has a 'package' tourist history dating back to the 1830s when steamboats linked the Dalmatian and coastal 'resorts' with Trieste (Italy) in the north and Kotor (Montenegro) in the south. It became a true 'international' destination with the advent of the railroads from Budapest to Zagreb and Rijeka, and from Vienna to Trieste (with a stopover in Rijeka) in the 1870s. Today, tourism is responsible for approximately 20 per cent of Croatia's GDP.

RUJANA JEGER: Zagreb

Tomislav 'Tompa' Zebić with Pero Lovšin. Ljubljana

Rujana Jeger is an esteemed writer and media personality in Croatia and ex-Yugoslavia. Less orthodox – but perhaps more in keeping with her punk personality – among her interests are canine archaeology and the *Pasji život* ('Dogs life') website she runs which seems to cover almost all conceivable aspects of canine behaviours. She first appeared in the public eye aged just fourteen but looking considerably older, when she was on the cover of the seminal, 1981, Yugoslavian punk compilation LP *Artistička Radna Akcija* ('Artists Work Action') which was re-released in 2014. Born and raised in Zagreb she spent a portion of her teenage years in Rijeka at the very time it was an undisputed creative hotbed of Yugoslav punk. Her mother is the famous writer and essayist Slavenka Drakulić. Our attempts to meet in Zagreb were thwarted by Rujana's travel to the United States to give a paper at an academic conference. At the time, I was unaware of Rujana's media profile and was a little shocked to see her on the cover of a glossy magazine at a kiosk in Zagreb central bus station before the journey to Pula. The postponed interview took place online in May 2018.

In May of 2019, Tomislav, Daniela and I met with Rujana at a terrace bar in Zagreb's Old Town. Tkalčićeva Ulica is a narrow, pedestrianised street, lined with decorous bars and cafés, the focal point of Zagreb's more 'urbane' nightlife – belying a hidden, much earthier, bloody and salacious past. Two small white terriers accompanied Rujana – 'Joy' (after Joy Division) and 'Pixie' (after the Pixies) – who was as irreverent and genial in person as she had been online. When she arrived in the late afternoon the sun was still above the red-tiled rooftops but when we parted several hours later the time was approaching midnight and the sky was that deep, Balkan, fig-black. By then we had been treated to an anthology of family eccentricities, bawdy social-faux pas, and tales of celebrated artists and literary figures – including her mother's close friend, the American 'Mother of Feminism', Gloria Steinem – all told without any hint of boastfulness.

Rujana Jeger and Joy. Old Town, Zagreb © Tomislav 'Tompa' Zebić (2017)

* * *

I was born in Zagreb in 1968 and I spent my childhood in Novi Zagreb, which is the part of town which got developed after the Second World War, in the sixties. I lived in one of those sixties buildings, not particularly pretty, but with plenty of greenery and parks and places to ride your bike. There was a hippodrome nearby and the River Sava where you could go hiking or biking for kilometres. We used to call the taller buildings of fourteen floors 'skyscrapers' but when I first came to New York at just seventeen, I became aware that they never scraped any sky. Only now am I aware that Novi Zagreb was very well designed, as opposed to those new parts of town being built now – buildings stuck close together, no trees anywhere, no common areas except for a shopping mall.

I was raised as a gender-neutral kid because my parents were hippies at the forefront of the new 'Age of Aquarius'. They wouldn't make a difference between girls' and boys' toys – ditto my clothes. I never wore dresses and skirts, and my first doll that represented a child – a baby – was black. I guess that's interesting as an experiment because I am very anti-racist today.

My parents were students. She was nineteen when I was born, he was twenty-one. He went on to study history and sociology and later became a sociology professor, and my mother went on to study literature and sociology. She later became a pretty famous journalist and the leader of a feminist movement in the '80s in Yugoslavia and subsequently a pretty famous writer who is well known for her books on the civil wars in the Balkans and the transition from Communism. Her name is Slavenka Drakulić and she is the most translated Croatian author in the last one hundred years.

I did not have a sister or a brother, but I was raised with a cousin who was just a year younger than me and he lived in the building nearby. He lived with his parents and my paternal grandfather and grandmother. My paternal grandparents were also very outstanding people – she (and her siblings) came from a long line of teachers, dating back to the nineteenth century, so the whole family has been teaching people for generations, and I guess it became a genetic trait. My grandfather was from a poor family, but they both joined the Partisan movement in the Second World War, and they were both very intellectually inclined, so this is how I have been raised. For example, they took me to the Zoo Garden in the Maksimir park and they would explain how humans have developed from the apes through the process called evolution. And then I would stare at the apes – I guess I stared at those apes for a few years. I would make my grandfather take me there and I would expect the apes to turn into people! In the end, I asked my father, 'OK, I am coming here over and over but they are not evolving into people. Why?' And then he explained to the five-year-old me: 'Oh, no, it's not those apes. It was other apes – long ago'. And I suppose this spurred my interest in anthropology and archaeology so that basically at the age of seven or eight, after watching a TV show about the Australopithecus Lucy, I vowed that I would be the one to find the 'Missing Link'!

As if we were not odd enough, we were also vegetarian. So, because I had a pet guinea pig, we had to pluck grass from the park and bring it home for it to eat. Then the rumours started that we were picking grass because we ourselves eat it – on top of that, the other kids thought I was weird – because I probably was. So, seeing that something had to be done about my socializing and knowing I preferred animals to people, my grandfather took me to the hippodrome and enrolled me in the riding club where I stayed until I was fifteen or sixteen. And then I discovered punk, and the boys, and the bands!

All the kids had to officially be members of the Youth Organisations, first the Tito's Pioneers (Pionirski Savez Jugoslavije), and then the Socialist Youth Organization – but the funny thing is that I managed to avoid both! I was born in November, which meant that I was still five when the school year started in September. But my mother managed to enrol me all the same – through a schoolteacher friend of hers because I could already read and write. So when I entered the First Grade after the winter break, everybody else had already finished one semester. I did not know anyone; I was a weird-looking kid and I had thick eye-glasses. Everybody else was already seated with somebody, had formed friendships and all of them were already enrolled into Tito's Pioneers. So I was cast in the role of an outsider where I think I remained – even to this day. At the end of Primary School, when we were all enrolled in 'gymnasium', I was almost expelled for doing damage to a teacher's car because he was unfair to a group of us – because we were punks. I was fourteen and the ringleader as we scratched his car. So, as a punishment, I was not enrolled into this other Youth Organisation which was called 'Socijalistička Omladina Jugoslavije'. So at the age of fifty, I can proudly say I was never a member of any organization or political party of any kind.

My paternal grandfather, who basically raised me because my father left when I was six or seven, was also very anti-authoritarian. After the Second World War, he was an Army Major and he could have had a career in the military, but he didn't want to. He'd had enough of war. He enrolled in university and he finished economy and went on to work. He was very anti-Stalin, but the very day Tito said 'No' to Stalin – which I think happened in '48 – my grandfather managed to say something bad about Stalin to a wrong person at work. If Tito hadn't had that speech on that particular day and clearly separated himself from Stalin, my grandfather would have possibly ended up dead, or imprisoned in Goli Otok – a prison on the island from which there was no escape. Also, my mother ran away from home when she was sixteen because her father was very different to this paternal grandfather of

Istria: Pirates and Punk Rock Heartlands

mine; he had the military career and was very strict with his kids. So, yeah, I guess I am the product of a bunch of 'anti' people!

My father's name is Slobodan, which means 'free man', a name chosen because he was born after the Second World War. He was raised much like he raised me – my grandfather and grandmother gave him a lot of freedom; he could do what he wanted. Apparently, he could do no wrong and, when he was about sixty, he gave a long interview for a documentary film *Generation '68* by Nenad Puhovski, saying that maybe this early freedom was not good for him later on because it didn't teach him responsibility. He was an interesting figure, the leader of the anarchist movement in Yugoslavia in the eighties – and he has been a legendary professor both here and then in Toronto where he later lived – but the fact is that he was never a responsible father.

He looked like Ché Guevara who later turned into the Maharishi. Once, I invited kids from school to my home to see my new guinea-pig and as we entered the apartment, my father is sitting in a 'lotus' pose, completely naked and chanting his Mantra. Of course, to me it was a normal thing – I thought everybody else's fathers are sitting naked in the middle of the room chanting, '*Omm*'. I mean, that's what fathers do – right? Well, it turns out it was not exactly what fathers did, not in Zagreb, and it turns out that those kids went home and told their parents that they'd seen my father naked. None of them ever visited me again. In retrospect, I am happy that was the only consequence – imagine what would happen today!

When my father left for another woman, my mother fell in love with this much younger guy. She was twenty-eight maybe, or twenty-seven, and he was twenty-one. His name is Mirko Ilić, and he is a graphic designer, illustrator and comic book author who later on became one of the best-known graphic designers in the world, currently working in New York City, teaching and writing books.[4] He moved to New York in '85 or '86 when they separated. He was one of the first punks in Zagreb. I remember he went to London in 1977 or '78 to buy graphic books and novels and came back with his hair cut short, his jeans ripped, studded leather bracelets, a pierced ear and a leather jacket – and when he left for NYC he gave the jacket to me. As well as his leather trousers, which was an utterly shocking item of clothing to wear to school. Which of course meant I simply had to!

He brought back *Never Mind the Bollocks* by the Sex Pistols, he brought back *The Clash* and he brought back the Ramones' *Rocket to Russia*. At first, I was shocked by the noise! He used to listen to the records really loud and we were living

---

4. In the documentary *Sretno Dijete*, filmmaker Igor Mirković travels to New York to interview Mirko Ilić who is one of the film's central characters.

in a 35 square metres apartment and neither my mother nor I didn't really like the noise. Once we asked him to turn the music down a bit and I remember him taking the *Rocket to Russia* LP and smashing it against his knee – two or three years later I bought the same LP and listened to it again and again – and Ramones are still my 'feel good band' to turn to, which is something he teases me about to this day.

We also moved house like six times, so I was always the new kid on the block and the new kid in school. Since I looked weird even as a small kid, in high school I started doing it on purpose. I moved to Rijeka, which is on the coast, to live with my maternal grandparents whom I hated, and I'm sure that the feeling was mutual because I was a kid that their horrible daughter had with this horrible long-haired guy who then left her. And then she managed to marry another horrible guy who dressed horribly. You know, it was all terrible for them.

So, that's when I turned very rebellious and cut my hair with a straight razor. I turned myself into an outsider on purpose. Then my stepfather came to Rijeka to visit me and took me to see Termiti, Paraf and Pankrti, which all belonged to the first wave of punk bands in Yugoslavia. So that also marked me pretty strongly – I turned into a punk. And this rebellion I think was very important for young females because it gave you a licence to be sexy – but in a threatening way! So basically, you wouldn't get the shit you would get on the street if you were dressed as a normal girl. If you were dressed in a normal skirt, and whatever, you would get catcalls and unwanted touches at the bus or the tram station, or on the tram. And, you know, punk girls seem threatening to men – and this is what appealed to me.

So basically – this is how I got into punk rock music, still at the end of primary school. My stepfather also brought a bunch of fanzines and stuff from London, and also comic books. He was a comic book author and his characters were all a little bit 'punk'. And I always tried to look like his comic book characters. When I was fifteen, my mother bought me an overall which was skin-tight with long sleeves and a zipper up front in a leopard pattern. I wore it with a leather jacket or a second-hand, fake-fur tiger coat from the flea market. And I had bright orange, spiked, short hair. I would go to school wearing black make-up, painting my lips with eye-pencil because there was no black lipstick. Also, I would do my nails with a black, felt-tip marker pen. Imagine what it looked like after a few days – there was also no hair gel, up until about 1984. We used soap and water, which was especially nice when it rained. Or you could put sugar water in your hair to get it spiked, and also hair lacquer. I would steal it from my grandmother if I was there or she was around, as it was very expensive.

I was in a band, definitely chosen for my looks because I really, really, couldn't sing. Maybe someone was in love with me for some reason, other than my voice! We used to play Iggy and the Stooges, and the Velvet Underground.

We were doing covers which were not really even punk, it was more proto-punk. And I was starring in some music video when I was fifteen. We listened to Termiti, Paraf, Pankrti, Šarlo Akrobata, Pekinška patka, Električni orgazam, Kaos – and these were the first wave of punk/new wave bands. Of the 'foreign' bands, my all-time favourites were Iggy and the Stooges, the Ramones and the Clash. I was always sensitive to the political message and the lyrics were – and still are – very important to me, but the Ramones had a lot of energy, and the Stooges were just visceral. I was also listening to Patti Smith – she's my all-time favourite female author. If you listen to 'Horses' that's a seriously fucked-up song. She was a poet and that spoke to me.

I don't think that punk died but it morphed into something else. It's a natural process – everything changes shape and reinvents itself. I don't think there is a timeline to it actually. Punk to me isn't only the music, it's the attitude – something that doesn't really die. This no-bullshit attitude is what makes someone a 'punk' even if they don't listen to the music. But I'm the wrong person to ask – I am not inclined to label things and put them into drawers.

Of course, I was a Goth kid too, later on. What appealed to me in the Goth scene is that it was incredibly tolerant of gay people – especially gay men, which was nice. I was never exclusively punk or exclusively Goth (we were called 'Darkeri' – the Darks), but sometimes it was nice to dress up in a dress and wear a black veil or something else – also shocking. But I don't feel that feminine, I always feel more of a tomboy. I am not particularly into kids and traditional 'feminine stuff/roles' and I prefer animal company. I always preferred climbing a tree to playing with dolls. I like to wear make-up, I have long hair and sometimes I do wear dresses or skirts, but I think punk helped show me the ways to dress that are not necessarily feminine but still are female – not necessarily 'pants' and sneakers … even though right now I am wearing black skin-tight jeans, black Converse and a black, turtle-neck t-shirt, and I have a tattoo sleeve I had done when I was forty because I always wanted one but knew it was not a thing for rash decisions.

I think that's what I am thankful to punk for; it released my sexuality, but it didn't make me a slave to it the way I see girls today are (or seem to be). You know, when I see them wobbling in fishnet stockings and those high-heels that are supposed to be for pole-dancing or lying on your back, and not walking? And a skirt the size of a maxi-pad, push-up bra, silicone lips and silicone tits … sometimes I think 'but they are half-naked', to which my husband (who was also a punk) tells me, 'Well you were half-naked all the time and I won't even mention your leopard-skin, skin-tight overall because everybody in the town remembers that particular piece of clothing. Especially all the boys!'

But I didn't feel exposed; I didn't feel at the mercy of a sexual predator. I felt empowered by those clothes and not restricted or victimised by them. But when I see those girls, well sometimes I think – it's not what we fought for. That's the type of woman that I feel pity for in a way because I think that in order for a woman to feel, and project herself as sexy she doesn't have to be stripped of her power to move, or to run, or to dance, or to do anything – anything she wants to. I don't really care if I'm a woman or if I should be feminine, or what I should be.

I had a feeling punk was against the system and there was much wrong with that system but you know, in the end we got what we wanted – or deserved! And that's liberal capitalism and I am sure that we had it better before. I am aware that we weren't behind the Iron Curtain so you can't call this country a 'communist' country, but I think 'socialism' is humane – especially if you practice it like Scandinavian countries do. And free market capitalism is completely inhumane. I have visited the United States twice in the last six months and I can tell you for sure, that's the country I would rather be caught dead than living in.

When I was seventeen, in 1986 or '87, my mother took me to spend a month with her in New York City and that was the first time that I'd seen people homeless – and eating from trash and garbage containers. That was in the US and I was shocked. I was shocked that there could be people so poor that they had nowhere to live and nothing to eat. My father was already living in Toronto, and Toronto didn't have the homeless people eating from the trashcan so I was deeply shocked. I will never forget it. Every time I see a person going through the trash bin I remember it. I have to say, except for it being a Tito dictatorship and a Tower of Cards – hell, the whole idea of socialism, I don't have anything against it. I think it's just, right. I think that Karl Marx was very much right when he said that capitalism is going to destroy itself. I would add that it's pretty obvious nowadays that it's going to destroy the world and the planet that we live on. There is no question about it. I'm really wondering how come that kids today have no anger in them? The state of the world that we live in calls for kids to react! But the point is that when you give people enough for them to think that they have a lot, then you have a problem. People get inert.

Nowadays, we have a turbo-Catholic state; almost not secular because the church is mixing in all the pores of society. We now have the same phenomenon as in America that if a girl goes to get an abortion there are people praying in front of the hospital and telling her [that] she's a murderer. And they are constantly trying to make abortion illegal. We have religious education at school, and you can opt for your kid not taking it but then your kid would be an outsider. Many of my friends opted for the kid taking it because they are unwilling to make their kid an outsider.

I think that's probably not so good for the kid because it doesn't teach independent thinking. But what do I know, being an outsider all of my life? In 91, I moved to Vienna, Austria and stayed there for some fifteen-plus years before returning back to my hometown, Zagreb.

As for my career, I've been writing for women's magazines for the past twenty-five years – for *Elle* magazine, *Cosmopolitan* and some others. I wrote a novel, published three books of columns and even had an 'Agony Aunt' column for some four years on a news portal, before deciding I had enough of humans. Then I wrote a book about dogs, after which I started a dog blog and now it grew to be an educational portal/site.

In the meantime, I started a Ph.D. in archaeology because I discovered that there is an archaeology of dogs. I wrote an e-mail to a person who wrote a very comprehensive study of dog archaeology and the dog–human relationship in prehistory, and I asked him to be my foreign mentor, so we started collaborating on scientific papers which got published by relevant scientific journals. We are particularly interested in the dog–human relationship; the why and how, as well as the timing of the dog domestication process.

To answer to your question about music today – I don't really listen to much you could call new. Basically, there is too much music and I don't have the time to listen to 'new' music. I am a person who needs to form an emotional connection to the music, to have … experience with this music, and to form a memory connected to this music – and there is no time to do that properly, like we used to. Really sit, listen and stare at the LP cover … I don't think anybody really has the time to listen to the music in that way. I prefer to read. So I listen to audiobooks when I'm walking the dogs, or doing the dishes, or some other menial task. If I choose music, I rather listen to something that delivers emotions and memories than trying to form new memories.

To conclude, I think I have a lot of attitude towards life that stem from punk. I do what I want to do if I possibly can. I don't judge others and I don't let others judge me. Hell, I even have a punk dog! I tend to like terriers. I do have two other dogs and I did have some other breeds, but I always have to have one completely crazy Jack Russell Terrier – the incarnation of punk, it's a punk rock dog for me – never scared of anything and always jumping around. Of course, I do get scared and mopey and depressed, but I think that punk rock gave me this fighting spirit, which I also inherited through my mother who is an incredible fighter – through life, through diseases, through divorces. Punk also helped with this sense of I can do anything if I want to. That helps a lot in life. So if I feel down or depressed, or I need to clean the apartment really fast, then I listen to the

Ramones or some other old-school punk band, and the music gives me strength, lifts me up and makes me face my fear. The other option would be to put on the Smiths or the Cure and think of ending it all – OK, I do that first. For a bit. Just to feel the difference.

Kaos. Ljubljana © Matija Praznik (1982).

TWELVE
Pula: Uljanik Calling

DAY EIGHT

Sale picks us up at the agreed time. As we drive – with Tomislav translating – he says he would like to give me a tour of Pula to see some of its history if that is OK with me. This sounds like a great idea. Again the weather is perfect. It is not yet mid-morning but the sun is warm and the sky virtually cloudless, thick and blue. As we drive, Sale apologises for not being in touch very much during the preceding months. He says he is 'not really […] a person for the internet, never buy anything from it and never use Facebook'. His first wife is a computer programmer. They had a computer twenty-five years ago but he saw then what was going to happen. Today he uses his computer only as a drop box: 'It may be old school, but I don't want to be online for twenty-four hours a day.'

Our first stop is Uljanik Rock Club. The club is in a central suburb of Pula, on a small, steep hillside. Sale parks up on the narrow road outside the club, in the shade of some mature trees still abundant with leaves. As we get out of the car, through the trees I see the cranes, workshops and perimeter wall of a huge shipyard just over the main road. The iconic Uljanik shipyard from which the nightclub, and so much more in Pula, takes a name. We walk across the road to take a look over the gate of the club. It has a large walled yard and the gate is locked. By chance, the club owner's wife appears from inside the club; she immediately recognises Sale and lets us in to take some photos and have a look around. The yard is an integral part of the club, it is a performance space, a hall with no roof. It resembles a primary-school yard but with an al fresco stage. At the back of the stage is a wall, painted with a larger-than-life reproduction of a 1950s, vintage crooner-style microphone. Above that, standing proud from the wall is the legend 'ROCK * ULJANIK * ROCK'. 'This is the summer terrace', says Sale, 'it holds two thousand people'. He adds that this place is legendary and has been open for more than fifty years, during which time numerous overseas artists and most ex-Yugoslav punk legends played here – Pankrti, Partibrejkers, Disciplin A Kitschme, Psihomodo Pop, Hladno pivo, Problemi and many others including, of course, KUD Idijoti. Outside Sale walks us to a shaded old stone stairway which leads up to a small park, 'This is Tusta's Stairs'.

On our way here Sale had pointed out the road on which Tusta lived. Tusta, Branko Črnac Tusta. No book about punk rock (or rock music) in ex-Yugoslavia would be complete without Tusta. Tusta was the charismatic and dynamic frontman of KUD Idijoti from 1985 until his death on 14 October 2012. I can well remember seeing the genuine grief and the earnest tributes from Croatians, Serbs, Slovenes, Bosnians, Italians and others on that day. At the time I had no real appreciation of Tusta's position as a figurehead, and in many ways talisman, of Yugoslavian punk. 'Tusta would have hated this being named after him', Sale says, smiling. 'But when he died the city council took a vote and ...' I had been wary of broaching the subject of Tusta with Sale. They had been bandmates and comrades through mercurial and turbulent times. I knew from our communications and advice from others that Sale did not like talking about KUD Idijoti. He told me it was my fortune to be 'Barry from Demob', and not a journalist – as such, the door was open to me.

At the interview, Sale would tell the story of Tusta's diagnosis with throat cancer in 2011 and how the initial prognosis was positive, one of hope, and of the band's response and his own personal emotions. I had seen videos and live footage covering twenty-seven years of Tusta's life. He was the first of my interview targets in Yugoslavia who we would lose during the process – but sadly not the last. Tusta, wearing a white vest, or a black t-shirt, sometimes his trusted black-leather motorbike jacket. Tusta, droplets of sweat dripping or flying from long, sandy-brown hair pushed back over his ears; stocky and muscular, prowling the stage, leaning over the mic-stand into the faces of the adoring audience. Them, hands outstretched towards the stage, and then fists clenched in response to Tusta's, or index fingers jabbing as they sing each anthemic word. For some he seems to have been a constant; barely ageing or showing signs of growing old. But there is something else. He is one of us. This is not fan-worship so much as love, brotherly love. And he smiles a lot. It is not difficult to see why some felt they had lost a beacon, an anchor, a reference point; someone who had helped them navigate the uncertainty of the post-Tito era, the break-up of Yugoslavia, a decade of wars and the downward economic spirals. A leader – albeit perhaps a reluctant one.

A documentary called simply *Tusta* is in production at the time I visit Pula. Among the filmmaker Andrej Korovljev's previous films is the award-winning documentary *The Years of Rust* which explores how the workers of Uljanik shipyard became victims of the murky and unscrupulous Croatian privatization process. By day, Tusta was a worker and trade union organiser at the shipyard. In an interview, Korovljev describes Tusta as 'a family man, father, worker, trade unionist, trade union leader, rocker, bar rocker, old hippie, punk [...] anarchist, antifascist'. I have seen him called 'The Che of Istria'. I cannot know for sure, but I suspect he may have laughed in the face of that kind of idolatry. Tusta once said,

> I have come to the realisation that political change can only be achieved by political means and political work, not by singing. Each activity has its

own implements. You plough with a plough, you fight a war with a gun, you carry out restrictions with laws. Songs against war do not stop wars, singing about poverty doesn't enrich the poor (perhaps the author of the song, ha, ha), songs about corruption do not prevent corruption. So, what do songs resolve? Nothing, for the most part.

We return to the car. Sale asks if we would like to see the castle and take in the view of the city below. We drive through narrow streets and up another steep incline. 'Parking is a problem', Sale tells us as he finds an off-road space. 'We will have to walk from here'. Pula has many places where the tourist trails and the working town are indivisible. This adds to its charm. We walk through narrow, pedestrianised streets, pausing for Sale to show us where he has a pitch for his record stall. High above us are the walls of a fortress. After a few more minutes, we climb some steps and arrive at the fortress site. From here I can see these ramparts are constructed on the vestiges of an earlier fortress. We clamber over crumbling walls and scramble up and down grassy banks. Sale moves quickly and smoothly, obviously at home on the terrain. Up another level, we are immersed in an even more distant past as we stand amongst the ruins of a small Roman theatre. Catching our breath for a moment, Tomislav grasps the opportunity to photograph the views of Uljanik below. The sky is now streaked with perfectly straight ribbons of pale white cloud. We climb again, dragged along by Sale. As we approach the summit Sale says, 'Pula was the main Austro-Hungarian port and most of the buildings here are Austro-Hungarian. You can see urban villas probably built for officers from the Austro-Hungarian military'.

Beneath us radiate tunnels dating from various times in Pula's long history: 'They say you can put forty-five to fifty thousand people in those tunnels and they would be safe' Sale tells us. Beneath the city we can see today, is a hidden city. Sale says that below this spot is where, in the 'old days', everyone came to hang out, drink, smoke pot or sniff glue. Tomislav laughs and asks, 'Does anyone sniff glue these days?'

Before embarking on this quixotic mission, I had not heard of Pula. A city with a history which pre-dates the Greeks and yet is linked with *Jason and the Golden Fleece*. A city which has some of the finest surviving Roman remains anywhere in the world. A city mentioned by Dante in his *Divine Comedy*. A city where James Joyce lived with Nora Barnacle. Where he is said to have written much of what would eventually become *Portrait of the Artist as a Young Man*. Joyce was not keen on Pula and was particularly patronising and demeaning about the locals. I suspect this is why Pula mutters rather than bellows its claim to a share of the Joycean heritage-tourism dividend. Pula was shuttled between Austria-Hungary and Italy, and then

Italian and German fascism; governed by the post-war allies as an occupied zone until 1947 and then subsumed into Tito's Socialist, non-aligned, Yugoslavia.

At the crest of this hill, keeping a benevolent watch over the town below, stands the Venetian fortress. On the landward side the city falls away dramatically, and we can see inland for miles. It is a magnificent view. In the foreground are grand Austro-Hungarian villas. The middle distance is dominated by a magnificent, three-tiered amphitheatre with its external walls forming an unbroken oval – the famous Pula Arena. Tomislav tells me that it is one of the largest Roman amphitheatres in the world. Beyond the arena are residential areas built into hills that climb away from the city centre. We are standing on a plinth of rock and closely cropped grass, at eye level with the upper windows of nearby stately Habsburg houses in sorbet yellows and pinks. The skeletons of walls from various eras outline irregular terraces beside and below us. As my eyes adjust to the panorama in front of us, what emerges is an intriguing kaleidoscope of Roman, Austro-Hungarian and Communist-era architecture co-existing shoulder to shoulder.

On the seaward side is the shipyard, harbour and bay. From here we can see that the city and the bay form a horseshoe bowl, tilted northwest with the city nestled in the curve. Two kilometres or so through the channel, at the open mouth, is the island of Veliki Brijun where Tito had his favourite residence. It was here that he met world leaders as diverse as Nasser and Nehru, Haile Selassie I, Eleanor Roosevelt and the Ceausescus. Here that, in 1956, he held crisis talks with Kruschev during the Hungarian Uprising. Here, famously, that he entertained Sophia Loren, Richard Burton[1] and Elizabeth Taylor, Gina Lollobridgida, Orson Welles, Kirk Douglas, James Joyce and Queen Elizabeth II. It was also here, contrary to the reports in hostile biographies that he was ashamed of his past as a metalworker, that he kept a lathe 'to practice his craft'. Here, also, that he kept a 1950s Cadillac.

At the crown is the Historical & Maritime Museum. This is the highest point in the city and the best view. It has been an observation point since Roman Times. We face the sea. From here the view is all about the sprawling Uljanik shipyard with which Pula is synonymous. Within its walls, four-storey, nineteenth-century warehouses butt against the Tito-era workshops and silos. It is seeped with industriousness and the dignity of labour. Just as Pula Arena commands the landward view, it is the cranes of the shipbuilding yard which dominate the seaward view. Perhaps a dozen of them, satisfyingly mantis-like, tower over the buildings below, and dwarf the sleeping T-bar, construction cranes. From here, it is easy to understand why Sale stressed that, at one time, everyone in Pula relied to some degree on Uljanik.

---

1. Burton was soon to play Tito in the Yugoslavian Partisan movie *Battle of Sutjeska*, for which Welles was a co-writer.

Sale used to work in Uljanik. He asks if we have ever seen a mega-ship launched. We have not. He says that to see a tanker or mega-ship launched live is a spectacular thing. He describes, with a writer's eye for detail, the launching process. He says proudly that it was from down there that the biggest ships built in Yugoslavia were launched. It was down there that a method of building a ship in two huge sections and conjugating them on the water was developed.

Pula's shipbuilding history is long and illustrious but less celebrated is its role as the link between the pioneering days of submarine warfare and *The Sound of Music*. Georg Johannes Ritter von Trapp was born in current-day Zadar (Croatia) in April 1880 and joined the Austro-Hungarian Navy, stationed initially in Rijeka. Submariner Georg married a wealthy, blue-blooded British lady named Agatha Whitehead, the granddaughter of Robert Whitehead, (arguably) the co-inventor of the modern torpedo – having established the world's first torpedo factory at Rijeka. The rapidly expanding von Trapp family lived in Trapp Villa, Pina Budicina 11, Pula – a short walk from our apartment.

In 1917, von Trapp oversaw the sinking of an incredible tally of eleven Allied cargo ships, including what was reputed to be the world's largest cargo ship at the time, the 'Milazzo'.

Agatha Whitehead died of scarlet fever in 1922 but not before producing seven children. So, Georg inherited a 'British' fortune just five years after sinking tens of thousands of tons of Allied ships and cargo. Forty-seven-year-old Georg then married the children's nanny, Maria aged twenty-two, lost the family fortune in a banking crash during the Great Depression and began a new career as the head of the singing von Trapp family. In November 2018, the legendary Slovenian dissident, industrial-post-punks Laibach released an album of covers from *The Sound of Music*. The typically perverse idea was conceived when they were invited to be the first rock band to perform in North Korea, where the film is apparently extremely popular. A documentary, *Liberation Day*, which tracks the band and their DPRK minders during the buildup to the Pyongyang concert was also released. Laibach alternated 'Maria' for 'Korea' when performing and recording the iconic track from the film, How do you solve a problem like …?

Sale points to the string of nineteenth-century properties along the coast, close to the shipyard, and tells us that nearly all of these were for military families. As my eyes acclimatise, I see that many buildings here are flying what Sale tells me is the Istrian flag – a horizontal blue stripe above a horizontal green stripe. On the stripes, set against a blue shield, is a yellow goat with red hooves and longhorns. Sale explains that goat is symbolic of Istria, since it represents an animal that gives a lot but asks for little. He says there is so much more we could talk about, but time is limited if we are to get started with the interview which is the main purpose of our visit: 'Let's go. Coffee time'.

Sale Veruda: Forum Square, Pula

Sale Veruda. The Forum, Pula © Tomislav 'Tompa' Zebić (2017)

Forum Square has been the heart of Pula since Roman times. For two thousand years this neat, paved square of perhaps twenty buildings has served continuously as the meeting place and administrative centre of Pula. Sale and I take a table at a café bar on the half of the square warmed by the ascendant autumn sun. Behind Sale, forming the northern edge of the square, is the handsome two-storey City Hall with its Gothic portico facing the main square. A City Hall has stood on this site since the ninth century. To the immediate left, originally dating back to sometime around the first decade AD is the Temple of Augustus. It was severely damaged by Allied bombs during the Second World War but rebuilt in 1947. Obscured from view by the buildings which form the west side of the square, the Adriatic is just 100 metres away to my left. There too is the manmade isthmus that connects the main shipyard to the islet from which Uljanik takes its name. On this tiny island stand fabrication workshops – and a single olive tree preserved as a reminder of its original state.

Sale was the first ex-Yugoslavian punk musician with whom I made contact, back in July 2015. It was, of course, Sale who had reinterpreted 'No Room For You' as 'To nije mjesto za nas' and recorded it with his band KUD Idijoti. It is he who is largely responsible for its rebirth and Balkan legacy. Without Sale the story would not exist, and without speaking with him the story could not be complete. KUD Idijoti's reputation as one of the few working-class punk bands in Yugoslavia added to the intrigue. As we sit at the table, drinking coffee and waiting for Tomislav to arrive to help with any translation issues, we find we have remarkably few problems understanding each other since we share the language of gear-heads as we compare notes about guitar set-ups and rigs, production techniques and the place of folk music in cultural DNA.

* * *

I have lived in Pula for almost fifty years. I was born in Belgrade. My parents were students. My Mother was a Meteorologist, and the only Meteorological school was in Belgrade. They met as students in Belgrade, I was born there but I'm not Serb. My father was a student of Law, but they divorced very quickly so my mother came to Pula.

Pula then was like you see now, the old city that you've seen. Times are changing everywhere and in Pula also. If we are talking about a period of forty or fifty years, you know that things must change in that period of time – sociologically, politically and in many other ways. It is inevitable for things to change. We had a change of two political systems; Yugoslavia – and this Balkan pool – was transferred from socialism to a period of 'capitalism'. Not totally the Eastern type of socialism, and not totally the western type of capitalism. You have to know that two systems changed during our time. So it changed politically, sociologically and in many other senses. Even within the framework of the same system – even if the systems didn't change – in fifty years even in one regime it could be a big change.

We didn't have a Russian type of socialism; we had a type of liberal socialism. Yugoslavia had valid money currency [sic] that was worth something, so we could travel all around the world. The living standard was much higher than the Iron Curtain countries; it wasn't like Romania or Bulgaria, or the whole Eastern Bloc, including East Germany. We were like a cross-fade between the West and the East. Especially if you look at it geographically – you can see that we are now just 100 kilometres away from Trieste in Italy. So the people from Istria were going to Trieste or other cities in Italy at least once a week. Some of them, even on a daily basis.

When I started actively to get into music I was fifteen and now I'm fifty-five. All of my life I have been interested in music, my father was a collector of music. In our family there was always a record player and we always bought records. Even today I have old records, old jazz records, from this collection. There are some great old records of my father's which still exist today. But you know what? We bought everything that was popular then. We bought folk music and funk music, everything. As a kid I even started going to music school. I have one grade of music school completed for accordion. Then I heard Bijelo Dugme; I sold my accordion, I bought a record player for myself, put that record on and that's how I started. I was listening to every kind of music. In my collection, you can find all kinds of music. Why? Well, in those days if you don't want to only listen to music from radio or television – if you want to listen to your 'own' music – you have to buy records and tapes. I was listening to everything between Abba and Mozart, Rubinstein and the Sex Pistols, the Ramones and folk music – to a cappella music from Dalmatia called Klapa.

Maybe I am being subjective, but it seems to me that Yugoslav 'musical intelligence' – let's call it that – was very progressive for the time. The older ones, the older generation, were telling me about Radio Luxembourg. They were all listening to Radio Luxembourg and everything that was hip at that time. Musicians at that time would be listening to Radio Luxembourg and hearing what's new, what's hip and what's relevant – and almost immediately they would try to cover it. And they would manage to cover it in a pretty short period of time. So, if they were in a band and they had a gig – let's say Friday night or Saturday night – they would be playing the things they heard on Radio Luxembourg on Tuesday. So it was pretty quick and pretty good. Bands even used to have competitions between themselves to see who would do it better, who would do it more precisely, and who would have the freshest material. Looking at it now, we didn't see it as something special, we didn't see it as something worth mentioning at that time. But as we grew older, we managed to see what a big thing it was for that time.

There were two big record companies in Yugoslavia. You had Jugoton in Zagreb and RTB in Belgrade. Jugoton, especially, had a great catalogue – even by today's standards – and you could find almost anything relevant in the world at that time on the Jugoton catalogue. Jugoton issued records of some bands that I find amazing that they managed to publish. Some of them, I really don't know how they ended up on the catalogue. For instance, let's say the Blasters and the Real Kids. The Real Kids were published by Jugoton! It was their first LP and it's a rare record. That record is widely known and widely appreciated all around the world as a rare record, and a good record. So the Yugoslav musical history of those two publishing houses – especially Jugoton – was really, really respectable. Yugoslav people really did care about what was being published in those two publishing houses. They knew what was happening in the world and they really did keep up with the trends. Plus, they travelled, so they could pick up records anywhere in the world. For [the] second example of this 'musical intelligence', the first punk band in Pula was called

Problems – or Problemi in Croatian. They had a show on the day of SKOJ[2] and that public holiday was on 10 October 1978. In relation to the world scene, I think that's quick to follow up. Another example would be that in those times I used to write a lot of fanzines and I had a question from a guy in East Germany. He told me that the first time he heard about punk was at some time in the mid eighties, and he started when someone brought him a Buzzcocks record that had been bought in Yugoslavia.

There were two factors that made KUD Idijoti. Problemi, the band, were the equivalent of the Sex Pistols on our scene in Yugoslavia – let's put it this way; it was a short and stormy career. So when this short and stormy career of Problemi ended, the singer was free. Me and my two friends already had a band called Nafta – Nafta means oil. In the seventies, there was the big oil crisis, so everything revolved around oil, so it was only logical to us to name the band 'Oil'. And since the singer of Problemi was free, he got into our band. That's how – from being a trio – we became four. So basically KUD Idijoti derived from the singer of Problemi and three of us from Oil. That was the first KUD Idijoti line-up. Sadly, we never had a gig with that line-up because the singer left the band after only three months. So, again, the first KUD Idijoti gigs we played as a trio – I was singing.

So then we became a four again with a new singer who was with us for some two-and-a-half years and then after him, Tusta came – it was 1985. We could say that '85 was the year that we established the final line-up, at least for a longer period of time. It was Fritz on the bass, Ptica on the drums, Tusta on the vocals and me on the guitar. And that line-up lived until 1999. Then we changed the rhythm section. In fact what happened was that the co-founder of KUD Idijoti came back. For such a long career we had a relatively small amount of changes of personnel in the band. And at the end of the circle we ended up as a trio again, because [in] the last few shows we had booked I had to sing because Tusta was too ill. So in a way I was made to sing because we were in a constant search for a singer.

When all of those things started in Pula – in '78, expanded in '79 and bloomed in '80 – we were a bit younger than the other people on the scene. We were, let's say, fourteen or fifteen while the others were eighteen and nineteen. The main thing is that most of them were already out of the army and that was the big thing because, at that age, two or three years difference made quite a lot of impact. So, we were not part of the first punk wave in this area; we were the second wave. The same as Stiff Little Fingers or Discharge are not the first wave of UK punk.

---

2. Savez komunističke omladine Jugoslavije (League of Communist Youth of Yugoslavia).

So, we had in Pula the compilation of *Punk & Disorderly Volume One*. And on that compilation is 'No Room For You' by Demob. I knew nothing about Demob. And then later in Switzerland when we played there, I saw a single which had 'No Room For You' on one side and 'Police Story' on the other side as a B side.[3] That's about it. For me, that song was just great, and the title was just great. In fact, the title was something I could identify with because I had already written my lyrics, and that song was a kind of a trigger for me. But you know in those days, copyrighting and stuff like that, we really didn't know anything about it. We were totally clueless. We began to get a grip on those kinds of things a relatively long time after we'd started. Not until around the time we were recording the album *The Price of Glory* – around that time we learned about copyrighting. That would be approximately somewhere around the summer of 1999. Until then we really did function only on the punk principles, the real punk ethos. At that time, we used to play in Germany and Switzerland a lot. But even though we did play in Germany and Switzerland, and even though it was wartime in Yugoslavia, we still managed to have bigger audiences and sell more records in our homeland – to be better in our homeland against all odds.

For me at that time, my favourite live experience was our concerts with the Ramones, I must say that. One concert we played with the Ramones in Hala Tivoli in Ljubljana.[4] And then also our first appearance in Serbia after the war, in 2000. It was a Sports Hall in New Belgrade. There may have been some Croatian artists and bands playing there before us but, if so, it was more like in a private arrangement, it wasn't a public event like ours. What's interesting is that the album *The Price of Glory* was the first album by a Croatian band issued in Serbia after the war. So basically, this gig in 2000 was the first gig, we can say, that worked on a normal level and it worked as a communication tool.[5] That means that no political party stood for us, and we didn't stand for any political party. I know that – because of the political views that our band was so obviously showing and because of our music. The fact is that KUD Idijoti had an audience – a following – in all republics in ex-Yugoslavia, before and after the war. It was the feeling that we were playing among the people like us, people that think like us. And we played from the heart and we played because we wanted to. There was nothing behind us, no hidden agendas. It was just for the sake of the music and the sake of our fans. At that gig we didn't have any people who were politically

---

3. This seems to be one of the many 'bootleg' singles released without the knowledge of the band and the flip side was probably Demob's first single 'Anti Police'.
4. KUD Idijoti opened for the Ramones at the Hala Tivoli, Ljubljana on 10 October 1994.
5. KUD Idijoti's performance in Serbia is widely viewed as the first performance by a major 'Croatian' band in Serbia after the war.

different from us. Anyone who hated the band didn't come, so we played among the people that loved us – and we loved them. So, it was the same for us if we played those gigs in Belgrade or Skopje, or Ljubljana, or somewhere in Croatia. It was really one great, domestic and pleasant atmosphere.

Nowadays I have a stall, a little stand where I sell my products (records, CDs, t-shirts, etc.). Many people don't believe it, but I really do check all of my second-hand stuff that I sell. Even today, some people who are DJs in the clubs are bringing records for me to clean up because I have my procedure – a certain procedure that really works. Let's say I have a secret method which does clean records really well; of course, if they are not mechanically interrupted or damaged – if they are, then I can't do anything. When I do those things with the records I spend about an hour-and-a-half to two hours on each record. I really spend a lot of my time doing that, so the music I am listening to most today is the thing that I am given to clean. Basically, we are talking about old records and old stuff. Actually, I started to listen more and more to old music. I was surprised, for instance, to hear how the Allman Brothers are a great band and Duane Allman is a great guitarist. The other specific thing about my stand is that I try to offer as much as I can of our domestic music, music from our country and this area. And, of course, I listen to all of it. So basically, it's anything from Croatian Jazz, Croatian a cappella – the 'Klapa' music – through to Croatian rock 'n' roll, punk and everything else. Also, I must say that I do even listen to notorious pop singers. It seems to me that nowadays I can find something good in anything.

What I'm most interested in now is the career potential of my band Saša 21; it's something that I'm totally involved with now and it's pretty much all I do. We're a band that started from scratch and that's a good thing. We started from zero. I don't play any of the old material – any KUD Idijoti stuff or anything. We are a new band and we act like a new band. That has a certain appeal to me. I don't use any old credits or merits, or anything like that. We are a new band. We are old perhaps in the number of years we have in total, but as a band we are as young as any band made by kids! And, of course, it goes really slowly and really hard – you know, the birth problems of a band. The only thing that I'm worried about is the fact that I'm not young anymore and now the biological clock is working against me. I'm just wondering if I will have enough time to record everything that I am thinking about now.

What can I say in summary? To change a world with music, well I got rid of these illusions when I was young. Music and musicians do change the world but not in a political sense – not in a political way of thinking – because music is just not the thing for political changes. If you want political changes, you have to do politics. You won't fix unemployment, you won't get rid of unemployment, just by singing about it. Let's say you're driving on a highway and you burst a tyre – you'll need a wrench

In Search of Tito's Punks

Number 13, not a song about it. You can write a song about wrench Number 13 but that won't change your tyre or fix your problem. The song is not the tool to change the tyre; it's wrench Number 13. So, I would say that if music and musicians do change opinions, they do it on an individual level. If you look at it, you can see how many bands in England tore their throats singing against Margaret Thatcher – from Crass to I don't know who – but she did all her terms almost to the end.

You know what happens, we all have in life a certain book that we've read; for someone else maybe it's a movie that he saw or a band that he met or saw or heard, and that was the thing that individually changed the person. So all of us will know at least a few people who will say that 'when I read this book or heard this song my whole world shifted'. That's this individual change that I am speaking about. And then after that you, as a person, function on a better level through your whole life. But the political systems around you didn't change. You did.

Branko 'Tusta' Črnac (left), KUD Idijoti. Novi Sad © Radovan Ristić (1989)

THIRTEEN
England: Back to the Forest

> When you lot get out/We're gonna hit the town/
> We'll burn it fuckin' down/To a cinder

Friday 8 December 2017; I am preparing to take a flight from Amsterdam Schiphol to Bristol. From there, I will travel up to the Forest of Dean, in West Gloucestershire, to spend a few days with my old friend and (several times) bandmate, Robert 'Miff' Smith, who wrote and sang 'No Room For You'.

For two days now, BBC radio has carried apocalyptic weather warnings about the 'Arctic storm' that is about to hit the United Kingdom and, quite specifically Wales and the West Country. This is not a good portent since the Forest of Dean is a plateau which sits between the rivers Severn and Wye. Such is the historical independence, awkwardness and quirkiness of 'the Forest' and its inhabitants that it is sometimes referred to as *between* Wales and England – not Welsh but, somehow, not quite English either. Even in the inter-connected, always-on, internet age, it somehow retains a certain remoteness – something which can be charming, or alienating or bewildering, or all three.

No matter, as I leave home in The Hague, the weather is normal for this time of year – perhaps a little colder than average but nothing exceptional. The trams and the trains run with their usual unspectacular Dutch efficiency. However, at Schiphol the departures boards are full of cancelled and delayed flights. Sure enough, KL1053 soon joins the list of those delayed. By the time we board, it is nearly an hour late. As we gather speed on the runway, the horizontal sleet shoots by, illuminated in the darkness by the flashing lights on the wing – classic aeroplane-disaster-movie material. The flight is not so bad, just some occasional turbulence, more than offset by the carrier being one of the few who still hand out free wine.

Another old bandmate and friend has offered to drive down to Bristol to pick me up. I have not seen Lar for nearly thirty years. I am quickly through check-out and arrivals and wait near the automatic doors, directly opposite a concession shop. Each time the doors open, bitterly cold air rushes in. I move towards the warmth of the shop and feign interest in newspapers and chocolate bars. Outside the night sky is leather-jacket black; it feels as though it has been like this for weeks. The wind whines as it grazes my skin. Lar texts to say he has been diverted but will be with me soon. I pass ten more minutes shuffling my hand luggage between the store and the concourse. Lar arrives, looking younger than he has any right to and we man-hug with the obligatory level of awkwardness.

Although we have only recently made contact again, the conversation is easy. Lar works as a self-employed, graphic designer these days (he was always a gifted artist) and is playing mostly local pub and bar gigs. But he has had a measure of success in the intervening years with one of his bands, Judy Speedway, getting a record deal and touring with the likes of the Stranglers and the Clash's Mick Jones. He also filled in as guitarist for a handful of dates with our old Forest of Dean friends, transatlantic 1990s chart-toppers, EMF.

We drive over the Severn Bridge which, since I last crossed it, has been saddled with the prefix 'old' – usurped by a newer Severn Bridge downstream. Exiting the motorway which runs across the Severn Bridge we drop down through the town of Chepstow – always one of my favourite towns in the area. As a child, my parents regularly took my brother and me to the spectacular ruin of Chepstow Castle which traces the jagged cliffs above the river's huge tidal rise and fall.

In the dark we cross another historic bridge – the Grade One listed, iron-latticed, Old Wye Bridge which has stood on this site since the early nineteenth century. We drive along familiar A roads bordered by farmland, and then deserted country lanes, roadside trees bending in the strengthening winds, and arrive in a small village which consists of little more than houses lining the main road. Not sure of the address, we take an educated guess that the house with a collection of 4 × 4s, including a restored vintage Land Rover, must be Miff's. Sure enough, we are soon sitting next to a real fire, beer in hand, whilst attempting to meet the demands of three rescued, 'scrapyard hounds'.

That night, Lar, Miff, his wife Sarah and I make the short journey into the nearby town of Coleford and two pubs which had not existed the last time I visited. Coleford is one of the two major towns in the Forest and was considered the 'capital' of the west Forest whilst the other, Cinderford, was the capital of the east Forest. Growing up there in the 1970s, it was impossible not to be conscious of a sharp rivalry between the two – particularly between young men from each. Perhaps the only thing which would unite them back then was their dislike for the punks – wherever we came from. Today, Coleford seemed considerably quieter and less testosterone-fuelled than in years gone by, but perhaps that was a consequence of us being older and less likely to attract trouble.

The following evening, Miff's band the Hickory Stick Boys are playing a gig in Cinderford. The venue is a pub which, back in our youth, had a well-earned reputation for low-level but high-frequency violence. It has long since been renamed and renovated. Sarah and I go for a walk around the near deserted town-centre (well, around the War Memorial which doubles as 'town-centre' in so many towns like this) and meet Lar for a quiet drink. When we get back to the venue the band is already on stage and kicking up a squall (the pub is not yet busy enough to kick up a storm) with their tight and spirited covers of songs by the Clash, Bruce Springsteen and the Specials. Miff's sister Deb is there with their Mum. In our teenage years, Deb had been the most 'punk' girl in the Forest (being a couple of years older than us) and had been with us at pretty much every gig we went to or played. During the band's second set things liven up and the dance floor fills. The locals clearly have a keen sense of their history and identity with at least two being ejected by security for varying degrees of aggressive misbehaviour and drunkenness – one after attempting to pick a fight with me, backing down and then coming back to apologise.

'Proper snow coming tonight mind', Deb prophesises as we stand in the arctic smoking area outside. We get home just after 1 a.m. Soon after that the 'proper snow' starts.

After a 4 a.m. finish, it was only to be expected that I would not rise until midday was in close touching distance. I do not even have to draw back the curtains to know that a serious amount of snow has fallen. What little sound there is outside is characteristically muffled. I resign myself to tomorrow's travel being at best hideous, and at worst abandoned.

That evening, Miff and I sit down to reminisce and fill in the gaps.

Monday 11 December; I am packed and ready to make the 275 kilometres trip to Bolton where I will be presenting at the 'Punk Scholars Network Conference' at Bolton University. This will be the first time I go public and expose *In Search of Tito's Punks* outside my circle of close friends and interviewees. I am a little apprehensive; what if they think it is a ridiculous subject? Worse still, what if no one is interested? In spite of the doubts, I am desperate to get there. The weather has been suggesting it might not happen and, even if it does, attendance at the conference could be severely hit. Miff, being Miff, says we should skip the idea of heading to the local railway station and he will drive me to the main station 35 kilometres away in Gloucester. He has the 4 × 4 so 'no worries'. The roads are quiet and the journey uneventful. At Gloucester, we say our goodbyes.

Suffice to say the onward journey is a predictably dreary, soul-sucking trial of standing-room-only trains; delayed trains; diverted or cancelled trains; trains that have that gag-inducing, ammonia-steeped, miasma in the vestibules; freezing cold platforms with the incessant, infantilised, public announcements about not leaving baggage, not cycling, not skateboarding, not smoking, not standing too close to the platform edge, not falling over on the wet floor, etc. I long to be back in the Netherlands.

In Search of Tito's Punks

Six hours later I arrive at a mercilessly cold Bolton and find my way to the hotel. It is situated on a deserted side street in a rundown former industrial area. A few metres from the hotel entrance I stop to give some tobacco and what coins I have to a homeless man whose cardboard sheets and bags are pitched against the foot of a low wall; I know it is a pathetic and largely futile gesture. It is 7 p.m. The air is icy and thin, the night sky is tar black and the temperature falling rapidly from an already low base. It is a little over seven weeks since I departed The Hague for ex-Yugoslavia. Everything looks different now.

Robert 'Miff' Smith: Coleford, Gloucestershire, England

Robert 'Miff' Smith. 'The Forest', Gloucestershire December 2017

How did I get to write that song? Christ! I never set out with a goal to write it and I didn't, at the time, imagine that I'd written the kind of song that it's become. It had to be easy because at the time I wasn't actually very good as a guitarist. So it was going to be quite simple; it was going to be three chords. The idea of the melody had come to me and it wrote itself because it fitted around the three chords. I was trying to write songs that meant something – rather than, 'La la, I love you'. Whitcombe Lodge had just closed down – and Whitcombe Lodge had been a very, very important part of my musical 'thing'. It was a total chance that place existed; it was a rundown motel on the outskirts of Gloucester. Some enterprising guys had taken over and decided to start putting on punk bands there. Any band worth seeing apart from the Clash or the Pistols played there. I went there quite a lot to see any number of bands. But the venue had been closed for various reasons. I think the police and the local council didn't really like the kids having a specific venue where they could congregate. I guess they thought that kids getting together was troublesome. I mean there were fights there but it wasn't like it was a real fighting, rough, venue. No worse than lots.

But yeah, there was definitely a police presence there. I mean it was a rough, tatty old place … holes kicked in the toilet walls and the cubicles never had doors on them. It was knocked down not long after it finished as a venue.

I think it started with gigs in October '78 and it lasted until about, early '80 I would say.[1] We played there as Demob must have been half a dozen times. We were never, ever, booked properly – apart from the last night when we were actually on the bill. We just turned up. One of the guys who ran it was a great big Rasta guy and the other guy was one of those characters who was like a 'hangover-hippy' dude who had turned punk. So you could go up there and they'd be hanging around on a Saturday afternoon and we'd say, 'Can we get up and play tonight?' And we'd invariably told, 'Alright, alright you can go on first. You can do twenty minutes'. The ethic in those days was that the main band would let you use their kit. So it was very much the punk ethic thing.

It was one of those songs that kind of wrote itself because the first line was so easy, 'Well we don't go there anymore'. It's only in the last fifteen years that I have realised it's infinitely more than I had thought it ever was. I was completely surprised that an American band had even known of the bloody song let alone want to cover it.[2] And then, of course, with the advent of YouTube in the next few years it became apparent that it was actually popular with lots of people from not only Britain but from Croatia, Poland, America, Canada [and] Australia.[3] And I had no idea the bloody single had got that far! Because Yugoslavia was then sort of 'behind the Iron Curtain', so to speak, I don't think that any of us really imagined that there would be punk rockers there – that the authorities would even allow there to be punk rock bands. So to find out that there actually were punk bands there and that amongst those punks and those musicians, 'No Room For You' was really popular was to me like fucking astounding!

I don't think we were really that aware of Yugoslavia. I mean we knew it was there because of geography lessons at school and things like that. I think that most

---

1. The first gig was autumn 1978 and the final gig was 15 September 1979 when the UK Subs played with a support bill comprising the finest local punk bands including Demob. During its lifetime, it hosted the Cure, Echo & the Bunnymen, the Damned, the Slits, the Ruts, the Cramps, the Pop Group, the Selecter, Madness, the Specials and many more. The Specials gig went down in local legend such was the violence. Violence was one of the main reasons why the promoter, Chris Garland, decided to call a halt to the gigs. Interviewed in 2015 he said, 'I stopped because it all became very unpleasant. A huge crowd of very nasty punks from Birmingham and elsewhere started turning up, and there was more and more violence'.
2. Defiance, street punk band from Portland, Oregon recorded it for their 2002 *Out of the Ashes* LP.
3. After this interview took place, we discovered a 2001 version by a Basque punk band which had 300,000 YouTube views and versions by two Mexican punk bands.

people of our generation probably only woke up and took notice of Yugoslavia when their 'civil war' started.

The first record – 'Anti Police' – sold, as I remember, about four-and-a-half thousand and the second one – 'No Room For You' – sold about seven-and-a-half or eight thousand. We had a number of re-pressings. We had a thousand done to start with and I got rid of most of those by carting them around in the back of my Triumph Herald and dropping off boxes. *Melody Maker* said it was, 'Typical, wet-soppy hippy. Punk rock is finished, and this record is by some band that is still stuck in the days of punk and awash with wet, soppy punk idealism!' I always thought, 'You fucking bastards!'

I like to think of it as a lament for a part of your life that you very much enjoyed, and you won't have it again. You know that it's finished – which it did quite quickly after 'No Room For You' was out. I realised that punk rock was finished for me, and ironically what made me feel it was those last couple of times we played at Malvern Winter Gardens.[4] When we should have been on an absolute high that we were playing one of our favourite old venues which meant a lot to us – a massive venue to us. And I remember distinctly feeling the difference between the venue and the audience from when we'd been there, just three short years before. The last time we played there I remember looking at the audience and realising that they were, on average, fourteen or fifteen-year-olds and yet three years before, most people seemed to be like twenty, twenty-four and twenty-five. And I thought that all those older punks had gone and it's all these kids wearing bondage-trousers and strappy-leggings and things, and I thought, 'It's gone'. I'd already written 'New Breed' which is on the back of 'No Room For You': 'We got the boots but no spikey-hair.' I felt punk died pretty quick for me. When we started going to Malvern Winter Gardens those were seminal times too. Because when we saw the Jam first time those boys were only a couple of years older than us, but they made the whole thing feasible.[5] You looked up there at Paul Weller and you thought, 'He only had his eighteenth birthday a few weeks ago […] Christ! He's already on a stage as big as this'. And I remember thinking, 'I've gotta do it by the time I'm eighteen', like he was. We didn't get the first Demob single out in time for eighteen but it wasn't far behind, so I thought, 'Yeah, that's OK, we're doing good'.

---

4. Malvern Winter Gardens was one of the best concert venues in the West Midlands which hosted many of the greatest rock bands between the 1960s and 2000 – AC/DC, Motorhead, the Undertones, Buzzcocks, the Jam, the Damned, etc. It was particularly popular with fans and bands because it was all-standing with a capacity of more than 1500 and was frequently sold out.

5. We first saw the Jam, at Malvern Winter Gardens on the In the City tour. It was 25 June 1977 and they were eighteen years old. Miff and I were respectively fifteen and fourteen.

It was that whole thing of that arrogance of the musical elite. I remember reading a *Sniffin' Glue* article at the time and it said about Rod Stewart spending more money on cocaine in a week than most blokes earned in a factory in a year, and Mick and Keith flying into Monaco on their private jet. And that kind of shit had no connection whatsoever to the ordinary boys and girls of sixteen, seventeen coming out of ordinary schools all over Britain. We were as divorced from 'Rodders' and Keith and Mick as we are from the bloody Queen. You know, they weren't real anymore, were they?

And I think the fact that it (punk) was younger and it also said, 'You haven't got to be able to play as well as they do'. You know, 'If you can play an "A" chord you can be in my band'. And it was bloody liberating. They were totally, totally remote from us. David Bowie with his knitted fucking jumpsuit on and his testicles hanging out, and a star on his face! I thought, 'You wouldn't catch me onstage with a big zig-zag eye and a knitted leotard, with me cock and bollocks on display!' We couldn't relate to them. I mean I could relate more at that age to Slade.

I was born into one of those classic British families that was working class and steadily clambered their way up to be what I'd say was lower, middle class – with a Labour Party, socialist, working-class attitude. I was brought up in a very typical, small Forest of Dean village. Nothing much there: one pub, one Social Club, one shop. The shop has long since gone but the pub and the Social Club are still there. The Forest of Dean in those days was very much a backwater. My Dad had done quite a time in the Army and he was a mechanic in the Royal Engineers. He had come out of the Army back to where he'd originally started his apprenticeship at a big engineering company. He mended trucks and diggers – bulldozers – and things like that and played the piano around the pubs at night. My Mum was an office worker, a book-keeper, at the offices of the same company. Dad got Mum pregnant before they got married, which went down really fucking well! They got married and my sister came along only six months after the wedding.

Dad was a fucking brilliant musician. Couldn't read a note, not a single note. He played the piano and my earliest musical memories of my Dad are of him being able to play the piano like a fucking demon – and the piano accordion. He could passably play the trumpet and the drums, and he was always going out playing gigs around the pubs and clubs of the Forest of Dean – of which, in those days there were many, many more. Most pubs in the early sixties still had pub pianos and Dad would play the pub piano. He would religiously watch *Top of the Pops* because he knew that, come Friday and Saturday night in whatever pub he was playing that weekend, he would be expected to play the Number One. Dad's ability, when you look back at it was staggering. He would listen to *Top of the Pops* then he'd go straight to the piano which was always in the corner of the front room, lift up the lid and play – Abba, Slade or David Bowie, or whoever. Jerry Lee Lewis was his idol, and I used to like it when Dad got a bit drunk because he always used to lift the lid on the top of the piano and reach in and turn the wood-keys – lift the front of the piano so you could see all the springs and he'd be banging this piano with his elbow and doing all the fucking foot up on it!

Our upbringing was pretty good though. They were fantastic with me about music. It was music or motorcycles for me all the way through my teenage years. I was utterly mad about music and utterly mad about motorcycles. I had a shagged-out old motorbike from when I was ten or eleven years old and I've still got a shed full of motorbikes down the garden!

I wanted to play piano. I wanted to play piano like our Dad. And one of the biggest, earliest, influences on me was nothing that you would have thought; it was *The Glenn Miller Story*, with James Stewart in it. I still love Glenn Miller big band stuff. And Glenn Miller wrote on a piano, so I thought I'd play piano. So a local piano teacher was enlisted to give me piano lessons but it definitely wasn't anything like Little Richard or Jerry Lee Lewis. It was, *Greensleeves*. And she used to have a big, long pencil and she would hit me on the back of my hands because the correct way to play is to have your hands arched. Well, I couldn't understand this because I'd seen our Dad playing the piano with his foot and his elbow. So I lost interest in playing the piano and it was decided that I wasn't taking it seriously; so the lessons finished. I was determined pretty much by the time I was fifteen or sixteen that I wanted to be a musician but I didn't have a clue how I was going to do it. And it had never occurred to me to try to sing, so I'd never bothered. The only reason I ended up as the singer in Demob was that Andy got sent down.

Andy was volatile in those days and got into a lot of trouble. It was like his third or fourth offence and it was decided that he had to be sent to Borstal – or what was called a Detention Centre – DC in those days. And he got three months DC, which was ironic because Andy and I had written a song called 'Three Months DC'. Andy wrote the lyrics and I wrote the music and we had written that only a couple of months before he got sent down, and it was quite a riotous number.

We rehearsed at an old church in those days and we turned up and Terry (Elcock – guitarist) said, 'We're in the fucking shit, Andy's been sent down'. And we had quite a few gigs coming up, one of which was supporting the Selector. Terry said, 'We've got a fucking support gig next week with the Selector and we've got no fucking singer, you can fucking sing'. I remember thinking, 'I don't sing, I haven't done any singing'. I don't know why they thought I could, but I did. I just started singing and I thought, 'I quite like this'. I did quite like the idea of being the shouty fucker at the front and the centre of attention.

Half of our success so far had been based on two incidents; the summer before I joined, Demob had played on a carnival float and it had ended in a mass punch-up with a load of Gloucester grebos – bikers;[6] then the year I actually joined we did it again and this time we entered as the 'Viking Youth Club' float because we were banned from ever being in the Carnival again as Demob. We filled the lorry with all of these kids from the youth club and we got on the float and played. It didn't end in a riot, but that was our PR.

My biggest regret about that Demob period is that I actually went back and did one more gig with them. Our last ever gig with you in the band was that one in South Wales which ended in a big fight. Well, that night was a continuation of what had started at a gig in Bristol – the mentality where some of the people around the band seemed to think that they were expected to have a fight at Demob gigs, and that we liked them having fights at our gigs. And I was pissed off with it.

I'd been speaking to the two lads that had organised that gig in Wales for quite a long time on the telephone and had got to know them. I knew that they were really looking forward to that gig. I remember one of the two kids coming up to me after, the police had just turned up and we had got the kit out, and he said 'Miff, I haven't got enough money. I've got about £170. I'm sorry mate. You'd better fuck off, the police are arresting everybody'. And I said to him, 'Mate, I'm so fucking sorry this has happened'. He said, 'Don't worry, it's not your fault'. So I asked him what was going to happen. And he said, 'I don't know. They've smashed the place up'. I went home and I thought, 'That's it. That's over'.

---

6. This was in 1979 whilst the media moral-panic in the United Kingdom still had momentum and the 'Gloucester Carnival Riot' made it as far as some national newspapers.

FOURTEEN
To Belgrade: On the Brotherhood and Unity Highway Again
DAY NINE (Part One)

It is 8:51 a.m. as the bus crawls out of Zagreb bus station and into the morning commuter traffic. We head directly east through the city's suburbs and, for the first time during my stay, I see the legendary Zagreb fog as the tops of apartments melt into the smoky white mists. Behind them, tower blocks have become murky silhouettes, barely visible ghosts. The city soon dissolves into semi-rural nothingness. Inelegant smallholdings and hamlets sit close besides the main highway. We leave behind the fog, or perhaps the sun has built up the strength to burn it off.

Soon after our arrival back in Zagreb late yesterday afternoon, Tomislav and I stood next to Slavonska avenija as the rush hour traffic jammed and loosened, jammed and loosened. He would not, after all, be joining me in Serbia and we were preparing to part company. Neither of us wished to prolong the event. Tomislav asked me about my impressions of Croatia; for one reflection of my first ever visit. There had been so many wonderful experiences, the friendliness and hospitality of the people foremost but also the beautiful landscapes, the wine, the rakija. Nevertheless, at that moment the most pervasive feeling was one of melancholy. If, to the south, Greece was becoming 'a warehouse of souls', it felt to me as though Croatia was – a little less poetically, for sure – the 'bus departure gate of souls'. The last thing Tomislav said to me yesterday was 'Goodbye my Balkanese brother. Say hello to Belgrade for me'. After that we 'man-hugged' – awkwardly. I headed home and packed everything ready for an early start the following morning.

That evening I went back to Sheridan's to have a drink with Dunja and say farewell to her and Tomi the barman. The pub was packed. Quiz night in Sheridan's is something of an event amongst the English-speaking young of Zagreb. Dunja arrived and presented me with a Tupperware container filled with small savoury pastries. 'These are kiflice od sira', she said as she peeled off the lid. 'Basically they are cheese pastries or rolls. I made them myself because I thought you might need some food for the journey.' Later we called at Dunja's apartment where she gave me further gifts of Croatian wine and jam to take back to the Netherlands. Dunja and I said our farewells as my taxi arrived and I headed back to spend my last night at Gruška 4.

Now we have a clear blue sky as we drive over an immense floodplain with fields and coppices stretching as far as the horizon. Once again I am journeying on Tito's Brotherhood and Unity Highway. There is standing water in many of the fields, although it has not rained in the city for the entire duration of my stay. Occasionally we cross rivers with the same mocha-brown shades as the soil around them. The ditches which line the road are thick with bare, brown, end-of-season bullrushes. The fields here are mostly exposed ploughed soil, last season's furrows now collapsing; or the remains of whatever was cropped here during the season – perhaps sweet corn. Smoke is streaming from the chimneys of many of the houses, although the day is not cold. Small cows and large sheep graze on opposite sides of the road. Here and there are deep-chestnut-red horses which resemble the horses of the Mongolian steppes. I open the container and eat a couple more of the surviving cheese pies.

This highway is the main link between Zagreb and Belgrade – neighbouring capitals and until recently the two primary cities of Yugoslavia – and yet traffic is virtually non-existent. A sign for Banja Luka seems to confirm that we are travelling in parallel to the Bosnian border a few miles to the south. Perhaps the mountains to our right are the border? I regret that I will not be able to visit Bosnia on this trip. So many people here have told me that it is a beautiful country. The mountains fade into the distance and now to our right is a vast expanse of level plain. It is 12:30 and the inside lane of the motorway is one long line of stationary trucks – I stop counting at one hundred – an indication that the Serbian border is close. A sign says, 'Beograd 113 km'. The LED above the driver's head confirms that this is yet another unseasonably warm day: twenty-five degrees.

The bus pulls up to the barrier. A border security officer gets onto the bus, takes the passports from all passengers and exits the bus. A second border officer gets onto the bus and calls out a passenger's name. A woman sitting just in front of me stands up, picks up her cardigan and walks to the front of the bus where the border officer waits to lead her away. Two guards escort the woman from the bus, walk her to an office and the door closes behind them. The bus moves through the security point and halts 50 metres further on. Twenty-five minutes go by. Our missing passenger returns accompanied by a policeman; her bags are removed from the hold. The two of them walk back towards the office, the policeman carrying her heavily-laden bags. Pausing at the office door, both burst into laughter. We move off once more, advance perhaps another 50 metres and a Serbian border guard gets on the bus and takes our passports. We sit, patiently waiting for the return of our passports or for someone to be detained, removed or turned back. It has taken nearly an hour to move less than 100 metres and we have lost a fellow traveller.

Immediately over the Serbian border the road becomes so uneven that I can no longer take even the scratchiest notes. We cross a broad and slow-flowing river with tree-lined banks. The trees give way to miles of level, black-brown soil, withered stubble and patches of wasteland where nature is slowly erasing failed attempts to build. Pylons stretch away to the horizon. An overhead sign points straight-on for Belgrade and right for Novi Sad and Budapest. We have been on the bus for nearly six hours now.

The agricultural landscape submits to closely-cut grassed areas and trees. Some way ahead I can see the tops of tower blocks – Belgrade. High-rises and low-rises line the expressway. They huddle around roundabouts. And then to our left I recognise the New Brutalist, 'Western City Gate', also known here as the 'Genex Tower'. The iconic 30-storey, twin-towers, capped with a rotunda which was designed to be a revolving restaurant. Sadly, the rotating mechanism has never been fitted and the restaurant has never turned – a cheap metaphor in itself. The smaller tower, which once housed commercial tenants, and the restaurant are now deserted. Today many people here call it, 'The ugliest building in Belgrade – or even the world'. Ugly or not, conceived in 1977 and completed in the year of Tito's death, it is a compelling monument to the end of an era.

We pass rapidly through the Belgrade suburbs, under numerous pedestrian and road bridges and then past a sports arena. Many advertising billboards are solely in Cyrillic. A particularly glossy billboard trumpets 'BELGRADE WATERFRONT' – in English. It depicts the city as a facsimile of Dubai; concrete, chrome and glass towers line a deep blue river on which passenger ferries and pleasure boats cruise. The expressway becomes a flyover and we are above the roofs of the city. We cross a wide river – I guess this must be the Sava. Iron and concrete bridges span the water, stitching the city like surgical staples. From our vantage point above the river, a patchwork of railway lines and sidings, moribund industrial sites and weed-covered no-mans-land sprawls below. Decaying, disused railway carriages stand abandoned in the middle of it all, side by side with piles of debris from demolished buildings. There is another huge billboard screaming 'BELGRADE WATERFRONT'. The brave-new-world of the future is brash and incongruous in the stubborn, old-world wasteland of the present. We crawl the last mile or so to the coach terminus, adjacent to the main railway and bus stations. It is now the late afternoon rush hour. At the very far end of the bus station, we come to a halt.

I exit the bus and wait for my suitcase to appear from the luggage hold. I drag it away from the bus and light a cigarette. As soon as I turn to walk away I am confronted with taxi 'pirates'. Fatigued and fraying I make it clear that I do not need a taxi. There are building works on every road. Even the side roads are carved-up and left abandoned with gaping wounds. Searching for a legitimate taxi rank I find myself in a loud and frenetic, suburban bus terminus. It is a white noise of engines revving, traffic fumes, street hawkers shouting and relentless streams of people released as the lights change. The last message – from Ned O'Millick – I received before we crossed the border seems prophetic:

> In Belgrade be aware on the streets. Belgrade is wild west. Lot of poor gypsies, drug addicts, junkies, lunatics. I mean nothing will happen. But just have in mind that Croatia and Slovenia is a calm sanatorium compared to Serbia. You will see […] Real East. And Balkan starts there. Love and peace. Your bud, Neno.

I spot a taxi-for-hire stuck in traffic and the driver acknowledges me. Two unflinching women hijack it as I attempt to cross the road. After a few minutes, I am sitting in another taxicab, pointing to the address on my booking confirmation. The driver is asking me questions in Serbian. I just keep pointing at the address. He appears a little reluctant to take me but, faced with my unwillingness to leave his cab, he acquiesces. We drive for a disorientating fifteen minutes, along broad main roads lined with shops and banks, through narrow, one-way streets where pedestrians have to press themselves against the wall to let us pass. We hit roadworks, and traffic snarled up by roadworks. In the shadow of a large, white-walled, domed church, to our left is a small street market selling fruit and vegetables. Elderly women with tight blue, or black, headscarves and dark floral dresses, and elderly men with flat-caps, white shirts, dark tank tops and baggy, belted trousers struggle across the construction site carrying plastic bags heavy with produce.

We arrive in a tree-lined residential suburb which clings to the side of a steep hill. Again the driver asks me something in Serbian. Frustrated with the lack of response from me he mutters to himself and takes a right turn. He pulls the car to a halt and says, 'I don't know where. This Internacionalnih Brigada. I don't know where you must be'. I tell him it's OK, I will find the apartment from here. I walk amongst grand villas set behind walls and wrought-iron gates, fences and trellises. Shrubs and flowers spill out over the walls from inside the hidden gardens and slide down the external faces like leafy-green and orange glaciers. Occasionally, there are deep-red vines snaking along the overhead telephone lines which cross from one side of the street to the other. Both sides of the road are lined with cars parked bumper-to-bumper, blocking the already inadequate pavements. I drag my suitcase down the middle of the street, halting every thirty seconds or so to squeeze between parked cars as a vehicle coming from the direction of my apartment passes.

The property is exactly as described in the welcome e-mail and I let myself into the building. I climb eight flights of stairs and, sure enough, my apartment is unlocked as promised. The fourth floor is the converted attic space and is a generous size. I have a view out towards the sun, setting over a residential hilltop suburb.

Within minutes it has become a silhouette dotted with the lights of houses and apartments.

I had originally booked an apartment in the central Museum District but changed my booking to get somewhere large enough for Tomislav and me. Now I have no need for this two-bedroomed accommodation in an area that I do not know. Nevertheless, when I received the e-mail confirming this new apartment and saw the address to be 'Internacionalnih Brigada' I felt it was a good omen.

Ljiljana Čenejac, Marija Katic. Novi Sad, 1981 (Courtesy of Ljiljana Čenejac)

FIFTEEN
Internacionalnih Brigada

DAY NINE (Part Two)

The very first Yugoslavs I met were the Yugoslavian veterans of the International Brigades who fought in Spain. It was November 1996. The surviving British International Brigaders were travelling to Spain to join their brigadista comrades for a week of commemorative events and the award of honorary citizenship to mark the sixtieth anniversary of the beginning of the war. Through the legendary 'Fagans' pub in Sheffield, I had become great friends with Dolores and Mike Wild, the children of Major Sam Wild. Sam was, by that time, no longer with us but had been one of the most illustrious commanders of the British Battalion of the International Brigades. Dolores and Mike welcomed me into the family, vouched for me with the Communists so that I could access archives, and even gave me a long-term loan of Sam's Civil War-related memorabilia.

In November 1996, I was broke. I was employed on a month-to-month contract and received a wage which did not even cover my rent. My brother paid for my flight to Spain and Dolores put me in touch with a family friend who was kind enough to allow me to use the sofa at her tiny apartment in Madrid. It was an unforgettable week; from Madrid the travelling party went to Barcelona, and took in Tarragona, Zaragoza and the battlefields of the Ebro Valley. I was with the Brigaders as they were awarded citizenship. To feed me and supplement my meagre budget, they smuggled me into official meals for which I had no invitation. 'Here, take my arm son', they would say as they stooped a little lower, chuckled and feigned a limp – delighting in the subversion and mischief-making. I walked with them and felt like a charlatan as young Spaniards shouted out, 'Thank you', throwing flowers, hanging garlands around our necks and embracing us. I stood on Hill 666 and talked with Jack Jones – the young British volunteer who became one of the most famous and respected leaders of the labour movement in the United Kingdom. But the most outstanding occasion was the celebratory evening of music and poetry at the Madrid Velodrome. Thousands of Spanish citizens came only to give thanks for the bravery of these men and women. *The New York Times* was one of many international media organisations to cover the story, under the headline 'Franco's Foes Return, With Wheelchairs and Memories':

> Soon they were showered with Spain's best: the laments of flamenco, poems of Garcia Lorca, folk music and battle songs. Before long, the

old men cried and saluted, raising clenched fists. Some of those fists trembled with age, but they went up anyway before a roaring audience estimated at 10,000 […] As old comrades recognized each other there were embraces, back slaps and laughter, and delight that friends were still alive […] Sava Ciprovac, 83, who had come from Novi Sad in Serbia, was looking for French comrades with whom he had spent time in a prison camp. He proudly showed a yellowed document issued in 1937 by the office of Josip Broz, then recruiting volunteers for Spain and later to become Marshal Tito, the leader of Yugoslavia.

Age had not dimmed the Brigaders sense of humour and it was not all tears. On the first evening, in the Madrid city centre hotel where the main group was staying, a welcome party was held. Only the hardest of hearts would not have smiled to see these septuagenarian, octogenarian and nonagenarian socialist, communist, anarchist, liberal and unaligned men and women conforming to our cheap stereotypes. The Russians were sat at the bar drinking spirits and giving no ground to anyone behind; the Americans were waving bunches of bills at the bar staff in an attempt to get attention; the British were queuing patiently and politely but quietly complaining about the impoliteness of everyone else; the Yugoslav brigadistas were a less visible group, huddled quietly at tables close to – but to the side of – the bar. At the time, I did not grasp that this courageous band who had fought for internationalism and socialism in Spain, and again as Partisans in the Second World War, had just witnessed the break-up of their socialist Yugoslavia – the one for which they had fought doggedly, side by side. And now war, and untethered capitalism, were rampaging across the Balkans annihilating all they had built.

This evening I am interviewing Petar Janjatović – journalist, music-critic, radio-broadcaster, occasional television personality and the man responsible for (among many publications) the touchstone *Ex YU rock enciklopedija 1960–2006* and one of the co-authors of *The Almanac of New Wave in SFRY*. We have been in e-mail communication for several weeks now and Petar has been an invaluable source of contacts and advice. I log into my e-mail for the first time in twenty-four hours and there is mail from Petar: 'My home is at Neimar. Hadži Milentijeva xy. If you are close come to me around 19:30 (I wanna show you something) and we can go later to eat something.' I put the address into Google Maps and it comes up as being just two streets from here. My last-minute relocation to Internacionalnih Brigada has turned out to be fortunate – serendipity is at play once again.

It is a little after 7:10 p.m. It is dark now and the streetlamps are lit. Within three minutes I find Hadži Milentijeva, at least I think it is Hadži Milentijeva but the street signs in Serbia are mainly in Cyrillic so I cannot be sure. I find the building. It is a tall, detached, Habsburg-era villa. There are no external lights, so I grope my way along a wall to a side-door. There is a list of residents and a bell-push for each. Unfortunately, most of them are written in Cyrillic and I cannot recognise any as Janjatović. Suddenly the door opens and an elegant lady exits the building leading a small dog. She looks a little surprised to find someone loitering in the darkness immediately outside the door. I attempt a reassuring smile, say 'Zdravo' and walk past her before the door closes. Inside the building is a curving stone and marble staircase off which there are several heavy wooden doors. I am not really sure what I hope to achieve by simply entering the building but after going to the top floor and checking every door I exit the building no wiser. I head back onto the lit street and call Petar. He tells me to wait at the entrance and he comes to collect me. We climb the stairs and enter a high-ceilinged and graceful apartment. There are books and magazines on shelves and coffee tables; it has the feel of a professorial lair. After a couple of minutes, the apartment door opens and the elegant lady and dog enter. Petar, white-haired and bearded, tall and slim, introduces me to his wife. We both smile; 'We've already met', I say.

Petar suggests we eat at *Gnezdo* ('Nest') – coincidentally one of the few places I visited in 2014. Tucked away on an upper floor of a huge abandoned Austro-Hungarian-era property with exuberant graffiti and murals splashed across the stairwells, it had been difficult to find; a little local knowledge would be advantageous. As Petar drives through the city centre, I am struck by the similarities between street-level Belgrade and Athens. Petar tells me that there is a great deal of historical and cultural empathy between the Serbs and Greeks. We leave the car and begin looking for 'Gnezdo'. I know it is halfway up a stone staircase on the road which runs parallel, and adjacent, to the River Sava. We walk near-deserted cobbled streets. But in the darkness, we cannot find 'Gnezdo'. We stop at one of Petar's favourite café bars high on the hill overlooking the river and the residential suburbs beyond. Petar goes in and I can see him in the half-light of the empty bar speaking with the two members of staff – it looks like a Hopper painting, except that all three are looking intently at maps on their mobile phones. From up here, I can see across the river. The lights along the bankside promenade below are reflected in the Sava's waters; so too are the lights of a riverboat bar. Scattered lights stretch away into the black infinity. Petar comes back out into the darkened street. We move on, renewed. But even armed with directions and the knowledge that it is 'two minutes away', we draw a blank. 'It's not a problem', Petar says. 'There is another restaurant just along here'. There is. But when we get there it is in darkness. 'There are other places', Petar says cheerfully.

Leaving the road which runs parallel to the Sava, we take a sharp right turn and climb a steep gradient. Petar seems to have a plan: 'There is a place here which I have heard is good'. I recognise this hill. I recognise this road. There is a restaurant here where I had the best meal – the best night – of my previous visit. It is in a ground-floor apartment in another, crumbling nineteenth-century residential building. From the outside there is little signage, and little clue as to what is beyond the heavy doors. It has capacity for perhaps 30 people. It will also be difficult to find.

I had been determined that I would return on this visit but could not see how I would find the time. Sixty seconds later we are standing outside. I tell Petar that I have been here before and how happy I am to return – this is 'Radost Fina Kuhinjica' (I am advised by native speakers that there is no meaningful translation, but it has something to do with 'joy' and 'little kitchen'). Once inside it is exactly as I remembered. Three small rooms have been opened out into one interconnected space. It is still recognisably a converted apartment. The lighting is minimal and the tables are heavy, dark wood, with tiled surfaces. Metal lampshades hang on long cables from the high ceilings so that they are low over the table – just above the diners' heads. There is an open kitchen. It could be in hipster East End London, Melbourne or Brooklyn – except without the 'hipster'. The waiter, or perhaps owner, comes over and speaks with Petar. In impeccable English he explains the entire menu and offers vegan options if required. We drink rakija and fine Serbian red wine; everything is as good as I remembered – and Petar's conversation captivating.

In Search of Tito's Punks

PETAR JANJATOVIĆ: Radost Fina Kuhinjica, Belgrade

Petar Janjatović. Raška (Courtesy of Petar Janjatović)

Radost Fina Kuhinjica is half-full when we arrive. Petar tells me that when the war in Croatia started he was, understandably, afraid that he would be sent there. And so he became 'a refugee in London'. Which goes some way to explain his understanding of England and the English – Britain and the British – and his command of the language. He is another born storyteller with an inexhaustible archive of stories and observations. A natural journalist. Ned had told me via skype that Petar 'had died' not so long ago, after a heart attack. I have no reason to doubt Ned's information, and early in the evening, Petar tells me matter-of-factly that he 'had a heart problem' and spent several weeks in hospital – during which time Bill Bryson books were his escape from the boredom. We bond over an admiration for the Des Moines curmudgeon. The nurses had told Petar he was risking his life laughing so much. But Petar shows few signs of fragility. It is easy to see that inactivity would be torture to him though.

* * *

I was born in Belgrade in 1956. My father was working in a hotel here in the centre of town and my mother was studying Comparative Literature at University, but also working in a hotel at the time. I had a twin brother; so when she had the two of us she left the job, [and] she started to think about the two kids. When I was eleven, or something like that, I heard rock 'n' roll on the radio and it was like, 'I'm in!' So strange, so different. At that time you had the first programme of Radio Belgrade, like BBC One, and they had new music. Especially because there was one guy called Nikola Karaklajić who was an international chess player, so he travelled a lot. And he brought back the records and started to make a programme of rock 'n' roll. And that became famous, really famous. We were running home from school to listen to the programme. So that was from the beginning, my first source of music. The older guys were listening to Radio Luxembourg – everybody will tell you that the Yugoslav rock 'n' roll of the sixties was born, thanks to Radio Luxembourg. A year later my brother sent a letter to Nikola Karaklajić to enter for 'Summer Vacation With the Listeners' and won; the person who sent the most original letter would be invited to go with them, so we met him. We went to the seaside and spent two weeks there. It was our first time without our parents, and all the guys and girls were into the rock 'n' roll. I mean can you imagine that? When you are fourteen?

It's hard to say rock 'n' roll was so popular, although most of the people in the cities listened to it. But when I went to the Armed Service in 1983, there were 50 of us in the barrack and 47 listened to folk music, and three of us listened to rock. If we had 22 million people in Yugoslavia, probably 1 million listened to rock.

When I went to University I started to work immediately, part-time, for that radio programme and then some magazines and stuff like that. I wanted to be a journalist, but I didn't have the idea to be a music-journalist. At the beginning I wrote about theatre performances, and books and travel, etc. I didn't really understand punk at the beginning. It seemed too simple to me and I didn't catch the sociological and political background of punk. I was sort of like a hippy. I'd hitchhiked across Europe and then I was hit by that. But then new wave came along, and new wave was my cup of tea completely. You had Johnny Štulić of Azra, and in one of his songs Balkan he has the line, 'I shave my beard and my moustache to be in Pankrti'. So he was also a hippy and then he saw Pankrti and he thought, 'Wow!' So it took me a time too.

I went hitchhiking across Europe: London, Amsterdam, Stockholm, Prague, Italy [and] Greece. All the time when we travelled, we would bring with us a cassette of the brand new Yugoslav rock 'n' roll scene. For us it was an excellent situation; somebody would pick us up and he would be into rock 'n' roll. We would say, 'We have some new Yugoslav sounds here, would you like to listen?' They would say, 'Yeah […] Wow!' So I felt like a cultural ambassador. And also, we Yugoslavs looked like any of the other guys on the street. And then they would ask, 'What will happen after Tito's death?' I said, 'A funeral'. Because we were proud of the country. And I felt insulted that they felt the country would fall down after him. OK, I was idealistic, but nobody will say, nobody will say, that, that kind of war is possible at the end of the twentieth century in Europe.

Something strange happened in the late 1970s Yugoslavia. In the same moment, something like ten or fifteen strong writers came out. And they came out at the time that those scenes in England and America gave you the opportunity to think about all kinds of stuff you have in your mind. And you don't have to be a great guitarist. So, if you have ideas for the songs and the lyrics you can jump on the stage. And in this Yugoslav punk – or punk and new wave scene – you have people like Jura Stublić and Johnny Štulić born in 1953, and you had kids who were born in 1962, '63 and '64. All jumping at the same moment. And we also had good 'soil' – clubs, radio programmes [and] youth press. So all of them worked together. The youth press was state-supported. The first fifteen pages were about the workers or the committee ideas or the 'great future', whatever. But the last part was about anything. So it was like, a completely schizophrenic magazine. But it was state-supported.

In 1981, we had the *Paket aranžman* LP ('Package Tour')[1] which featured Belgrade bands. Those people had the idea to do the same thing with the next generation of punk bands who were from Belgrade. So Jugoton put out the LP, *ARA: Artistička radna akcija* which means 'Artistic Work Action'.[2] Because 'Omladinske radne akcije' (ORA – Youth Work Action) was a government programme for youngsters where they would be building a highway or something like that. It was a really Soviet Union way of doing things, but it was great fun for them. They were mostly from rural places and they didn't get to go to the seaside during the summer, and the bands would be playing at those camps, etc. So that was kind of the joke. So we had two days with all of those young bands playing at a stadium with the main bands Idoli, Šarlo Akrobata and Električni Orgazam (from the original *Paket aranžman* LP). And there were so few people – the stadium was for 10,000 people and we had maybe 2000 people. I still don't have an answer to that. Probably a lot of people thought it was a lie that Idoli, Šarlo Akrobata and Električni Orgazam would come and they didn't care about the small punk bands. Actually, punk was for the 'club'; the stadium is not for punk. I think that was our mistake. And it was the best sound, everything. We had a budget; we didn't have to make money. We had state

---

1. *Paket aranžman* was a scene defining, eleven-track new wave compilation album released in 1981 and featuring three young Belgrade bands Idoli, Šarlo Akrobata and Električni Orgazam. It remains influential to this day.
2. *Artistička radna akcija* was a twenty-track compilation featuring ten Belgrade bands, the best known of which is (arguably) Urbana Gerila. Released in late 1981, the sleeve features the teenage Rujana Jeger.

money; we made a big stage. It was our opportunity for the kids in the bands, to show them to the audience. It would have been much better if we had gone to the club and made ten gigs!

After Tito's death in 1980, they introduced the new conscription age. When you finished grammar school you went immediately to serve Army. I followed the old rule because I was already a student in 1980, so I went when I was twenty-six years old. But at that time there was an Army psychiatrist, a doctor who – if I am not wrong – fell in love with some young girl from that rock 'n' roll circus in Belgrade. So most of them – rock 'n' rollers – never went to the Army. He gave them an exemption. Can you imagine? Nobody wanted to go to the Army, but you have to have big balls to play that you are crazy! So, you will not find a lot of songs in punk and new wave about the Army Service. But also, it's quite interesting that most of the big, famous musicians – not only punk musicians – in Yugoslavia, their fathers were officers in the Yugoslav Army. Probably, this is how to fight authority, with a guitar and a song.

The punk bands had an enemy too; like you had in the UK: 'Fuck off Bijelo Dugme. Fuck off YU grupa. We're gonna show you something'. That was also important because if you have an enemy it's much easier to express yourself. Bijelo Dugme were playing in the football stadium and there were 70,000 people there. The punks were in the small club showing that they have the balls. And the Sex Pistols were huge among those kids, really huge. Most of the local guys didn't speak English so it was the fucking energy and anarchy. The Gang of Four played Zagreb and it was an excellent gig; that gig became legendary. For ages, all of us who were there would say to people that it was a great gig and the legend was correct. Their records were released here by a local record company, so it was easy for people to get hold of them and to understand. I think their popularity in ex-Yugoslavia was only because of that Zagreb gig. If they had not come, they would be seen as a cool band but not the legend. Most of the people in those audiences didn't have a lot of experience of live gigs – if we are talking about English and American bands – and seeing a band like the Gang of Four was a great experience. First of all, they were fucking strong. They were a machine. With only three instruments and it was like, 'Wow!' I remember when they started to play it was like, 'Jesus Christ'. The evening before, the band Classix Nouveaux played – the English band – fake new wave and people recognised that! Nobody talked about Classix Nouveaux after the Gang of Four Zagreb gig.

We didn't have a lot of international gigs at that time. I guess the first may have been Mungo Jerry for example in 1971 and then Santana with Earth Wind and Fire, and Clapton, Deep Purple, Jethro Tull, Tina Turner and then the Ruts. That

Ruts gig in Belgrade was also a big trigger.[3] Film, the band from Zagreb, was the support band and it was the first time they had been here in Belgrade, so there was also great interest in them. Talking Heads were big here also but, of course, they were much more into the arty scene. They had great gigs in Zagreb and Belgrade in the summer of '82. The Stranglers came to Ljubljana in maybe 1978?[4] In Slovenia they had a good promoter with good connections and also it was much cheaper to travel from Munich, or Vienna, to Ljubljana than to go to Zagreb or Belgrade. Not so many gigs here but a few of them are legendary.

A lot of things came together in a proper moment. You had Idoli, for example, one of the most sophisticated bands of the new wave, with a completely strange record like *Odbrana i poslednji dani* ('The Defence and the Last Days', released 1982) with songs about Marshal Tito, with songs about Russia. There is a lyric in that song called Russia; that was sort of a love song, 'She had stronger arms, I could not fight with her'. So it was a love song about the Soviet Union. It was clever and people recognised that. They had a song about a guy who was a 'guy' but inside was a female and is thinking about changing sex. I mean nobody thought about that, at that time, in a poetical way. That record made other kids say, 'I can sing about anything that's in my mind'. And two or three years earlier, editors on radio programmes were asking for the lyrics of the songs we would play. In just a few weeks the atmosphere changed.

Some of the lyrics were changed and some of the record covers but nothing big. That's my point. The authorities didn't understand punk. And, a very important thing, Tito died in May of 1980 and the next day they started to fight for power. And they were fighting each other under the radar. It suddenly became easier for us. Three months after his death you could write a lot of things; you could say a lot of things on the radio, nobody gave a shit. It's the same as with Milošević. Milošević was supporting an image of Tito until 1989. And then suddenly you can say all kinds of bullshit about Tito because he decided, 'Right, now I'm not a Communist anymore. Now I fight for the Serbs'. They fought each other, and for punk and new wave that was great.

Did anyone tell you about Kugla glumište, from Zagreb? Very strange group of people, excellent. Very strange performances. I think they started in the late seventies; they were based in the Student Centre and most of the bands – Haustor, early Azra, Sexa – had a rehearsal room in their theatre and they were together in so many different ways. So the brass section from Haustor used to play very often in Kugla glumište's performances. They used to make performances in the street;

---

3. Pinki Hall, Belgrade, 29 January 1980.
4. The Stranglers played in Ljubljana on 30 June 1978 with 999 as support.

so you would follow them, for something like 5 kilometres and they did all kinds of stuff. Excellent, supported by the Government. One of them (Kićo)[5] is now a well-known actor in Denmark, with a movie career. Most of them moved to Amsterdam when the war started but unfortunately nothing much then happened for them. It was such a nice feeling – you would go to Zagreb and Kugla glumište had a new play and it was great.

We had this 'BITEF' – 'Belgrade International Theatre Festival' – which was very, very popular and very alternative. All the important underground plays were in Belgrade from 1971 until now. In 1981 or something there was a punk theatre performance at the International Festival. It was a nice feeling – you could write about the scene from different angles. We had what were called amateur theatres for people who didn't have an education but liked to act; we had three or four of these quite well-organised amateur theatres in Belgrade. Some of those actors were in the punk bands and that was kind of the same scene. They went together to the parties and everything, and some collaboration was quite normal. And we also had that kind of street theatre too.

After the Second World War, the Government organised 'KUD', 'Kulturno Umjetnicko Drustvo – Cultural Artistic Societies'. They were performing folk dances and they would travel around the world. Every country has this kind of thing: Russia, China has this, then you have the Irish dancing. Under that (KUD) umbrella people started to form theatre groups and that was also financed by the Government – and, of course, it was a great place for people who liked to do something creative. Most of the people were also in bands at that time. So if you are making a play and you need music it's good to have original music – so it is so logical that it should go together.

In Yugoslavia, there was something perhaps very unique within the global rock 'n' roll scene. All of the punks or new wavers went to university – middle-class families or above. And also you had these 'Mannequin Punks' – guys with wealthy fathers – going to London, to Chelsea, buying very expensive punk dress. Nobody remembers them now. Some of the people in that scene were 'living in high-hills'. We had this hill called Dedinje where Tito and all his Ministers lived. And some of the kids of those high-positioned people – the politicians – were in punk bands, or were in the audience, and they held the parties there. When Tito died, the first President after him was a politician from Bosnia living in Belgrade – Mijatović. His daughters were very much

---

5. Zlatko Burić aka Kićo, Damir Bartol Indoš and late Željko Zorica Šiš were the nucleus of the Kugla Glumište radical theatre group from Zagreb. Burić moved to Denmark in the nineties where he indeed had serious mainstream succes as an actor. Recently (2016), he acted in the brilliant Croatian movie *Quit Staring At My Plate* (awarded Best European Movie at Venice Festival 2017) directed by Hana Jušić and British film *Teen Spirit* (2018) directed by Max Minghella.

into the punk scene.[6] They used to hold parties. So Mijatović would be sitting in the next room when they were having parties. And the legend says that one time he went to ask them, 'Could you turn the music down a little because I have to make some very important telephone calls'. I don't know, but it sounds good.[7] So most of those people, it was a hobby for them, which doesn't make the music of lesser quality. But KUD Idijoti didn't play for a hobby. I mean, the working-class heroes were KUD Idijoti – the only working-class heroes in punk and new wave before the wars. That's one of the reasons why people love them so much. Pula was like a small town with not so many possibilities. They played in the band but they still had to live. And their parents were not wealthy. So this is why people trust them when they sing about working-class rights. They know what they are singing about. This is not a pose.

After the Second World War, all of the Italians who lived in Istria moved to Italy because they were afraid of revenge. So Istria was half-empty. Then the Yugoslav Army, or Tito or whatever, replaced them with a lot of people from very poor areas of Bosnia and from all across Yugoslavia – or kids who lost their parents during the war. So Istria is multi-national and multi-cultural. When you look at Sale's (Veruda) building, and you look at the doorbells, there is every kind of surname that you could imagine – Croatian, Serbian, Bosnian, Macedonian, Slovenian. So Istria was an excellent background for a band like KUD Idijoti because they were anti-fascists. They are anti-fascists; they are anti-nationalists. So they had a proper audience and during the nineties they were very much against Tuđman. They couldn't play Croatia; they played only Slovenian, Macedonia and Istria. I was so proud when KUD Idijoti were the first Croatian band to play in post-war Serbia because they deserved to be the first. And they asked me to announce them at the gig. They had never played to 5000 people in Belgrade and most of the kids had never seen them live. It was a great gig. A great gig.

---

6. Cvijetin Mijatović had two daughters, Mira and Maja. The elder sister, Mira, was a founder member and lead vocalist of the Belgrade band VIA Talas (which became Talas) who were part of the *Artistička radna akcija* LP project. In 1983, Talas released the LP *Perfektan dan za banana ribe* ('A Perfect Day for Bananafish' – taking the title from a J. D. Salinger short-story). Tragically, Mira died of a heroin overdose in 1991. Maja died that same year – apparently also as a result of substance abuse. There is talk of the Mijatović curse since the girls' mother had been killed in a car crash in 1970 when they were still young children. Their father remarried – this time to the famous Serbian actress Mira Stupica, whose nephew Srdan was also a prominent new wave musician with Ekaterina Velika and Disciplin A Kitschme as well as being a well-known actor. Two of the other four members of VIA Talas also died before the end of the millennium.
7. A story is told that VIA Talas would rehearse in the basement of the family villa in Dedinje and one day Cvijetin Mijatović went down to ask them not to hit the crash cymbals because he was trying to have a telephone conversation with Russia's President Brezhnev.

Tusta was a very simple and straightforward man. Simple in terms of always being friendly, with a smile. And a man who was really behind what he was doing. He still worked at the shipyard and he managed to take care of the workers – all the time working with the band too – a nice guy.

This German guy – Rüdiger Rossig[8] – came to Belgrade in June of '92. He gave me a ring and he said, 'I am writing an article about Serbian rock 'n' roll and oppositional issues, I would like to do an interview with you'. Waiting for him I got the idea to write a letter to KUD Idijoti and to ask him to send that letter from Berlin because there was no post between Croatia and Serbia. There was no nothing. No telephone. Nothing. It was the middle of the war. I was expecting one of those journalists who know nothing. We met so many of them, with a lot of prejudice. They worked for big companies and they went to a so-called war zone – so there was big money in it. I prepared a letter with an envelope addressed to KUD Idijoti, Pula, Croatia. He rang the bell and he had earrings and Dr Martens shoes, and I started to laugh. I said, 'Come in'. And he sat down and I said, 'First, can I ask you something, could you please send this letter when you're back in Berlin?' He said, 'Wow! You know KUD Idijoti? They are my favourite band!'

My favourite – sort of – new band is Repetitor, but they have existed for something like ten years. They are for me, some kind of incarnation of those early new-wave Belgrade bands. It is a guy playing guitar and singing, a lady playing bass and a lady playing drums – and they have this kind of original anger, original frustration. They are playing in Russia, Europe, China, etc. There is, I think, a Dutch documentary – Dutch and American – called *Do-It-Yourself* about the small bands who are connected and help each other in organising these low-budget tours. If you ask musicians in former Yugoslavia, I think they helped each other a lot. You know, somebody had a problem with an instrument so they would give you an instrument. Vuja from KBO! will tell you a similar story. You know, sitting in Kragujevac, in the city where they had one of the most popular hippy bands in Yugoslavia – Smak – everything was under the umbrella of that hippy band. And he was a kid who was playing punk, so it was like, 'You idiot'. So he was the rebel. He got it together and helped all kinds of kids from around Kragujevac with his studio; he's been the leader of the scene for ages. So he's a really good source of a 'completely under the radar scene'. He is punk from the very beginning, I love him!

And also those bands in Belgrade during the early days of new wave were quite similar. They were friends and they helped each other. And, of course, they

---

8. Rüdiger Rossig is an author, journalist, blogger and Balkanologist who has written widely on ex-Yugoslav rock, and pop-culture.

remained friends. There was the anti-war project of Partibrejkers, Ekaterina Velika, Električni Orgazam, etc. In the middle of the war, just a few days before the war in Sarajevo started, they did this record *Slušaj vamo* ('Listen Here').[9] It was a very big possibility that all kinds of gigs would be closed to them; the media of course would be. But they didn't give a shit because the media was bad in many ways. Radio B92 was actually the publisher of *Slušaj vamo* and they decided one day that they would drive around Belgrade playing the song live from a stage on the back of a truck. But we didn't have gasoline, you had to buy gasoline on the black market. People were selling it in plastic Coca-Cola bottles – it was Romanian, very bad gasoline. And they ran out of gasoline! The name of the ad hoc band was Rimtutituki which is slang for 'Turim ti kitu' which means, 'Oh fuck you', or something like that.[10] It's a completely idiotic name for a band which was doing such serious stuff!

After the war in Bosnia, I went for the first time to Sarajevo in 1997 when U2 had a gig. I was afraid. I am coming from Serbia, from Belgrade. It was only two years after the war and you do not know how people would react. And I was made so fucking welcome it was pathetic. Some of them told me that when they heard about the song made by members Ekaterina Velika, Partibrejkers, Električni Orgazam during the war, 'We realised that Belgrade is not completely mad. There is hope'. So this is a huge song, a really huge song. And this is punk. Really. I mean, it can be hippy also, but it is a statement where you are against everybody. And that was big. The anti-war song was a political statement but the lyrics were about, 'I don't want folk music to win, I don't want a gun, I want pussy [...] young pussy', something like that. This is good. This is simple and straight into the target. They made the song in one afternoon. They were in the rehearsal room and it was one-riff, and Cane[11] started with the singing, and the whole thing was excellent. I don't know if there is film. At that time it was not so easy to get a camera, cameras were expensive.[12] We had a problem; I mean it was so easy to be against Milošević because he was pure evil. This guy Vučić – our current Serbian President – is a lizard, he's not a pure enemy.

---

9. *Slušaj vamo* was the single and it was co-published by Radio B92 and the PGP-RTS record label. The collective involved members Partibrejkers, Ekaterina Velika, Električni Orgazam and Rambo Amadeus and several of these bands would take the anti-war message abroad playing concerts under the banner of *Ko to tamo pjeva* (*Who's That Singing Over There*) named after the famous Serbian movie.
10. Another translation is 'I put my dick in you'.
11. Zoran Kostić (aka Cane), originally a member of Urbana Gerila but more famous as the front man and one of the creative impulses behind Partibrejkers.
12. Footage of the live show and protest is on YouTube under the title Rimtutituki – *Mir brate mir* – *NE RACUNAJTE NA NAS* – *(Live 1992)*.

Novi Sad punks (centre, the late Dragan Radosavljević aka 'Dragus' of the band Van Kontrole, also fanzine creator)

SIXTEEN
Lost in Belgrade Central

DAY TEN (Part One)

My intention today is to sleep late, lie around, write up some notes and generally take it easy. This afternoon I have an interview scheduled with the famous Serbian journalist and novelist Branko Rosić. And tonight I am meeting Belgrade street-punks Pogonbgd. Pogonbgd have recorded a brilliant version of 'To nije mjesto za nas', and as a younger generation of ex-Yugo punks, I am keen to hear what they have to say. A little ominously, their message of yesterday said,

> We can meet in 'kafana Mornar' (kinda old-school pub, balkan way). Place is across the street of 'Dom Omladine' (Belgrade Youth Center), everybody knows about this place. It's downtown of Belgrade [...]
> The plan is to drink few rounds till about 21:30/22:00, and then to go to our studio. Band squad will not be full, but friends will join us, so maybe we can have a little jam session and barbecue.

I have seen film of their gigs, band videos and promo photos. They do not look like the kind of people who do things by half measures. Friday night in Belgrade with these people? Factoring in recuperation time seems wise.

Alas, at some time around 8 a.m. I am woken by a diabolical symphony of drills and circular saws, of lump hammers and sledgehammers, from outside and inside the building. I cover my head and try to sleep through it all. Eventually I give up, get dressed and make the first of several coffees. I scour bus and train timetables for tomorrow's trip to Novi Sad. The logistics are thorny. The bus trip takes one hour and forty-five minutes. Many of the places I want to visit are well out of the city centre and local bus services patchy – so I will almost certainly need to take cabs once I get there. I need to allow at least three hours for the interviews. And I have to be back at a reasonable time because I have an early start on Sunday for my overnight trip to Kragujevac.

After a telephone call with my long-suffering wife, she offers to transfer some money to me if I can find a driver for Novi Sad. In desperation I e-mail Radomir, the Airbnb host, to see if he can point me in the direction of anyone. A few minutes later he replies to say he has a cousin, Ivan, who is a very good driver and is free tomorrow. Within an hour we have agreed on a very reasonable price; Ivan will pick me up at 10 a.m. the following day.

I am to meet Branko at 5:30 p.m. on the terrace at the famous Hotel Moskva. On my last visit, I had taken a walk to see the Hotel Moskva because of its iconic status – or something the *Rough Guide* had said. I even vaguely remember what it looked like. I leave at 4:30 p.m., with my route traced in black biro over my crumpled Google Map printout of central Belgrade. I climb a steep hill up Čuburska, pass the mini-market and keep climbing. At the top, I hit a bustling shopping suburb with cafés, the ubiquitous shifty-looking currency exchanges and shops. Rush hour is in full swing again, and crossing the roads at busy intersections, whilst trying to read the map, is hazardous. I head confidently down Makenzijeva.

The weather is once again exceptional. Even at this time of day, there is still warmth in the sun and I take off my jacket and stuff it into my rucksack. The gradient levels off a little, although I am still heading downhill until I find myself on the fringe of a huge building site. On the map it is marked some kind of square, Trg Slavija, with a green space at the centre. I guess that once it was a large roundabout – perhaps with a small park at its heart. I find the exit I need, Kralja Milana, and from here it is a straightforward 1-kilometre stroll along one of Belgrade's best-known commercial and administrative thoroughfares.

Reaching the point on the map where I have marked an asterisk in biro, I see no sign of the Hotel Moskva. This is not as I expected it to look. I spend ten minutes exploring each of the roads radiating out from this square. Still, I can find no Hotel Moskva. Rush hour is now hitting its peak. There are hundreds of pedestrians waiting at lights, weaving in and out of the traffic and queuing for buses. The traffic is snarling-up just as it had the previous evening. I text Branko to say I am lost. He texts back to say he is stuck in traffic. Then he asks where I am. He tells me to stay put and 'wait next to the statue'.

Beneath the towering verdigris sculpture of Prince Mihailo astride a magnificent horse, I sit on the bottom step and light another cigarette. From this precise spot, during the freezing winter of 1996, the three leaders of the 'Zajedno' ('Together') opposition gathered daily to lead hundreds of thousands in peaceful marches against Slobodan Milosević. The President, they said, had 'stolen' the November elections. Milosević teetered momentarily but steadied himself and prevailed. International support for the protestors had not been forthcoming and disunity soon set in amongst the fragile and conflicted coalition. However, their efforts seeded and informed the subsequent mass protests which finally forced the tyrant from office in 2000 and cleared the way for his prosecution at the ICTY in The Hague. By this time though, another battlefront had been opened in Kosovo during which almost 14,000 had been killed and hundreds of thousands displaced, NATO (under the clear direction of the United States) had bombed Serbia in return and the fate of this diminished 'Yugoslavia' was irrevocably sealed.

After ten minutes I recognise the figure of Branko heading towards me. He is hurrying, smiling and reaching out to shake my hand. Dressed in a black leather jacket, dark maroon shirt and dark jeans with black trainers, his hair is cropped short and his beard the same length. Average height, stocky and broad-shouldered, smart and casual, he could be a businessman or a reformed football hooligan. His cheery bearing matches the mischievous nature of his e-mails and messages whilst planning the meeting. He apologises for making me wait and is at pains to find out what sort of venue would be best for the interview. Branko clearly has much more experience as an interviewer than I do. He has the gravelly, full-toned voice I have come to expect from my Balkan interviewees; as if a Shakespearian stage actor spent all of his free time, smoking cigarettes and drinking rakija from the bottle, with his friends on the wrong side of the railway tracks. But he speaks with a staccato machine-gun pace.

Branko leads us across the square and into a narrow pedestrianised street with shops, café-bars and restaurants on each side. The streets are busy with Friday late-afternoon shoppers, homeward-bound commuters and straight-from-work revellers. We take seats outside of a smart, modern café bar and, after asking the waiter to take a couple of photos for posterity, we begin the interview.

After completing the interview, Branko offers to walk me to 'Kafana Mornar' (Kafana being the generic name for a traditional Yugoslav café-bar serving meze snacks, and 'Mornar' meaning Sailor), where I am due to meet Pogonbgd. It is just two or three minutes' walk. From outside I can see that it is already busy. Branko knows this place well. 'Kafana Mornar' has long been part of Belgrade's punk rock tapestry. It was here in January 1980 that members of Hipnotisano Pile ('Hypnotized Chicken') – a band named after the line from Iggy Pop's 'Lust for Life' – plotted with another local musician to form an ad hoc punk band which would become one of the most famous in the ex-Yugoslavian punk pantheon – Električni Orgazam. Legend has it that; it was after attending a concert by the Macedonian rock band Leb i sol ('Bread and Salt') at the 'Dom Omladina' across the road that the band wrote the song 'The Waiter' here whilst waiting for table service. Električni Orgazam would go on to write and record the song which is said to best describe Belgrade's gilded youth of the late 1970s, 'Zlatni papagaj' ('Golden Parrot'), in which they attack the privileged individuals whose 'Daddy pays all the bills', who carry pressed and scented feathers and consider themselves too fine to travel by public transport. The ones Petar Janjatović calls 'Mannequin Punks'. Električni Orgazam were a fundamental part of the Rimtutituki anti-war project with Partibrejkers and Ekaterina Velika. Their lyrics were considered of such literary worth that ten of them were included in the Janjatović anthology of ex-Yugoslavian rock poetry, *Songs of Brotherhood, Childhood & Offspring*.

Branko has heard of Pogonbgd but declines my suggestion that he come in and join us for a drink. We agree to try and meet again when I return to Belgrade after the weekend. I enter the bar and see immediately why Sale from Pogonbgd had described it as 'old-school'. Tables are set out in straight rows, with wooden chairs neatly placed around them. Every table has a sharp-white tablecloth. The waiters are smartly dressed in white shirts, dark trousers and aprons. The walls are freshly painted in white and cream. Pictures depicting events in maritime history are framed by decorative wall mouldings. Almost everyone is smoking; a reassuring, if injurious, smog hangs briefly in the air before being extracted. Directly to the right of the door as I walk in is a group of five or six short-haired, athletic young men, most of whom are wearing black t-shirts. As soon as I turn to face them, one smiles, stands, reaches out a hand to shake and says, 'Barry? I'm Sale'. Over the next two hours beers are brought with regularity, and then carafes of red wine. These boys take no prisoners.

In Search of Tito's Punks

BRANKO ROSIĆ: Belgrade café terrace

Branko Rosić. Central Belgrade

Branko first found fame in 1980 when he was a founder member of Belgrade punks Urbana Gerila. Branko and his bandmates were all aged fifteen years or younger. There can be few bands subsequently proven to be so precocious. His co-founders were – the now legendary – Zoran 'Cane' Kostić (Partibrejkers and Rimtutituki), Slobodan 'Loka' Nešović (Defektno Efektni) and Vladimir Arsenijević who at just twenty-nine years of age became the first – and only – debut novelist to win the NIN Yugoslavian Book of the Year,[1] for his critically acclaimed 1994 anti-war novel *In the Hold*. *The New York Times* critic described Arsenijević as 'the amazed, sardonic and eloquent witness to the spectacle of a country devouring its own heart'. Several other later-to-be cultural luminaries would drift into and out of the band before it evolved into Germanic dark-wavers Berliner Strasse, with Branko and Arsenijević still at its core.

* * *

---

1. The most prestigious Yugoslavian, and now Serbian, literature award, established in 1954.

I was born in Belgrade. My dad was a poor child and he worked in the Yugoslav Army as a lawyer, but he always wanted to be an engineer. The family didn't have the money for the Technical University, but they had enough money for the University of Law. He was a strong man; he was a nice man; he was a 'Dad'. He died ten years ago – but he liked the idea that I would be a mechanical engineer. And I finished my studies as a mechanical engineer, but I never worked as an engineer.

In the early days I knew that I had a talent for writing because I won a prize in Belgrade for children's writing. But it was socialism, and in socialism, two universities were the most important – engineering or industry, and medicine. And, you know, your parents always want you to be a nice guy with money, with a house in the village, a house in a fantastic neighbourhood. My father was a straight man and my generation felt that our parents were like our grandparents, because these were people born before rock 'n' roll, before films, before important books. Today you can be a 'modern father' but my father didn't go with me to concerts when I was a child. In those days, he was younger than I am today! They are parents from another millennium.

My mother died years ago; she was a nice woman, but she didn't have a big education. In Yugoslavia, you had eight years in primary school and four years in gymnasium (high school) – and after that twelve years you would go to university. My father went to university but my mother didn't. She was a civil servant, working in a textile industry factory. I had a nice childhood. I had problems with my parents because they hated my clothes, my hairstyle – sometimes I had red hair; sometimes I had green hair. The socialism was not the problem, the parents were the problem! We had another kind of socialism and many people today are nostalgic for the socialist era because life was much better – much better for ordinary people. Ordinary people could buy a house, could buy a good car. But today, it is like India – many rich people but mostly poor people. In socialism you didn't have these differences.

We had a different kind of socialism then to Russia and the other Eastern Bloc. We could go to London – I could go to the Kings Road to see the punks. I could go to Amsterdam. We had Interrail and we could travel all around Europe. I went to London – London was more interesting then than it is today. I have always liked London because England is in my blood. I started by listening to teen-rock, glam-rock like Sweet. This is our roots. The Sweet were a good band, Slade too! Slade played in Belgrade, in the big hall. I was listening to all the punk bands – Sex Pistols, the Clash, the Stranglers and after that Stiff Little Fingers, some Oi! bands like the Cockney Rejects. All the old punk bands played in Serbia – UK Subs, the Exploited, Cockney Rejects.

I was one of the first Yugoslavian punks featured in the *New Musical Express*. In 1981, the famous journalist Vivienne Goldman came to Serbia, to Belgrade, and wrote an article about 'Punk in Socialism'. And took a photo of 'punks with Lenin' ha ha ha ha. I was also the first person in Yugoslavia who had an interview with Crass; I published it in my fanzine. I did an interview by letter. I remember, one day I had a high temperature and I was asleep in bed, and my mother said, 'Hey you have a letter from England' and I saw the 'Essex' postmark and it was the Crass answers for my interview. I was only fifteen or sixteen years old. The fanzine had the same name as my band Urbana Gerila, and I made it with Vladimir Arsenijević the guitar player from the band. He is a writer, an author, today. All of the members of Urbana Gerila are famous today – not famous like a VIP but famous in art or something similar. Because the punk kids, I must say, it's very different to England; it's without social context – you don't have the classes within socialism, but we are the youth from the middle class. We didn't have rich and poor people, but we did have poorer people.

The Yugoslav socialism was different, and we had private shops, etc. It's different from Russia and the other countries – and we had rich people in socialism. But what is true is that we were people not from the higher class but from the middle class. This is important. We went to study, but everyone could study. My father was from the village and a poor man, but he finished university – but not only university, he became a Doctor of Law after university. You know Lars Von Trier – his mother was a fan of socialist Yugoslavia and she cried when Yugoslavia went to war. Because many people, and many foreign people, thought that Yugoslavia was a good society; with pride for workers and pride for poor people, poor people could study. The son of a miner could be a university professor.

We were very young when we started Urbana Gerila – fifteen years old. I had a dream, to be a rock 'n' roll musician because I started listening to music when I was very young – twelve years old. I went to concerts and when I saw the dark in the hall, the sound engineer, the red lamps on the Marshalls – I only wanted to be a rock 'n' roll musician. And punk gave me the chance. Maybe I wasn't a good bass player, but punk gave me a chance. Punk invited you and me to enter the stage. But we had to have ideas and good songs – if you are not a good player you must have good songs. We started very young and we started very quickly. I remember the first gig because Pankrti played that evening in Belgrade – it was 1980 – we didn't play with Pankrti but on the same day. We played at some festival – not a socialist festival but a youth festival. The singer from Urbana Gerila was Zoran, now from Partibrejkers, and he was a showman. Fifteen years old but a showman, the showman was born!

So we had a good singer in Urbana Gerila, but he had a conflict with the guitar player, and he left the band. We couldn't find a singer like him because he was a trademark for Urbana Gerila. We were still good, but the frontman is the most important for a band – and when you start without your frontman you are shit! Pulp without Jarvis Cocker. The Smiths without Morrissey. But we tried with another singer and it was not good. After that we tried to change style because we had a new drummer who liked Joy Division, Bauhaus, [and] the Pop Group. We had the same name but changed the style and all the fans at the gigs were like, 'Fuck off!'. Because they wanted the old songs, the punk songs from Urbana Gerila. We had depressing bass lines like Joy Division, an atmosphere like Joy Division, but we still had the old name. One day we said we must change the name; we have other songs, another style, we must have another name. The new singer sang in German and it sounded fantastic. So we had a gig, as Urbana Gerila, with Paraf and we changed the name to Berliner Strasse – new singer, new band, new life.

But it was hard for punk bands in that period – it was hard to record and hard to make videos – but it was not because of the politicians. The top bands like Pankrti, Paraf, Pekinška Patka made albums but Urbana Gerila only made compilations. It was hard to make vinyl. New wave bands could, but punk not so much, and Berliner Strasse couldn't because we were not commercial. You must be commercial, commercial in socialism! It's another kind of socialism! Socialism where the labels must sell records. It's like in capitalism, they must have big names and big records with an audience. But some editors at the labels thought that punk was not commercial. We did not have independent labels like in England – like Rough Trade. In this period we had only five state labels. It was a free time after Tito's death. Yugoslavia was very interesting – but we didn't know that war was coming, we didn't know. We lived in Disneyland – we went to sleep in Disneyland, and we woke up in the apocalypse.

After Berliner Strasse, I had some problems because I didn't like mechanical engineering. I was a bad pupil and I had bad marks. If you had bad marks you couldn't go to study philosophy, economics or law but you could go to study chemistry, biology and mechanical engineering. You paid, and you could study. It was not a university for bad pupils, the best pupils also went. But it gave a chance to other pupils if they paid. So I paid and studied mechanical engineering. Under socialism it did not cost big money. But I was a lost person – I did not know what I could do, what I could be.

And in socialism you had a problem with the Army service. Once you finished gymnasium school you had to go into the Army. I was eighteen years old and had to go into the Army, came back from the Army and another band member went into the Army – the fucking band lost the music, lost everything. The band lost two members and two years. The Yugoslav Army killed Yugoslav Punk and new wave – the Army was catastrophic.

I was sent to Slovenia and I had a problem because I had a Laibach fanzine, and Laibach was the most dangerous thing at the time. Laibach were not allowed concerts because the name was from the Nazi regime – Laibach is Ljubljana in

German. Some officers found the Laibach fanzine and the cover of the fanzine was Hitler in a museum, and this is a socialist Army.

> What is this? Who gave you this? Did you know that they are a dangerous band in Yugoslavia?
> Yes, I know.
> Who gave it to you?

So, they sent me to the frontier, with twelve people. I lived in a hut on the frontier with twelve people for one year. I didn't see a woman! I didn't see anything. Only twelve people and one dog! It was 1982. It was a fucking danger for me. And now, I just had an interview with Laibach last week! And next week we will see the film which was just recorded in North Korea – Laibach in North Korea – at the film festival in Belgrade. The first day of the festival will be Laibach in North Korea!

I started with journalism, sometimes freelance, sometimes working for someone. I didn't have the idea that I would be a professional journalist because I hate working in an office and I hate working to deadlines. I worked in a daily newspaper and I hated daily newspaper jobs. When I worked in a daily newspaper I went to a psychologist – because I can't fight with that everyday stress. All fucking day I worked. I started in the morning with a conference – because I was the Editor – and all day you have bullshit on your head and you think at six o'clock, 'Fantastic, I've finished, I will go home.' And then they shout, 'Hey, do you know what is happening in London?' Or, 'In Berlin, a car has killed ten people'. And it starts again. Amy Winehouse is dead, and I must change the copy and write an article about Amy Winehouse but I only have one hour. I knew that working in a daily newspaper was shit and I did not want to become a machine. I wanted to be at a distance and be a freelance journalist.

So I did the freelance work; I worked for *Playboy*, *Cosmopolitan* [and] *National Geographic*. My favourite animal is a bear, so I wrote an article about bears in Serbia. But it is a sad story because Gypsies had bears for dancing. I did articles for *Playboy*; I wrote articles about TV shows, about *The Sopranos* and about many things in pop culture. In *Cosmopolitan* I worked for money. I was the male writer in the women's magazine! I had my column where the Editor would send me some letters from readers. A woman would ask, 'Why doesn't he call me? He said on Friday he would call me and doesn't call me Saturday, Sunday or Monday. Why? Why? Why?' And I must write about this shit! And some articles for *Elle*. I am not a journalist for women's magazines – I only did that because the Editor is my friend. So I worked freelance for many magazines and papers, but after a few years I couldn't work as a freelance anymore because there was no money in freelance. The times had changed.

I have changed through many styles [and] interviewed important people. I have many chapters in my life. Many punks from my generation still live in the seventies or the eighties, but I don't want to be like that – I am in this time. Journalists come to me and say, 'Can you tell me something about Urbana Gerila?' and I say, 'Fuck you! I've published a book. You came to do an interview with me about a book!' I want to talk about the book and they want to ask about Urbana Gerila but I'm not selling a disc about Urbana Gerila or making a film about Urbana Gerila! They live in the past.

In Serbia, it's a big problem because new people are not interesting to people. The readers like old stars, old stars from former Yugoslavia – some actor or something. I hate many new things but I also like many new things – great TV shows like *The Sopranos* and *Breaking Bad*. You have good new things; you have bad new things. In the old times it was the same. I had a problem when I published my book because it's a new book about a new era. My hero is in advertising and politics. You see, all newspapers and magazines in Serbia are connected to politics because newspapers can't exist without advertising – and advertising can't exist without politicians. You have journalists, advertising agencies and politicians.

So I write about an advertising hell. I write about this character and he's like Faust in these times. But it's not an intellectual book; it's a good novel. It's not cheap literature but it's not philosophy – it's fiction. My hero is a man who sold his soul because he worked with a political party, a political campaign. One day he thinks that he could fight the system and take the money and take his girlfriend to travel. They take the money and he doesn't do the campaign for the party. He finishes in the zoo, in a cage – with bears!!

Serbian politicians became advertising men – this is a continuation of Tito and Milošević. In the advertising world, they say black is white, and in the past twenty years Serbian politicians say black is white and white is black. So, I say, advertising and politics are now the same thing. I think that Tony Blair is an advertising man too and in Serbia we have only advertising men. A guy from Idoli, the band, was an important advertising man in Serbia and worked for Saatchi and Saatchi. Two members are important advertising men in Serbia. Today the only industries that exist in Serbia are betting offices and advertising houses.

I did an interview with Morrissey – it was important for me because he didn't know who I was. The agent gave him questions from twenty people from all over the world, and the newspapers gave out the news that he had cancer. He gave a tour and said he didn't have time for all the interviews with journalists. He said he would look at the questions and choose which ones he would answer. And he said [to] my questions, 'It's interesting. I'll give him an interview'. He didn't know if I was twenty years old or fifty years old, [or] if I have a big name or a small name.

It's a good interview because I asked him not only about music but about David Cameron, about Labour, about the situation in the world. It's interesting because it is not about music – I had a fear that if I asked a lot of questions about the Smiths he would say, 'Fuck off!'. I asked about animals and the political situation in the world, and it was a big percentage of my questions.

Goran Bregović,[2] he's a clever guy and one of the better people I interviewed. The music is shit; I hate his music because his music is not interesting for me. But he's a fantastic guy. He's very clever and has fantastic words. I asked him about migrants and he said, 'If we didn't have migrants, we wouldn't have Apple because the father of Steve Jobs came from Syria'. When I asked him about Islam in Europe and al Qaeda and ISIS, he said, 'Islam is a young religion and you have many porn sites. If the Crusaders had the Internet' He talked about his career in striptease bars during socialism. And his drug history because he used LSD, and he said that LSD destroyed his brain. He has an interesting story. He likes to present himself like an ordinary man but he's not an ordinary man.

I still watch football and I still like Partisan because my childhood was near the Partisan stadium. In my childhood Liverpool was the dream team because I liked Dalglish, Souness and Ian Rush. But I support Chelsea. Why? Because of the goalkeeper Borota. Petar Borota is my first idol. I am a supporter of OFK Belgrade. I was young, and my father took me to a football match of Red Star against OFK Belgrade. My father was a supporter of OFK Belgrade and we went to see them. Borota came and he was like a rock 'n' roll star! He was different to the Yugoslav players – he had an image. After that, he went to Partisan and after that he went to Chelsea. I liked Borota and Chelsea. Chelsea is near the Kings Road; I am a punk fan, Kings Road is Vivienne Westwood's 'Sex' boutique, the place the Sex Pistols was born. Borota is a controversial person. He went to prison because there was a robbery in a museum – he didn't take part in the robbery, but the robbers worked for him. He died a poor man. When he died, I wrote an article about him and his sister called me – I didn't know her. She read my article, called my newspaper, asked for my number and called me. We went out for coffee and she showed me some old pictures and some new pictures. But his sister said it wasn't true about the robbery.

---

2. Perhaps the most famous and commercially successful Yugoslavian rock-musician and composer, Bregović was an integral member of Bijelo Dugme. Over four decades he has journeyed through Balkan roots and classical music, as well as writing numerous film scores and contributing to many movie soundtracks – including Sacha Baron-Cohen's *Borat* movie and *Arizona Dream* (1993) which starred Johnny Depp, Jerry Lewis and Faye Dunaway, and featured Iggy Pop singing Bregović's co-composition 'In the Death Car'. Bregović has Bosnian, Serbian and Croatian roots and declares himself to be a Yugonostalgic.

Lost in Belgrade Central

Termiti. Ljubljana © *Vojko Flegar (1979)*

But I don't go to matches nowadays anyway because I hate the crowds – the nationalism. Some supporters killed a young man from France, Brice Taton;[3] they killed him, and I made a decision not to go to football matches. The fans in Serbia are very dangerous. You won't have a problem at the stadium; we could go and not have a problem, but you have racism against Black people. These are mad people; we don't have black people in Belgrade except for a few! But not all are hooligans – they are a small part of the football fans. I am not racist though, and I hate nationalism.

It's not the only reason why I don't go to football anymore. The football is bad. Because we live in times when we don't have any dreams anymore. Today football is not a romantic story. You see, I like dreams but today you don't have dreams – you have big money. I like dreams, like the Nottingham Forest story, it's like a film. It's like rock 'n' roll. One against all.

---

3. In 2009, a twenty-eight-year-old Toulouse fan Brice Taton was attacked and brutally beaten as he drank at a Belgrade bar before the Europa League match with FK Partizan (Belgrade). In 2011, fourteen Serbs were handed sentences of up to thirty five years; some in absentia, but numerous appeals over the years reduced these significantly and there is a general feeling that 'justice' has not been well-served.

SEVENTEEN
Kafana Mornar: Belgrade Is Drowning

DAY 10 (Part Two)

It is a little after 7 p.m. In Kafana Mornar we do a round-table introduction. There are two members of Pogonbgd; Dovla (Vlad) and Sale (Saša), plus members of Trnje (Thorns); Lule (Luka), Džigi (Igor) and Ive (Ivan), plus the irrepressible Laki (Andrija) who is introduced to me as 'a friend of both bands'. It is soon obvious that my technical limitations, the logistics of speaking with a group of people around a rectangular table, these background noise levels and the constant flow of beer and red wine are likely to prove too much for both the recorder and my interview technique. Undaunted, I soldier on.

POGONBGD, TRNJE and FRIENDS: Kafana Mornar and Studio Mašina 23

Pogonbgd is a neat play on words. It stands for Pogo New Belgrade, but also for Pogon (which in Serbian also means machine/engine) and Bgd (Belgrade). The band have been together for thirteen years now and consists of Đinko (guitar/backing vox), Dimke (guitar/backing vox), Dovla (drums) and Sale (guitar/vox). These people around the table are sharp; the sense of humour is a giveaway but also the nuance of their English. Sale has a music studio and works as a sound engineer and music producer, Dovla does sound and video tech at conferences, Dimke works in a press-clipping firm and Đinko is an architect but owns – and works in – a printing shop.

Sale is talking about 'To nije mjesto za nas/No Room For You':

> To me it has that meaning. I never really knew what the song was about. I just liked the KUD Idijoti version. I liked the song. I didn't know really what it was about. But after two or three years I discovered that the song is a Demob original and then I started to find out about that song. If I'm not mistaken the song is about that club that closed. To me that song has a different meaning. It's about some ex-Yugo nostalgia shit, but that's just my opinion about KUD Idijoti's version.

He and Dovla look almost insulted when I ask if they are interested in the 'history and tradition' of ex-Yugo punk. To me it is not an unreasonable question since not so many of their generation in 'the West' seem particularly invested. I fear that it may be the nostalgists of my generation artificially keeping the flame burning, or smouldering.

> But we have a rich history. Punk showed up in Britain in 1975 or '76 and here it was 1977. It's an amazing thing because we were a Communist country – a different kind of Communist country, we were not in good relations with the Russians but we were in good relations with Americans. And back in the day, the Government said, 'OK, kids can do whatever they want, they are not making any trouble so it's OK you can play punk.' Ex-Yugoslavia was a big country and that was a big deal because of lots of things. One of those things was Punk and Rock 'n' Roll because Rijeka in Croatia was in ex-Yu, and because of that we had influences from all around; from Slovenia, from Croatia and from the West, from Europe and from America. Now it is different. But that is why we already had in '77 the first punk bands in ex-Yugoslavia, which was a big deal.

Today there are existential challenges for Serbian bands (and bands from Bosnia and Herzegovina, Montenegro and Kosovo), challenges which are accentuated when the prefix 'punk' is involved. Luka explains,

> We are playing a big venue next week – over a thousand people and this is going to be the second big gig in our career. We have been together since 2015 and we now have a great, great band. We are published and we have a video soon, and everything is going great for us at the moment. We have played a lot outside of Belgrade, but in Serbia. Last year we had about ten concerts outside of Belgrade and that's a lot for a punk band here. Of course if you have Serbian passports it is much more difficult to play in the EU, because you have to pay taxes and declare that you are making profits in the EU if you are Serbian. It's kind of like a work-permit but it has additional tax returns that you have to file. If there were more people in the EU trying to get bands from Serbia it would be easier I guarantee you, but right now it's just turbofolk bands and that's real shit. That's shit quality music, it's made on PC and nobody is playing. Even the singers, they correct them – autotune. When they play live, they use play-back and they just open their mouths.

Their appetite undimmed by the barriers, these men are compelled to take punk to new and uncommon audiences. Whilst 'rokenrol' is well established in the urban centres at the extremes of the Balkans – Belgrade, Novi Sad, Kragujevac, etc. in the

179

north, Athens and Thessaloniki in the south – there remain vast swathes of the rural 'Wild East' as yet unconquered. There have been gigs in the Bulgarian countryside where the entire village turned out to see the young punks and the event became a celebration of the community. The villagers' clothes may on occasion be things of wonder – such as when the mayoral robes comprised a garish, 1970s suit and a 'kipper' tie – but even there 'you could see the beginning of punk'. Northwestern Bulgaria is the poorest region in the European Union (EU) and shares depopulation as severe as anywhere in the afflicted areas of the bucolic eastern Balkans, but everyone agrees that these places, whether they are in Bulgaria, Romania or rural Serbia, are the best to play:

> Their culture, when they go to a gig, is they don't care, they just want to have fun. That's great. And when that combines with a band that likes to play, that's a phenomenal energy. It's better than Belgrade or London or whatever because it's the whole village. They know each other and it's all positive energy. We used to play those kinds of villages here in Serbia. Crazy. Crazy.

History may not actually repeat itself but perhaps it does, after all, rhyme; forty years ago Pankrti, Šarlo Akrobata and Električni Orgazam took punk rock into the communist Eastern Bloc countries to the north and west and today a new generation is taking punk rock to the forgotten fringes of the European Union to their south and east. Perhaps the countries which made up Yugoslavia were not on the *fringe* of the Iron Curtain after all, perhaps they were actually the *hinge* between East and West? And in some unheralded way they still fulfil that function.

Rock bands as gangs is a well-rehearsed trope and one which rarely reflects the realities of hothousing a handful of, often colossal, egos. My impression in this company, however, is that it seems to ring true. They tell me how these friendships were formed, bands emerged and the record collections of older siblings were raided for inspiration. Sale's girlfriend Mia has joined us and lets it be known that we should start thinking about moving on to the studio. One last round of drinks is ordered and delivered to the table. Demonstrating a grasp of English working-class culture well beyond that of many native English, my young companions applaud veteran punks the Cockney Rejects and Cock Sparrer for staying faithful to their East End dockland heritage. We talk about these blue-collar communities and how their 'traditional values' have been denuded by decades of shiny consumerism, instant gratification and the cult of the individual-above-all. 'Look at West Ham United, man', Sale says citing his admiration for West Ham's fans and their unequal fight:

They ripped the heart out of that community when they knocked down the Boleyn Ground, for what? Some flats, some retail outlets, some leisure places? One hundred years they had watched their team play football there. Some families, four, maybe five generations will have walked the same road to get there, drank beers in the same pub before the match, and stood in the same place at the ground. And now what? They play at an athletics stadium a few miles away. And none of them asked for that. The owners, the football authorities, the money-men, they are the ones who wanted that.

It is inarguable that, for much of the world, football in the Balkans is often synonymous with hooliganism. The western media's shrill reports of mass brawls are often exaggerated when compared with events in our own countries – racism and exceptionalism come in many shades. To some eyes, Dovla, Luka, Sale, Laki and others may fit a stereotype of Balkan football hooligans but they are united and implacable in their contempt for those who defile Serbian football. Partizan Belgrade's last three or four games have been played behind closed doors as a punishment for the errant behaviour of their supporters and the next match is against an Albanian team with an equally notorious following; trouble is expected once again. Sale leans forward towards me over the table, his manner suddenly much more solemn: 'All of us, we support our teams'. He leans back and motions around those at the table pointing at each of his friends and alternating the two sworn rival clubs: 'Red Star. Partizan. Red Star. Partizan. But we are all against the Nazi fans. That's not good. We don't like them'. Astonishingly, they tell me that 'To nije mjesto za nas' has been adopted by a group of Partizan fans who were forced off the South Stands after a schism between generations of the club's supporters. I am not sure if this is true or if they are having fun at my expense.

As we drain our glasses a young man, perhaps in his early thirties, enters the bar to be greeted with smiles and handshakes by my associates. They tell me, only half-jokingly, that this man is the 'leader of our political movement'. One or two dissenting voices vouch a distaste for politics. But it seems that all do have an interest in this kind of politics. It is politicians and not politics per se that they detest. Lule is the most vocal and active when it comes to politics: 'Yes but this is guerrilla politics. They organise themselves'. Someone interjects, 'This is different. This is social politics'. Lule elaborates, 'Yes, social politics. We don't want Belgrade to be ruined like this. We really care about our city. So everything like this Belgrade Waterfront, it's disgusting man. They are building Belgrade Waterfront like "this"'.

> He holds his hands in front of his eyes, forming a wall, 'so that nobody can see the river. You know the song "London's Burning"? Well, for us, Belgrade's Drowning. That is our movement. But it's also like London Calling; "Belgrade's Drowning, I Live by The River". I'm drowning too'.

I say that I have seen the glitzy billboards. There is considerable indignation and headshaking: 'You will see a lot more of that'. The wasteland I saw as I arrived in Belgrade yesterday, the place where the billboard dream so jarred with wasteland reality, is Belgrade Waterfront. In 2012, Serbia's then Deputy Prime Minister Vučić first floated his ambition for the project whilst sailing down the Sava on a pre-arranged photo opportunity with none other than Rudi Giuliani. The entire process surrounding the $4 billion development was mired in a staggering lack of transparency. There are accusations that Vučić had acted unilaterally when he agreed the deal with the billionaire Emirati businessman behind the development in Dubai of the 'world's tallest building' and the 'world's biggest shopping-mall'. Today, Vučić is President of Serbia. National laws which were broken have been altered retrospectively. Some sources have reported that the $4 billion investment evaporated to become $160 million investment and a $300 million loan. Families and businesses have now been forcefully evicted and protestors threatened, intimidated and beaten up. The promise that Belgrade Waterfront will be the site of Europe's tallest building and biggest shopping-mall falls on land as barren as the development site. A local architect was quoted as saying, 'It's like a bad joke […] It's just another shopping mall in a country that has no money to buy anything'. The average wage in Belgrade in 2017 is around $480 per month.

Desperation drives exploitation. Two construction workers died on Belgrade Waterfront in the months after my visit. The pictures, mock-ups and models have an obvious and fundamental flaw; unlike the billboard illustration, in reality this part of Belgrade is comprised of steep hills formed of rock. There is the added jeopardy that much of Belgrade is geologically unstable and susceptible to landslips. In 2016, anger at the whole undertaking led to the biggest anti-government demonstrations in the history of post-war Serbia. This was the 'Don't Let Belgrade D(r)own', movement of which I am now learning. The people were clear; gated communities may be acceptable amongst the oligarchs and extended royal dynasties of the Middle East, but they have no place in the heart of their Belgrade.

A waiter places the bill on the table. When I try to offer to pay I am firmly rebuffed, 'You are our guest'. When I attempt to hand over a modest amount which I calculate will at least cover my consumption and a little for the collective kitty, the response is even less equivocal, 'We can be polite, or we can tell you to go fuck yourself. You can choose'.

The bill is settled and we leave, splitting into two travelling groups. I am ushered to a car with Sale, Dovla and Mia, who is as charming as Sale had promised. We drive to a supermarket in the centre of the now darkened city and collect some food, some beer and some wine. Back in the car the conversation is as animated as before. For perhaps fifteen or twenty minutes we climb away from the city centre, through commercial and residential districts. We skirt around the darkened silhouettes of a number of sprawling four and five-storey buildings. At a corner block on the far side, we pull up at an unlit side entrance. It is deserted and dark here but we seem to be surrounded by a brown belt of undeveloped land and beyond that are residential tower blocks and houses. Two more smiling young men appear from within the adjacent building and hold open the doors as we carry in the provisions and head down a brick corridor into what may be a basement. Another door opens and my new friends stand aside as they wave me through. I find myself in an unexpected rock 'n' roll sanctuary; a subterranean punk rock grotto hidden under southern-central Belgrade. I am introduced to the remaining two members of Pogonbgd: Đinko and Dimke. We are standing in the Control Room of a studio. It has the dimensions and feel of an old-fashioned, English street-corner pub; in the corner is a bar, with four bar stools. Framed photos and posters decorate all the walls, with movies, TV and music the constant themes – *Reservoir Dogs* and, of course, *Only Fools and Horses*. The only thing lacking is a poster for *Good Vibrations: The Movie*: 'I saw that movie. Fucking great movie!!'

Sale tells me that this part of the city is called Voždovac. The studio is located in what was the basement garage for this block. Sale rented the space and put his heart and soul into developing the studio for his band and the musicians of Belgrade – even sleeping here whilst it was under construction. In May of 2014, soon after completing his labours, Belgrade (like much of the Balkans and Central Europe) was hit by catastrophic floods. The impact was felt even up here on the hillside. The studio – the entire building development – was flooded by underground water and badly damaged, although Sale and his friends salvaged the gear. It took months for the waters to subside – as I saw when I visited the city in September of that year. But still the water did not leave the building. The studio remained closed and the building's owners were losing tenants. After six months, Sale and his father devised a solution which involved getting specialists to divert the underground streams. They even raised the money to fund the work. Their strategy was a success and the studio rebuilt. The added pay-off was that the owners were so grateful the studio space is now rent-free for Sale.

In Search of Tito's Punks

In front of a sizeable mixing desk is a viewing window onto a spacious studio live room. It is beautifully decorated; opposite the window is a three-dimensional wood-block wall, another entire wall is covered in a Rose Damask, the floor is a light-wood parquet. In the far corner is a dark-stained drum kit with the Pogonbgd logo on the front kick-skin. A full band back-line is arranged around the perimeter. A PA system and three vocal microphones are set up. Over the next few hours we drink steadily, eat heartily – a huge spread of freshly prepared food is brought out and consumed – and talk freely. Later, we all decamp to the live room where Pogonbgd crash through an incendiary, but (given the alcohol consumption) astonishingly precise, six song set which I record. They finish with their version of *To nije mjesto za nas*, and it is exhilarating. I could not be more honoured. I am humbled. But extremely happy, and proud. And quite drunk.

Rebecca West had written, 'It must be admitted that this city, with its starved professional classes, its lavish governmental display, and its pullulation of an exploiting class, sometimes presents an unattractive appearance. I did not like Belgrade that evening'.

Well, I do like Belgrade this evening. Even more than I ever had before.

Pogonbgd and friends. Studio Mašina 23, Belgrade

EIGHTEEN
Novi Sad, Vojvodina: Words and Bullets

DAY ELEVEN (Part One)

9 a.m. I don't feel great. But not as bad as I should do. When the drinking finally ceased last night Mia and the guys drove me back across Belgrade and dropped me at the near end of Internacionalnih Brigada. Unfortunately for me, I somehow got lost between there and my apartment. I walked for fifteen minutes or more, getting increasingly concerned that perhaps I was in the wrong suburb. It was well after 2:30 a.m. Eventually, I saw a lone taxi-for-hire idling at the side of the road. I got in and told him the address. Two turns and three minutes later he deposited me at the end of the road where Mia and the guys had dropped me twenty minutes previously. This time I recognised it. It was less than two minutes walk to the apartment from here.

I check my e-mails and there is one from Radomir, the Airbnb owner, telling me that his cousin will pick me up at 11 a.m. Breakfast makes no great appeal this morning. Cigarettes make me tremble. I shower and pack my bag, remembering to bring the two bottles of water I had put aside. Another e-mail arrives from Radomir:

> Hello Barry, Good morning, I just wanted to tell you that my cousin is in front of the building, car is grey skoda. Take your time. Have a nice day! Please feel free to contact me at any time if you need. Best regards, Radomir.

I have been particularly looking forward to my trips to the provincial cities of Serbia. I am unashamedly provincial. My literary fellow travellers are not wholly in agreement with regard to today's destinations. Claudio Magris wrote that 'The countryside is superb', while Rebecca West described Novi Sad as 'very agreeable', saying it reminded her of her birthplace of Edinburgh. Were it not for the animosity of a travelling companion, the journey from Belgrade 'might have been pleasant, for the train ran beside the hallucinatory landscape of the misted Danube floods' – exactly how I had imagined my quixotic railway adventures before colliding with the harsh reality of long-distance Balkan coach-trips. In a 1994 magazine article, Geert Mak was more equivocal, reflecting on '(the) rich, fertile Vojvodina, where, according to the writer Aleksandar Tisma, the people hang themselves on the rafters "as others say goodnight", because the wide sky above this flat land will never offer anyone peace and tranquillity'.

I take each at face value and make allowances for Mak having recently returned from wartime Novi Sad just as escalating UN sanctions had slashed incomes, driven millions of Serbs into poverty and led to severe shortages of fuel, power and pharmaceuticals. And being Dutch.

Out in the street a man in his thirties is standing by a silver-grey Skoda. I smile, wave and walk towards him. He tells me his name is Ivan. I get in, fix the seatbelt and Ivan says, 'OK? Let's go to Novi Sad'. As we drive, we chat. Ivan is reserved and speaks mostly when spoken to. I force the conversations, conscious that I have only one chance to make the most of this day and just three days of this trip remain. Ivan is an articulate, educated and industrious individual. His English is excellent. By day he works at a senior level for the Serbian equivalent of the British AA or RAC, or the AAA in America. He likes his job, but he says it is hard to make good money in Serbia, so he is always vigilant for extracurricular opportunities to earn.

As we leave Belgrade, Ivan asks what my itinerary is for the day. I am hoping to meet my interviewees at 3 p.m. but I have to contact them when I arrive in Novi Sad. Before then I would like to see Petrovaradin Fortress, the Old Synagogue, and some of the sites hit during the NATO bombings in 1999. I read out my list, scribbled in the grey exercise book open on my lap: 'The bridges over the Danube. Varadin Bridge or the bridge which has been built to replace it. Liberty Bridge. Žeželj Bridge. The suburbs of Sremska Kamenica and Šangaj. The TV station at Mišeluk'. I pronounce these poorly and unconvincingly. I apologise. Ivan nods for each. He asks me to repeat a couple: 'OK. I think I know most of these places'. He taps the addresses into his satnav and says, 'I have a route, let's see what we can find'.

Low, white clouds are scattered against another deep blue sky. The landscape – flat and given over largely to arable – is much like that I saw during the bus trip from Zagreb to Belgrade. That is to be expected. Then I was travelling eastward across the great Pannonian Plain on the southern edge of the province of Vojvodina. Today, I am travelling westwards across the same great flat plain – still in southern Vojvodina. Whilst most outside of ex-Yugoslavia have heard of Kosovo, I venture few (at least in the West) know much of Vojvodina. In Tito's Yugoslavia, each of these provinces was home to approximately two million people, and both were autonomous within the federation. Over the centuries, both have been shuttled between rule by hostile occupiers and both have experienced ethnic bloodshed. But whereas Kosovo's deeply entrenched, toxic and incendiary ethnic prejudices endure, Vojvodina – despite the upheavals of recent decades – has not yet atomised into monocultural ghettos. Today, there are 25 ethnic groups listed as living here, and ethnologists say there are many more.

Ivan checks the route again and says, 'We will go first to Petrovaradin Fortress'. In a little more than an hour, we reach the outskirts of Novi Sad. We go over a narrow canal and are on an inner ring road, lined with auto-workshops, café-bars and small shops. A few turns and we cross the Danube on the new Varadin Bridge. We bear right through a quiet residential suburb and up a steep, tree-lined and cobbled road which arcs relentlessly to the right. We park up in the courtyard of the Petrovaradin Fortress complex, there are just a few cars and a single tour coach here. Ivan points me in the general direction of the best views and most notable features, and I leave him alone to make some 'business' calls and have his lunch.

I round a corner and find myself on top of a huge rock promontory. Laid out in front of, and below, me is the entire city of Novi Sad. Between here and the city is the magnificent Danube. Imagine a letter 'S' turned anti-clockwise until it lies on its back, and you have the way the Danube shapes the city. Petrovaradin is on the inside of the right-hand of the two bends in the reclining 'S', where the river sweeps dramatically back onto itself before changing course again and moving westwards and upstream. Upstream, in the distance, I can just make out the towers and suspension cables of the Liberty Bridge. Below and to my right is the understated curve of the Varadin Bridge we crossed earlier. Further still, in the mid distance, are the elegant, twin-white arches of the new Žeželj Bridge. On the quay of the opposite bank, I can just make out the outline of what I am sure is the beautiful 'Monument to the Victims' of the 1942 massacre of Jews, Roma and Serb civilians. The urban canopy of Novi Sad fills most of the view. Only two or three tower blocks and the spire of a cathedral penetrate the surface like stalagmites through a sea of red roofs. The Danube is the hue of the eels I caught as a boy – a translucent, sparkling, silvery-green-mud colour – but also the deep blues and brilliant whites of the sky above. In front of me are the three, stone pillars of a destroyed bridge. Immediately beneath the north wall of the citadel is the Lower Town of Petrovaradin – a historic enclave where a patchwork of sloping, red-tiled roofs fills the spaces between the maze of narrow streets.

The museum is open and I pay the small entrance fee at the desk. The first room is a long hallway divided lengthways down the middle to form two exhibition spaces. The right-hand wall is lined with glass display cases housing a collection of typewriters through the ages. Immediately I am nostalgic for the solid black cases, the damp, metallic thud of the keys and the physical slap of the 'Return'. The first exhibit is an 1892 Frister & Rossman. There are Adlers and Klein Adlers. There are wood-encased, clam-shaped machines from the 1880s. There are Underwoods, Remingtons and Mercedes, including one from the 1920s which seems to epitomise the bohemian sexuality, glamour, abandon and decadence of Weimar Germany – if that is not too much to infer from a typewriter. These wonderful relics are from the collection of 500 owned by a local pensioner. Present also are some names less familiar to me, those of models manufactured in former Yugoslavia, such as Sava, UNIS and Biser. One of today's interviewees, Stevan Gojkov later sends me a photo of one identical to the 1971 UNIS model in the museum, with the explanation 'most of my fanzines were made on a typewriter like this one […] being the cheapest thing on the market, it was probably in wide use by Yugo zinemakers'.

On the left, the display is more in keeping with the setting. The first cabinet contains a long-barrelled wooden rifle with a fixed bayonet, from the late nineteenth or early twentieth century, several more bayonets, military swords and cutlasses. The backdrop of the cabinet is formed by a triptych of life-size monochrome photographs of First World War troops of the Serbian Army. In the central photograph an unshaven soldier wears a traditional Serbian uniform of light-coloured trousers and tunic, and a pale, Šubara – the cylindrical hat which later became synonymous with 'Draža' Mihailović's Chetniks during the Second World War.

In the next display case are three heavy machine guns of various vintages including a British Vickers-Maxim. Maxim was an engineer and inventor of some repute. Amongst other things (he held 271 patents in his lifetime) he had invented an unforgivingly effective mousetrap, hair curling tongs and longer-lasting carbon filaments for the electric light bulb. The Balkans, however, played an unwitting but not insignificant role in the ascendency of the invention which was to become *literally* synonymous with his name. It was here that his future business partner, perhaps the least scrupulous and most successful arms dealer in history – Basil Zaharoff – cut his teeth as the representative of a British–Swedish arms company which manufactured utterly useless submarines. In a 1915 letter to *The Times*, Hiram Maxim told the chillingly banal and prophetic story of his greatest 'success',

> In 1882, I was in Vienna, where I met an American whom I had known in the States […] He said, 'Hang your chemistry and electricity! If you want to make a pile of money, invent something that will enable these Europeans to cut each other's throats with greater facility'.

Fifty years after Maxim's eureka moment, Zaharoff was quoted as saying, 'I make wars so that I can sell arms to both sides'.

Intrigued by the military displays I have lost track of time and now precious little remains to explore the rest of the museum. I hurry past display cases exhibiting a selection of artefacts which evidence the continuous settlement of the Petrovaradin site from the Stone Age through the Early Metal, Bronze and Iron Ages.

Long and claustrophobic brickwork tunnels lead to subterranean wells, all clues to Petrovaradin's past. There are many kilometres of tunnels which provided hiding places and escape routes in times of siege and the wells provided access to drinking water. I check the time; I must leave if I want to get to my other destinations.

I have been in the museum for nearly two hours and have seen just three other small groups and a lone Japanese tourist. On such a sleepy afternoon it is difficult to imagine the scene in early July each year when Petrovaradin hosts EXIT – one of Europe's most celebrated music festivals. Originally staged as a student protest against the Milošević Government in 2000, EXIT now hosts around 200,000 people annually to see the likes of the Sex Pistols, Beastie Boys, Manic Street Preachers, Nick Cave & the Bad Seeds, Morrissey, Iggy Pop, Pulp, Massive Attack, Patti Smith and Portishead, or ex-Yugo, new wave legends KUD Idijoti, Darko Rundek, Partibrejkers and Novi Sad's own Obojeni Program, Pekinška Patka, and Atheist Rap – two of whom I will meet later this day.

NINETEEN
Novi Sad: NATO Bombs and Jew Street Ghosts

DAY ELEVEN (Part Two)

Back at the car Ivan asks, 'Are you done? Where now?' I reiterate that I would like to go to Sremska Kamenica and Šangaj – residential areas targeted in NATO bombing raids. I have no interest in apportioning blame. I have spoken with Serbs who say there were good reasons why NATO bombed Serbia, and Croats who think it a despicable act of inhumanity against innocent Serbs. I want to try to better understand why these particular places were singled out – and civilians, including children, were killed or injured in my country's name. Sremska Kamenica is a typical Serbian small town. We pass a cemetery where there are huge stone angels, a football-pitch, two churches, large brick-built detached houses and smaller orange, green and pink pastel-shaded houses. There are a number of flower stalls beside the road. A flatbed pick-up truck is piled high with cabbages. There is nothing here today to give me any clues as to why the town was targeted. Its only distinguishing feature seems to be that it has long been home to one of Serbia's (and Yugoslavia's before) biggest and best hospitals. If the bombs which fell here did so in error, we can only be grateful that the consequences were not much more dire.

We leave Sremska Kamenica and head towards Šangaj. We cross the Danube again and pick up the inner ring road. Skirting closely around the city to our left we go back the way we came this morning, over the narrow canal and away from the city. A right turn off the main highway takes us onto a poorly maintained two-track road. The road follows the perimeter fence of a huge oil refinery and we then bear right into Šangaj. This is a very different place to Sremska Kamenica. The entire settlement is wholly on one side of a minor road which passes on its way to a thermoelectric power plant – where it ends. Passing traffic is rare. Šangaj is cut off from the rest of Novi Sad by the canal and the Danube to the west, and its only neighbour, the oil refinery, to the north. The entire enclave is less than 250 houses laid out in a geometric grid system of just six blocks by two blocks and dominated by the refinery which must be at least ten times the size. Šangaj is the Serbian translation of Shanghai, but the similarities escape me. It is difficult to see any purpose to Šangaj other than to house the lowest-paid workers for the oil refinery or to quarantine an entire community. Of course, I may well be wrong. Perhaps Šangaj was here first and the oil refinery built right next to it.

Some of the houses are tidy and well-maintained. Others look as though they have never been completed, consisting of bare breeze-block exterior walls and corrugated roofs which could be made of asbestos. Cables criss-cross the streets strung like loose boot-laces from lampposts on the skinny pavements either side. Lone women carry shopping while groups of men stand around cars. There is another flatbed pick-up loaded with cabbages. And one loaded with chopped wood. We have to stop to allow a car to pass and a group of men stare warily at us. The older ones wear Trilby hats and black or brown trousers and sports-jackets. The younger ones wear tracksuits and have baseball caps or sharply cut jet-black hair, closely razored on the sides, the crowns and fringes heavy with glossy wet-look hair-gel. Graffiti on the wall of an elementary school seems to say 'KOSOVO. SERBIA'. We tour the entire enclave in the space of ten minutes. The overall impression is of a less prosperous and rather isolated place, but not one which is destitute, or irrevocably abandoned. I ask if this is a Roma area. Ivan laughs, 'It is a Gypsy area and it could be poor. But look at the cars'. I see what he means. Some are slightly battered old Yugos and others early 1990s VW Golfs, but there are also gleaming new coupés and a not inconsiderable number of new BMW, Mercedes and Audi 4 × 4s.

We drive back towards Novi Sad and Ivan tells me that this oil refinery was formerly a wholly state-owned enterprise but just 10 per cent is now the property of the Serbian Government and 90 per cent is in private hands. 'Gazprom', he says, 'maybe the biggest official Russian investment in Serbia'. Gazprom Neft now owns over 56 per cent of NIS (Naftna Industrija Srbije), making it the Russian giant's biggest overseas asset. By NATO's own admission, it was targeting the oil refinery in 1999 when it hit Šangaj. I have no reason to doubt that. But it does lead me to question the public face of the NATO campaign which boasted of its 'surgical strikes' – and wonder if such surgery is possible? I have to question every 'videogame' report broadcast by western media which sought to portray the bombings as both a humanitarian act and a technological triumph. The distance between the perimeter of the NIS refinery and the nearest residential property of Šangaj is less than 50 metres. The elementary school sits helpless on the no man's land between residential Šangaj and the oil refinery – perilously close in the event of hits and misses alike.

When Geert Mak visited Novi Sad in 1999, he also crossed the canal to visit Šangaj:

> We walk past the big gleaming headquarters of the NIS, Milošević's, state-oil company close to the bridge. It had not been scratched. In Shanga, however, a Gypsy neighbourhood, we end up by the ruins of a hovel that did take a direct hit. The woman next door is willing to talk to us and invites us in. Her name is Dragica Dimić, she's twenty-three, she has two children and her world consists of a leaky roof, a

dark room that measures three metres by four, two brown, lice-ridden beds, a wood stove and a little flickering TV.

Dragica tells Mak about the night the NATO surgery went awry:

> Late in the evening we were standing outside talking to the neighbours across the fence. They'll probably come after the refinery again, we told each other. We heard the planes coming. There was a bright light. We went inside. Suddenly there was this sound: ssssss. We were thrown against the wall, everything shuddered and burst. More explosions, we threw ourselves on top of the children, covered them with our bodies. Then we raced out of the house, it was all dust and smoke. Our youngest son was covered in blood. Water was spraying out of the pipes, power lines were hissing and popping. We ran out into the field. I could hear my neighbour screaming in the distance. Their house had been hit, her husband was bleeding to death.

I get a text from Stevan Gojkov to say he is in the city centre now and we can meet when I am ready. Ivan says to tell him I will be dropped at the main square. Within ten minutes we are there. Ivan tells me to text him when I need picking up.

I had heard that Old Novi Sad is beautiful and this main square – Trg Slobode ('Freedom Square') – does not disappoint. Around the perimeter, people sit next to small ornamental trees, chatting and enjoying the mid-afternoon sunshine. In the centre of the square is an imposing statue of Svetozar Miletić the leader of the Vojvodina Serbs and Mayor of Novi Sad. Again it is the work of Ivan Meštrović – responsible for the Strossmayer statue I had admired on my first full day in Zagreb. In the Second World War the people of Novi Sad hid this statue away from the Nazis, erecting it again only when they left. Today, the locals often use the vernacular 'Miletić Square' after the statue, rather than its official name.

The square is beautiful. Behind me the sand-coloured Gothic Revival cathedral, in front the neo-Renaissance City Hall whilst all around is rich with pastel browns, yellows and pinks, bell roofs, dome roofs, pillars and porticos, stone balconies and masonry balustrades.

But for all of their aesthetic value these are not the buildings which I am most excited to see. I turn around and look back the way I came. And there it is 'jutting into Main Square, one corner rounded like the stern of an ocean liner'. I had entered the square by walking the length of the building I was seeking but – under its concrete awning and next to its store windows – I had been unaware. This has to be the 'Mercury

Building' – home of the eponymous Marislav Blam in Aleksandar Tisma's *The Book of Blam*. It begins, 'The Mercury is the most prominent building in Novi Sad'. Today it is called Tanurdžićeva Palata after Nikola Tanurdžic, the rags-and-riches merchant who bought the plot of land on which the Munich Brewery stood and financed the building of the six-storey Bauhaus 'Palace'. Construction began in 1933–34 but was not completed until during the Second World War, after which it was nationalised under the communist rule. Thus, Tanurdžić never saw a return on his investment and, his dream only partially realised, struggled financially until his death in Novi Sad in 1969. The building had its place in modern, popular and punk culture too. The cinema in the building was called Narodni Bioskop ('People's Cinema') and Stevan recalled that its celluloid staples were 'mostly Kung-Fu, Spaghetti Western and erotic movies', until it closed sometime around the middle of the 1980s. A newsagents shop in the ground-level parade was the spot where Vojvodina's punks could get the latest copy of the *NME* or *Melody Maker* during the late 1970s and early 1980s. There was even a venue in the hotel basement where punk concerts were held, thus cementing the place of Tisma's Mercury Building in local punk rock folklore.

I see Stevan approaching me from the City Hall side of the square. Black hair, blue jeans, a blue hooded anorak and a green sweatshirt. We walk back across the square the way Stevan has come. He smiles and says, 'Do you know they call Novi Sad the Serbian Athens? Is there anywhere you would like to see before we interview?' I would very much like to see the Synagogue if possible. 'Ha, no problem, we are walking past it to get to my place'.

As we walk, Stevan tells me that his brother worked for many years at the ICTY and Stevan would spend one month each summer in The Hague. 'Scheveningen is one of my favourite places to be', he tells me. We stop outside a branch of the ubiquitous 'Idea' supermarket chain, situated on the ground floor of a panel-clad, shopping-centre. 'I want you to see this place', says Stevan. I recognise the modest 'square' as the site of a legendary Pekinška Patka concert. When I first saw the fourteen-minute video of that gig it was a game changer. Here was a Yugoslavian punk band, playing at a Novi Sad shopping precinct, in 1979. A handful of the band's punk friends pogoed and generally showed off for the camera, whilst shoppers stood three rows deep looking on with expressions of bemusement, disdain and boredom. It could have been a scene from any suburban shopping centre in 1970s Britain. It really could have been us. A little later Sava Savić tells me that he was at this very gig.

'The Synagogue is just along here, two minutes', says Stevan. 'This is Jevrejska, Jew Street'. We walk along a broad commercial street, solid and unpretentious nineteenth and early twentieth century shops and apartments on either side. One side is lined with silver-barked trees planted so closely that the branches touch.

193

In *The Book of Blam*, Tisma weaves fact and fiction so tightly that it is sometimes difficult to know where one begins and the other ends. His imaginary characters walk on real streets and are press-ganged by real events. Jew Street itself is almost a character in its own right as Tisma casually introduces us to the inhabitants of the properties between number 1 and number 13. Amongst them is a bookseller, a watchmaker, a leather merchant, a lamp merchant and a morphine-addicted lawyer who – the victim of mistaken identity – is tortured as a Communist and 'went home and immediately asphyxiated himself and his wife in the kitchen'. The tragic fates of these individuals – perishing in raids at the hands of Hungarians or Nazis, or in the camps, or of the cold on the Eastern front, or simply of cancer – are told with a detached indifference. At number 4 Jew Street lived the tailor Elias Elzmann with his wife and four grown up children, two sons and two daughters. The Elzmanns were German Jews so the Gestapo ordered the Hungarian occupiers to arrest them:

> When the Hungarian soldiers went to Jew Street to round them up, they amused themselves by making the Elzmann daughters dance naked in front of their parents and brothers, who had to sing foxtrots and waltzes and clap in rhythm.

The Elzmanns were later gassed to death in the Nazi concentration camps of Serbia.

It is Saturday and the Synagogue – which retains the address '11 Jew Street' – is closed. It is no longer used for Jewish religious ceremonies since there are just a few hundred Jews left in Novi Sad today. Around the main entrance a wedding party of perhaps a dozen people loiters taking photos. A memorial plaque in Serbian commemorates the date in 1944 when the Jews of Novi Sad were deported to the death camps. A wreath of blue and white flowers and a ribbon of red, white and blue hangs beneath the plaque. In April of 1944, Novi Sad's Jews were herded into this synagogue which had been designated a 'transition camp' by the Hungarian authorities who 'did not give much thought to the choice'. The synagogue had to accommodate not only the Jews of Novi Sad, but all of those Jews driven in from the surrounding countryside. It was large enough only because so many had already perished, or disappeared, during the three years of Axis occupation.

Mass detention and murder, of Serbian and Jewish civilians alike, had begun immediately after the occupation in 1941. But from early January 1942, in the guise of crushing Partisan activity in the Bačka region of Vojvodina, the Hungarian gendarmerie and military launched what became known as 'The Raid'. Their intention was to curry favour with the Nazis and tighten Hungary's grip on territory to which it considered it held historical claims. They swept through the villages and small towns slaughtering men, women and children, and stripping them of valuables. From January 20 three days of hell was visited on Novi Sad as Jews, Serbs and Roma were rounded up and murdered. The search was systematic, the city sub-divided into a grid and purged block-by-block. Families were executed on the streets. Bodies were collected and tossed into the Danube from the public beach – still today a popular bathing spot. Thousands were forced to form a column and slow-marched in the direction of the Danube. As they marched, they could hear bursts of machine-gun fire ahead and the sounds of wailing – but fear and threats, desperation and hope, kept them moving towards their fate 'like a human conveyor belt, like grain walking to the mill'. It was midwinter in the northern Balkans, snow had fallen on compressed ice, the temperatures approached −30°C. Witnesses described seeing victims being forced out onto the frozen Danube where artillery fire would then shatter the ice; or stripped naked before being shot, or simply thrown – still alive – into the river. Some 1400 civilians died in Novi Sad in those three days. During three weeks in January, 4000 were murdered in the Bačka region. After the war, one of the main protagonists on the Hungarian side, László Deák, was extradited to Vojvodina to stand trial for war crimes. He was found guilty and executed by hanging in October 1946.

We leave the synagogue and within minutes, through a side alley, we approach a low-rise apartment block. We climb some stairs and enter Stevan's apartment: 'This belonged to my aunt and when she died it became mine'. Stevan motions me to sit down and says he will put on some coffee and get something stronger if I would like. Coffee is perfect for me at this point.

The interview lasts for a little over three hours and then I walk back across the city centre, over the beautiful square – now floodlit – and meet Ivan at the same point he dropped me earlier. Before we leave Novi Sad, Ivan says we must go down to the Danube so that I may take in the sights from river-level at night. We stroll along a freshly refurbished riverside walkway. Rangy young men are playing basketball in the newly erected courts alongside the riverbank promenade. Elsewhere, young women sit on benches or low walls, playing cool and out-of-reach, whilst gaming cigarettes from the 'boys'. Downstream, to our left, illuminated by single strings of lights which reflect in the black of the water, is the superstructure of the new Žeželjev road and rail bridge. Ivan tells me it is due for completion in 2018 and is needed to replace the one destroyed by NATO bombs in 1999. We get back into the car and I ask Ivan if he thinks Serbian people want to be part of the European Union? He smiles, 'Fifty-fifty', he replies. The journey back to Belgrade is uneventful.

Unsurprisingly weary, and anticipating tomorrow's trip to Kragujevac, I decide once again to remain in the apartment. That evening I sit by the open window, occasionally distracted by sounds from the streets below, and continue reading *The Book of Blam*. I re-read the text concerning the 1944 detention and deportation, thinking now of the Jews from my own street in Scheveningen. Tisma's description is one of the most achingly beautiful and heart-breaking texts I have ever read.

When the Jews of Novi Sad were rounded up, their pet dogs 'trotted alongside their masters to the synagogue and […] remained outside when the guards refused to let them through the gates'. They faithfully waited beyond the gates for three days and nights. On the fourth day, the Jews were gathered in front of the synagogue to be marched to the station for deportation to the death camps. It was then, in the darkness, that the dogs 'rushed up and filled Jew Street with joyous yelps and fawning whimpers'. They walked loyally alongside their masters – children and adults – and at the railway station some were fussed and even finagled a scrap of food as a treat.

> But soon they were alone on the tracks. For a while they ran after the train, but they stopped when their noses lost the familiar smells. They stared in wonder at the fields and ditches where they found themselves, their long, red tongues hanging from their mouths, and started back, one after the other, in the direction of the city.

STEVAN GOJKOV, VLADIMIR 'RADULE' RADUSINOVIĆ and SAVA SAVIĆ: Central Novi Sad

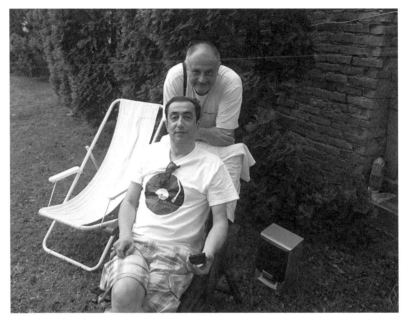

Stevan Gojkov (front) and Sava Savić. Novi Sad

It is mid-afternoon and Stevan tells me that we are waiting for his old punk friends – the journalist Sava Savić and founder-member/guitarist with Atheist Rap and Protektori, Vladimir 'Radule' Radusinović. Stevan was also a founding member of Atheist Rap. Before we begin the interview Stevan hands me three well-thumbed Clash albums from his vinyl collection: the American release of the first, the Clash, album, a copy of *Combat Rock* he bought in Germany before it was released in Yugoslavia, and the Yugoslavian licenced, Suzy Records version of *London Calling*. Amongst the ex-Yugo fanzines and books he leaves me with whilst he fetches the coffees is an encyclopaedia of Novi Sad punk co-authored by Sava Savić. There is also an evocative snap of four very young teenagers playing a gig at a house-party.

> The first band I formed was this one: Crkveni pacovi – Church Rats. These people on this picture are all between twelve and fourteen years, and these are my school friends [...] I was in the band on-and-off because

> I never had any money to buy an instrument. So they needed a singer and I sang on their first concert, in this house. It was a sort of half-practice, half-gig and I was the singer. Then we had one gig with Pekinška Patka. Then I was the bass player and on the third concert with them – somewhere like fifty kilometres from Novi Sad – I was the drummer! So I was playing all the instruments in this band except the guitar. These two are brothers; this one is dead and this one is an ex-junkie and not functioning so good now.

STEVAN: I was born in Novi Sad in 1966. My parents are from a village nearby, but they came to Novi Sad in the early fifties. My father was a normal working guy and my mother was a teacher by education (profession), but she worked as an office worker all of her life. Novi Sad then, when you go outside of the town centre, was like every socialist city in that time; concrete blocks instead of buildings, not many trees, not many places to play, not many market-shops. You had one shop that was covering the whole big area for groceries, coffee and the everyday things. And there were record shops – wherever they were selling the records I was there buying records. I bought my first record in 1974, when I was eight.

STEVAN: We (Stevan and Sava) are the same age, born in 1966 but he was born in January, so he went to school one year before me. So he's like an 'older' because he was with the guys one year older than me. We grew up in the same building. We played in the same bands, his story in many places is exactly the same as mine.

SAVA: I was ten and he was nine and we saw our first rock show together. It was Bijelo Dugme.

STEVAN: The records he bought I didn't buy because I could always borrow them from him, and he could borrow them from me. If he buys the Saints, I buy the Vibrators, if he buys Public Image Limited *Metal Box*, I buy Pankrti or whatever. But some records, mostly domestic bands, we had to own for ourselves.

STEVAN: We soon discovered Cob Records from Wales, a mail-order company which was working with Yugoslavia and you could send Yugoslav money. By 1978 we were already ordering records from the UK but they were much, much, much more expensive than the licensed stuff we could buy here, like three times as much. So you have some pocket money, you have some birthday money you have everything you can collect – like three red 1000 dinar banknotes. You put it in an envelope, you send it to Wales and you get your records in a week or two. Also Better Badges in London, we used to order from them. We had the catalogues because here in the centre of the city, in the late seventies you could regularly buy *New Musical Express, Melody*

Maker – and even *Sounds* for like a year or so. We were thirteen, maybe fourteen years old and not so good at English.

SAVA: And magazines too. He bought *Melody Maker*, I bought *New Musical Express*. We would exchange them and cut out the pictures.

STEVAN: But we also had *Džuboks* magazine. That's where punks put classified ads, 'I want to be pen pals with …' for punks from all over Yugoslavia. I found pen pals from Mostar, from Ljubljana, from Zagreb, from all over. So we were exchanging music, we were recording tapes. There were people who were recording tapes for money – home-taping and pirating – and they would regularly put ads in *Džuboks*. I would record music on tapes and there would be some guy from Zagreb who had a nice collection, so we would put the money in the envelope and exchange.

RADULE: I was born in 1968. Somehow, I ended up in totally the other part of town. So I had the opportunity to hear a lot of the bands who were playing in Detelinara,[1] and it was like a working-class part of town. My parents were so-called 'intellectuals', my father was an Engineer and had a pretty good career as he was an important part of the economic structure so to speak. But on the other hand, he was a Communist in his mind and he didn't use his position for himself. And so he taught me be to be such a person.

STEVAN: The 'Boom Festival' in 1978 was very important. 'Boom' was the biggest Yugoslav rock festival; it was held in Ljubljana, then Belgrade and Zagreb. And the last two years of the festival – '77 and '78 – it was held in Novi Sad. So we had this great opportunity on the last of the Boom Festivals to see these new forces of rock – Paraf, Prljavo Kazalište and the first major gig for Pekinška Patka. It was like the whole Yu Rock scene in two days. My parents – since I was twelve-and-a-half years of age – allowed me to go just one day, until 10 p.m. But the gig started at 4 p.m. and Pekinška Patka played first. Just the day before the gig we saw a small poster which said 'Pekinška Patka Punk' and we saw a picture of four funny guys, one with glasses, one had a wig. We were laughing like hell, 'Who are these idiots? They are not real punks they are fake'. And then we went to see their first major gig and we were blown away. It was great. The first punk band we ever saw.

SAVA: A couple of thousand spectators. But punks? Maybe twenty! Maybe.

---

1. An inner-western suburb of Novi Sad.

STEVAN: I don't remember any, I was so impressed with what was going on, on stage.

SAVA: I was a little boy of twelve-and-a-half years and I saw the band, and around me were hippies with bad fur coats and flares. It was a predominantly hippy crowd. Before punk I didn't care much about music and with punk I first caught the emotion.

STEVAN: We were lucky, we were living just across the street from the festival. So our parents let us go to this big concert because you would just cross the road and you were there – and you could come home at the right time. Here you could drink beer at fourteen years and nobody cared!

RADULE: Yeah, the first punk band I heard was Pekinška Patka. And I was like, making some jokes and a guy bought a single by Pekinška Patka and I was like 'yadda yadda, that bull shit'. After a few months, on a famous radio show, he played 'Narodna pjesma' ('Folk Song') by the band Paraf from Rijeka, the uncensored version, which was like wow! 'The thieves aren't stealing. The killers aren't killing. There's no one better than our police'. I was like twelve and with my father. He was talking and there was something on the radio I wanted to hear. We were putting the volume up and down and I said, 'Sorry, Dad can I just listen to this song and then we can talk again'. He said, 'OK' but he didn't pay attention to the lyrics. I was like, 'So, this is fucking punk! Wow!' Then I went to a neighbour whose older brother was born in '66 and the guy had some punk friends and I asked them, 'If I gave you two ninety-minute tapes – Philips – can you record me something?' So the first few tapes were like, the Vibrators first album, Stiff Little Fingers *Nobody's Heroes*. Then the Dead Kennedys and Discharge. And it was like, 'Wow!'

Vladimir 'Radule' Radusinović. Novi Sad

SAVA: My friend Boris Mišković brought me my first original punk LP, from London – *The Image Has Cracked*, by Alternative TV.

STEVAN: In May 1979, I went to London, as a tourist with my relatives, and bought the American pressing of *Never Mind The Bollocks*, and the Clash, 'White Riot', and one more single by the Clash, and Generation X, *Valley Of The Dolls*, on coloured vinyl. Woh! For a kid of thirteen years old to go to London and buy a coloured vinyl seven-inch it was fascinating! I knew a lot of things about London through music but I was really just a kid who was into punk for like a year and into music for longer. In my childish imagination I thought there would be punks everywhere. I stayed in a hotel somewhere near Kensington High Street but I never saw any punks there the first time! Because it was not fashionable by that time – no punk graffiti, nothing. The New Romantic fashion was just starting then I think. I only saw four punks in Hyde Park; poseurs probably, taking photographs for tourists and that was the only punks I saw. I was surprised, I thought everybody in London would be a punk!

STEVAN: Pekinška Patka did it for kids here with no money to follow the high-street fashion in London – because it was obligatory to have a black motorbike-jacket at first.

Pekinška Patka took the old coats and jackets from their parents, and the neckties. They made an idea of fashion where everyone can be a punk. I took my grandfather's old jacket and some big baggy pants, torn apart, and some old shoes. I put on a couple of badges. For the first year of being punk rockers we never knew about the small, button badges – we only knew about the big ones, we called it a 'saucer'!

STEVAN: In the eighth grade of the elementary school on the last day, all of the kids who were into punk decided to go in full gear with torn shirts and everything. So, of course, after one class they took us to the Principal and we all got some kind of detention-punishment for being dressed like punks – 'not respecting the school rules' or something. But we had all our t-shirts torn because we had no original t-shirts from London, so we had just written 'Buzzcocks' or whatever. I had a guy who was a comic book writer and he wrote a big Buzzcocks logo and I tore the shirt. We had self-made badges where we cut the photo from the magazine, put it on some cardboard and then fixed a safety pin with a bit of duct tape. Those were our DIY badges until the industry came along … and Better Badges. We have more in common with you because it's more like a provincial scene than a big London scene or New York.

STEVAN: Yugoslavia was a very big country at that time (the late 1970s) with 22 million inhabitants.

RADULE: It was liberal.

STEVAN: Our communism was much softer than the Eastern Bloc; we were not part of the Warsaw Pact. We were Non-Aligned.

RADULE: I still cannot describe it as a dictatorship.

STEVAN: But you had to know what you can and can't do. You were always aware of that. But not forced – like you did not walk the streets afraid that the cops would come after you for being dressed as a punk. It was a much more liberal society at that time than all the other socialist countries. I remember when we were full-fledged punks there were Hungarian tourists coming to buy their first Beatles records! We were like, 'Oh fuck you, you're […] years late'. We were listening to some new stuff from Manchester or wherever and they were still buying Beatles records here.

RADULE: Everybody was forming bands, and every band was different from each other and there was so much energy in that stuff. It was probably something which actually pushed me into punk – I switched to punk immediately I heard it. I was listening to my parents' tapes, Ray Conniff and some shit like that, and some 'good stuff' like Paul Anka, then a little bit of the Beatles, then Sweet, Kiss, some Uriah Heep; and then came *Fresh Fruit* … by the Dead Kennedys. Punk totally erased everything from the past for me.

STEVAN: Punk is the only thing that did that to people. Completely changed people in one day. I heard a lot of stories about people listening to Sex Pistols records and the next day they cut their hair, or sell their records or ….

RADULE: Yes, overnight.

STEVAN: A famous Novi Sad guitar player who was later included on Pekinška Patka's second album was a heavy-metal kid into Deep Purple and Rainbow. He went out onto his balcony with a guitar and an amp played 'Smoke on the Water' for the last time – the whole song with the solo and everything – and went to the barber shop, and from then on he was a punk rocker playing with Pekinška Patka. And he never looked back; he played in Pekinška Patka when he was sixteen or something!

RADULE: I loved that time in Novi Sad you know. When some record would appear here and then switch from crew to crew, around town. While recording it we were scanning the covers and the lyric sheets and stuff you know. There were not many punks then but a significant number, maybe 50 people.

STEVAN: The first, like '78, '79, '80, '81, they were beautiful years; no violence just quiet. Never had any trouble with passers-by just because we were wearing leather jackets or whatever. Once a guy hassled me verbally for one hour but he didn't beat me up – he got bored. It was just because I was wearing a brand-new leather jacket from London. There was some sporadic violence but not like there was in London or places like that in '77.

RADULE: We had some small stuff, kid's stuff you know. Some bullies would come up to us, but they would bully anyone – you know, we were different.

STEVAN: They would bully the heavy metal kids, the punks, anyone.

RADULE: It came after.

STEVAN: Maybe with the skinheads in '82 or '83.

STEVAN: We started the fanzine *Punk Process* and we put out four or five issues, and then everybody had to go to the Army at a certain age. It was like a normal thing, you go to secondary school, and then the Army, and then to university. That was the path for millions of young men in Serbia and Yugoslavia. So, every band suffered from that. Thirteen-and-a-half months I was in the Army. They sent me to Macedonia, right to the Bulgarian border – 90 kilometres to the nearest settlement! But it was good. It was beautiful nature, nothing dangerous but hey, you couldn't be at home and you couldn't listen to your music. For thirteen-and-a-half months in the Army the one so-called 'punk' tape was the only rock 'n' roll we had! All the other people on our unit were listening to folk music. Or maybe commercial Yugoslav rock but for anyone to be into punk and new wave was very rare. I never met any punk for thirteen-and-a-half months in the Army.

RADULE: We had a band before the Army and there were three of us – and in '87–88 the bass player and me went to the Army, and the next year the drummer went so we had two years of pause.

RADULE: And after, some guys were organising some concert for the Novi Sad underground scene and us dumb fucks said, 'Hey we have a band and we want to play'. The organisers said, 'What's the name of the band?' We said, 'Atheist Rap' and they said OK! And then Pećinko and Diša came to me and said, 'Hey do you wanna play in a band? We have a concert booked in a week'.

STEVAN: We booked our gig first and then we started making a band.

RADULE: So in that week before the concert we made some stupid songs. We were trying to sound like something that, in my head, was like Culture Shock.[2]

STEVAN: To mix punk with Rap and Ska.

RADULE: And we appeared there and played these two songs, and the third one was a song we made up on the spot.

STEVAN: We would do 'sampling' by playing it, not by taking actual sample from records but by recreating them with instruments. That's the 'rap' in the name of the band. He (Radule) just borrows perhaps a small guitar lick from the Dead Kennedys, but he always cites it on the lyric sheet or the liner notes, 'These are the songs that influence us, or we borrowed from ...' or whatever.

RADULE: We would buy whatever shit instruments were on the market.

STEVAN: East German stuff. Czechoslovakian stuff.

RADULE: I never had a proper (branded) guitar. Mine was totally Novi Sad stuff. Someone made the guitar. Some guy made the amplifier.

STEVAN: You could not buy Fenders, Ludwig drums or Gibsons, or whatever. You just had these cheap Czechoslovakian Telecaster copies, with the same body for a bass as a guitar, and that was it.

---

2. English ska-punk-reggae band of the mid 1980s.

STEVAN: The original bass-player for Pekinška Patka was a self-taught instrument-maker, so he took a lamppost made out of wood, and he took that wood and made two guitars that were played by Radule.

RADULE: And he also handmade the pick-ups! I built some 'fuzz' inside the guitar which just had a switch, nothing to fine-tune it, just to switch it on and off. And it sounded really powerful. But this guitar was heavy – eight or ten kilos! After a while we cut it to make it five-and-a-half kilos. Totally, totally, totally handmade guitar and it was so hard to play it with the action like a centimetre and a half (between the strings and the fretboard), so I had to squeeze it and to bang it – so after that I switched to a Telecaster. But it was the reason why I shaped my style of playing, because of the guitar. I never played solos because it was impossible to play solos on it.

RADULE: When they opened the border between Serbia and Croatia after Milošević, we went to Croatia for the first time and we were fucking popular! They'd been releasing our stuff all through the nineties. And we had a huge base in Croatia, and still have. A new generation, a third generation of people is coming to our gigs.

RADULE: Back in '94, Atheist Rap and Chumbawamba appeared on the same compilation[3] – Crass were also for me one of the most important bands on the world punk scene.

STEVAN: Back in 1994, a guy from America was making a compilation of bands who combine rap and punk in all forms.

RADULE: Chumbawamba, Credit to the Nation, MDC.

STEVAN: So we sent them a fun song – all the other bands were so political – because we didn't know what they intended to do with their compilation. And that was our exposure to the wider world.

RADULE: *Blu Trabant!*[4]

STEVAN: The first Atheist Rap album was put out in, I don't know, 500 copies but the pirates who were really big in Serbia in the nineties sold about 20,000 or 30,000. Just cassette tape and Xerox covers, they sold 20,000 or 30,000 copies. We had one or two, let's say, national hits.

---

3. *Delete the Elite* on Eerie Records.
4. Tongue-in-cheek paean to the East German mass-produced 'communist Volkswagen' famed for its basicness – now a cult, collectors' item.

RADULE: For our second album we signed to some government-owned label because it was the 'Year of Culture'. Milošević – the real dictator – declared the 'Year of Culture' and because of the contract they had to put us on the TV commercials. So all around Serbia people watching a news programme, the commercial break comes on and it's, 'Atheist Rap, New Album'. And, actually, we signed the contract just because of that part – to break in the homes of all Serbia so that we can schedule our shows there. And we used it. I was reading a book about punk in Novi Sad and realised that there is some hole in my memory somewhere between '95 and '96. Then I realised that from '95 to '96 we had three gigs per week, for the whole year. And I wasn't in Novi Sad, so I couldn't be at the gigs there, because I was always playing somewhere – for two years – it was crazy. And we were playing all around you know, all the shitholes and all the venues of Serbia. We played bars and shows at every fucking hole that you could put on a show.

STEVAN: Discotheques, bars, or in a house – a festival in a house-yard! Some old village house and you would play on a stage that's part of the house, you play to a crowd in the yard. You have to do that because small villages don't have youth centres or other places to play.

RADULE: Still we do it from time to time. The last show was in some small town in Croatia and we played in front of some 40 people. There were two guys from Ireland, or somewhere, there and they were totally like, 'Wow!' because it was like a punk bar – two times the size of this room – and Atheist Rap is playing! I like that. One night we played in Kovačica; it's a village near Pančevo near Belgrade, for some 120 people in a pub and then the other day we opened for Dubioza kolektiv in Belgrade Arena, and, by the time we hit the stage, there were seven-and-a-half thousand people inside. But for me, the better concert was the day before!

STEVAN: We had this way of political thinking in the early days. We were changing parts of the songs to sound like a terrace-chant from football fans, 'Slobodan Milošević is not normal', to the tune of 'Jingle Bells'. So we had these little things, but the real political lyrics started, when I left. Especially on the fourth album.

RADULE: That was released in 2005. The country went not just two steps back but more and more. It was too much. We had wanted to change Tito's system to something better.

Atheist Rap. Petrovaradin-Novi Sad (first show) © Radovan Ristić (1989)

STEVAN: Even though we learnt from an early age that it was the best system that there is!

RADULE: I still feel like some anarcho-communist, I wanted the best conditions for every person. In Yugoslavia it was never like communism the way Karl Marx described. Communism is sort of a Utopia.

STEVAN: But it's probably not suited for countries like Russia and Yugoslavia. Communism is possibly suited to countries with high industrial societies when you can produce everything you need. But what can a poor country like Yugoslavia produce and build with for communism? This capitalism I see here now is quite different to something I would see as a kid in France or England. Now it is capitalism mixed with nationalism at the same time; the two forces united.

RADULE: And a third, the Church. Actually the main difference in the punk scenes between Serbia and Croatia is that in Croatia most of the time they've had a government that has been ruled by Croat nationalists, capitalists and so on. So the punks stayed punk as I see it, a social movement. And in Serbia, Milošević was acting like some socialist and most of the punk scene turned right. They turned patriotic, nationalist or so on – like the skinhead movement but not real skinheads. I'm not talking about the whole scene turning right, but just a part of it, and the quality part stayed punk and hardcore as it is.

STEVAN: Yugoslavia already had a healthy rock scene. Germany had its thing and Krautrock, but most countries had nothing. In '48 Tito broke his pact with the Russians, so we had to turn to America and western states because we were shunned by the whole Eastern Bloc, and we were the black sheep of the 'Socialist' countries. So, we had this kind of communism that was still true to his roots but was making contacts with America. Instead of Russian music, in 1948 and 1949, what suddenly became popular was Mexican music![5] Everything Russian was thrown out of our lives, so it was Paul Anka and then rock 'n' roll and then the sixties of course, and the rest is history.

STEVAN: Our national music has crazy rhythms in fifths not in fourths, completely different sections – that's our national music.

RADULE: With bands like KUD Idijoti you feel that Istrian lunacy of some discordant melodies. Then you listen and you hear tamburitza, you can feel that Slavonian tamburitza everywhere.

STEVAN: That's also the national instrument in this part of Yugoslavia.

RADULE: We also have tamburitza bands here. You have some totally crazy stuff, like a band called the Spins, from Negotin. They are forgotten because they are on the Romanian border in the far east, where the nature is like Switzerland. They play some kind of hardcore but mix it with like crazy psycho-mania parts. I'm talking about when you are listening to a band from Belgrade, like Unison, and some guitar parts sound like some Macedonian artist – but totally, totally hardcore. This is like subconscious. It's not like doing some replica stuff but a style of playing in totally different genres.

STEVAN: Even if you don't listen at home to that kind of music, it's everywhere around you in pubs, bars, and especially when you go to the Army – then you realise.

---

5. Yu-Mex was a phenomenon stemming from Tito's break with Stalin's Russia in 1948. With the cessation of Russian cultural imports (specifically movies), Yugoslavia looked for a non-aligned replacement and found the perfect partner in Mexico. Mexico's movies were cheap and often proudly revolutionary. With the movies came Mexican music and a wave of Yugoslavian Mariachi performers was born – singing in Serbo-Croatian.

I went to the Army thinking that Yugoslavia was full of young people who like to listen to new wave, who buy 501s in Trieste. But when I got there 90 per cent of those people, mostly from the villages, were listening to folk music only. Maybe some folk-rock-pop crossover also but they had never heard of punk, or new wave or anything. You had new wave bands on TV, you had *Džuboks* magazine, you had *Start* magazine which was kind of like *Newsweek* or *Time* but with interviews with rock bands. You had it everywhere. Because that's what you got from the media, from Belgrade TV. But it was just on the surface. The rural part never got it.

TWENTY
To Kragujevac: On the Brotherhood and Unity Highway Once More

DAY TWELVE

I leave my apartment soon after 10 a.m. in order to catch a bus direct to Kragujevac at around midday. The bus journey should take about three hours. The weather is perfect for walking to the station – dry, a little sun, cooler than previous days. Kragujevac is high on my list of places to visit. Tonight I will be interviewing Vuja from KBO! – a man about who I have heard much. However, I have also been warned that Vuja is incorrigible, an inveterate joker and wind-up merchant particularly given to puncturing egos. My trepidation is heightened by a brief reconnaissance of the bus station a couple of days earlier and exacerbated by the online tales of travellers. Timetables and destinations in Cyrillic only, unhelpful ticket sellers who speak no English and an impenetrable system involving multiple tickets just to get to the bus. Throw in the stories of the diabolic powers of the local pickpocketing gangs and the temptation is to call in sick. Despite all of this, I am genuinely looking forward to the day ahead.

    On arrival at the central bus station, I smoke a cigarette and check that I have most of my money hidden, but sufficient to hand so as not to reveal my modest reserves when I purchase my ticket. The ticketing hall is busy; several tellers are engaged in animated conversations with travellers. To my north-European sensibilities most of these sound as though they may erupt into full-blown conflicts at any minute, but they all seem to end with smiles and thanks on both sides. Then it is my turn. I attempt, 'Zdravo', and the young lady responds in kind but without any smile, or any change in facial expression whatsoever. Through the combination of mime, pointing to the name 'Kragujevac' on my printout, and monosyllabic English we progress reasonably well. She says something unintelligible to me and points to a desk further down the concourse. I have no idea which one until another young lady at the desk looks up and acknowledges. This young lady speaks a little English and before long I have a single ticket to Kragujevac in my, by now very sweaty, hand. There is nearly an hour until my bus is due to depart so I reconnoitre the departure gate for 'Крагујевац'. This done I head out in search of coffee. Ticket and coffee secured; I feel inordinately proud of my 'achievements'. Now an expert in the Serbian public transport system, I calculate that the ideal time to head to my bus would be about fifteen minutes before departure. Any earlier and I could board the wrong bus. Any later allows insufficient time to rectify slip-ups or the unexpected.

Precisely fifteen minutes prior to the appointed departure time, I make my way through the increasingly busy, single-storey departures building. At my gate there is a turnstile similar to those which plague public washrooms in bus and train stations across western Europe. I attempt to nonchalantly push the barrier open; holding my ticket at shoulder height, clearly visible and proving that I am not a fare dodger. The barrier does not budge. I push again and still it does not budge. Now there are people in the queue behind me. The looks on their faces tell me that they have no concern about whether I am wilfully mischievous, dishonest or just stupid. They just want me to get out of their way.

An overweight, bald man in his sixties shouts at me from across the barrier. Repeatedly. He waves me back with his hand as though shooing a dog, or a pigeon. I stand my ground and show him the ticket. He shouts at me again and points me towards another barrier, further along the platform. I gently push back past the irate and growing queue of travellers behind me and make my way to the other barrier. A tall man who looks like he may be ex-military, dressed in camouflage combat-trousers, paratrooper-boots, t-shirt and a ripped waterproof jacket is standing next to the gate. He has seen the commotion and he says nothing as I approach. I gently push the barrier whilst waving my ticket in his direction. The barrier does not move. Now he shouts at me in Serbian. I have no idea what he is saying. I can see passengers boarding my bus and there are now just ten minutes until it is due to leave. He shouts again, this time in English: 'Coin! Coin! Coin!' On the turnstile casing I see a slot for the coin. I fumble around in my pockets and extract different denominations. I select the one most likely to fit and attempt to insert it into the mechanism. It does not fit. I knew it would not. 'Ne! Ne! Ne!' he shouts, growing increasingly angry. 'Medal! Medal! Medal!' In the scheme of things, we are not getting along so badly then. This is practically a conversation. He shoos me away just as the other shouter had, now pointing me back to the ticket hall. I push my way, once more, gently past the exasperated travellers queuing behind me.

Back in the ticket hall I approach a desk where there is no queue. It is the young lady who sold me the ticket. Clearly she has observed much of what just happened. 'I have this ticket, but I cannot get to the bus'. Impassive, she explains in broken English that I need to buy a 'pass' to get onto the departure platform. That is helpful, but perhaps she might have explained that to me when I bought the ticket. For a few pence I purchase a token which, sure enough, proves to possess the magical properties necessary for me to reach my bus. I ask the driver if this is the bus for Kragujevac, remembering to put the emphasis on the 'Kra' and then tail off for the 'goo-yuh-vats' and he nods. I board the bus and find a seat towards the rear.

In Search of Tito's Punks

Once again, I find myself travelling Belgrade's inner-city arteries, tramlines to the left of me, railway to the right with the Sava river 100 metres beyond that. For the first time in my journeying to-and-around Belgrade, today I will not cross the Danube which is behind me to the north, or the Sava which is on my right, to the west. Progress is relatively smooth; Sunday traffic being considerably lighter than on previous days. We are on the same A1 autoroute that took us to Novi Sad yesterday but today it is not northwest we head but southeast. Once more I am following the original route of Tito's 'Brotherhood and Unity Highway'. We pass grey, or off-white, eight or ten-storey tenement blocks with peeling paint and crumbling masonry. Rusted railings leak ochre stains down the outside walls. It is a snapshot of every 'concrete communism' western stereotype. Some windows are open and people are leaning out. Some have washing hanging from the windowsills to dry. The shutters on many windows are down despite there being no sign nor forecast of rain or bright sunlight. The impression here is one of partial desertion. There is yet another billboard advertising 'BELGRADE WATERFRONT'.

Over the tops of the roadside trees, half a kilometre or more away, I can see the peaks of the 'Eastern City Gate' or the 'Three Sisters' – the brutalist echo of the 'Genex Tower', 11 kilometres to the west. The three concrete, pyramid tower blocks stand twenty-eight storeys high as both monument and millstone. Constructed in the 1970s they fell into disrepair after the fall of Yugoslavian socialism saw them privatised. From that point onwards, residents elsewhere in Belgrade, struggling to pay their newly private rents, did not feel inclined to contribute to the upkeep and maintenance. Even more pointed was the attitude of some of the building's occupants. Those on the second floor did not require lifts to work as far as the 27th floor and were not disposed to 'subsidise' their neighbours. Those on the twelfth floor were similarly reluctant to contribute to the repairs required to maintain the pumps supplying water to the upper storeys. In 2008, action was taken by the municipality to restore essential services. However, an estimated €4m is urgently needed just to repair the crumbling facades which were never fully completed. Lumps of concrete as large as 60 kilograms have been reported as falling from the structures. Once again, the fantasy of the new world sits uncomfortably with the reality of the old. The LED clock at the front of the bus says 4:40. I check the time; it is actually 12:16.

Our route takes us through miles of languid hills, sage-coloured with a patchwork of dark-green bushes. There are small pastures where sheep graze and irregular empty pastures. There are tennis-court-sized rectangles of ploughed slopes and what seem to be tiny vineyards. In the distance, over the roadside scrub, a red locomotive creeps along, pulling twenty yellow freight trucks behind. Further, much further away are the outlines of low hills and behind them dark mountains cloaked in white clouds.

A hawk on a dead tree is silhouetted against the thin, smoky sky. In almost every field stands a dirt-red raptor. We pass a large roadside sign which says 'Bosphorous Hotel, Istanbul'. I worry, momentarily, that I really may be on the wrong bus. I convince myself that it is a crazy thought. This is the well-travelled route from Belgrade, past Kragujevac and on into Bulgaria to Sofia, Plovdiv and crossing into Turkey at precisely the contested point where Turkey, Bulgaria and Greece coincide.

We skirt by a traditional village on our left-hand side. A man dressed in blue overalls and black wellington boots stands on a small village green while a dozen fat sheep graze it. An elaborate hide stands on stilts facing a large copse of trees; this is clearly hunting country. At a tollbooth in the middle of nowhere we leave the highway. A man on crutches stands by the booth, taking most of his weight on one crutch. He is unshaven and wearing a torn, checked lumber-jacket, drawing on a cigarette and talking to himself. The bus driver appears to hand him some dinar notes. We pass numerous tractors standing motionless next to piles of wooden pallets. Departing the main road we arrive in a deserted village. At the bus station no one gets off, or on. An old man sits alone on a bench, smoking a roll-up.

Returning to the four-lane highway we crest a low ridge and enter a natural bowl, surrounded by dark-wooded hills. After two hours of farmland, scrubland, villages and hamlets, now tower blocks rise from the densely packed, red roofs of the residential streets at their base.

On the city inner-ring road is a roundabout with a huge Fiat grille badge. Yesterday, Ivan told me that Kragujevac had been the centre of the Yugoslavian auto industry and the Zastava-Fiat factory here was the centre of that. During its peak years, in the 1980s, almost 250,000 of the largely interchangeable Zastavas, Fiats and Yugos rolled off its production lines annually. Whilst 'sophisticated' consumers in the late twentieth century 'west' may have considered the 'Yugo' primitive to the point of being prosaic, or even a joke, it was the kind of heavy industry which demanded and rewarded a skilled workforce. It was also a symbol of an economically forward-looking country. Not only that, parts for the Yugo came from across the federation: the seats came from Macedonia, the electrics from Bosnia-Herzegovina and Slovenia, and the plastics from Zagreb. Each car produced was a manifestation of brotherhood and unity across the nations.

But then came the wars. In 1999 NATO bombed the factory. Local press reports told how workers formed a human shield, held themselves hostage and camped in the factory in an attempt to prevent the region's main source of employment and income being destroyed in the name of peace. They even sent out e-mails and faxes saying 'Please don't bomb our factory. Please don't take our jobs away'. For three days, the NATO bombs fell and more than 130 workers were injured. The factory was left, at best, standing but fatally damaged; the mangled shells of red Yugos hung like lumps of meat from a butcher's hooks. At worst, it was a blackened tangle of metal girders and pipes, the floors beneath flooded with oil, chemicals and water.

In 2008 the Serbian Government announced that the plant would be privatised. Fiat came forward with an offer to rebuild and re-tool the plant. In return, the Serbian government had promised Fiat they need to pay Serbian workers just a third of what they paid Italian workers. Just to sweeten the deal further, Fiat would receive subsidies and ten-year tax breaks.

A few weeks before my trip, Zastava workers had been on a month-long strike in protest against 'starvation wages and terrible working conditions'. Workers were said to be labouring up to sixty hours per week for an average monthly wage of just €320, whilst the workforce had been reduced by 700 the previous year.

There is a tragic footnote to the Zastava story – and sadly one which also illustrates some elements of the collapse of Yugoslavia. Cars and trucks were not the only items for which the factory was famed. There was a 'proud' history of manufacturing small arms; one which dated back to the middle of the nineteenth century. Rocket launchers, guns and grenades, and even military vehicles were said to have been produced during the earlier Balkan Wars. By the late 1990s, the management denied responsibility for anything more than rifles for hunting or target shooting. However, in November 2015 it was reported that the weapons used in the Paris terrorist attacks which claimed 130 innocent lives (with over 350 injured) were manufactured by the Zastava Arms factory. The serial numbers of the M70s had been passed by the police to the factory and confirmed as being part of a batch which was sent to military depots in Bosnia, Slovenia and Macedonia. The BBC reported the Director of the factory as saying, 'There's no doubt they were produced by us, we were the only producer then, and we have serial numbers of everything we ever produced, but in the 1990s anyone could get a hold of them in army depots'.

The bus station is away from the city centre on the edge of what seems to be an old industrial estate. The terminus itself is basically a pot-holed carpark around which three-metre metal fence panels have been erected. Outside this compound is a smattering of unsubstantial single-storey buildings – cigarette and confectionary kiosks, cafés and a ticketing hall. I disembark our bus and exit the almost deserted bus station. I walk past a low-rise tenement complex and across a small square; an unfussy café is the only establishment open here on this drowsy Sunday afternoon. I cross the bridge over a small river and within minutes I am in the city centre. By now the sun has burned off most of the clouds. It is a pleasantly warm, late-autumn, Sunday afternoon. Just across the deserted main square is a taxi rank with three Fiat Yugos and no sign of any queue. I walk to the head of it and knock on the driver-side window. A young man in his late twenties winds down the window and looks at me slightly warily. I guess there are not so many foreign tourists on foot in Kragujevac out of season. 'Zdravo', I say. A little suspiciously he replies, 'Zdravo'. 'Jadranska, dvadeset sedam', I risk. He looks blankly at me and gestures for me to hand him the folded paper I had just read from. He reads it and says, 'Jadranska, Twenty-Seven. Yes. No problem'. We drive for between five and ten minutes and he drops me outside a two-storey house on a narrow residential street: 'This is the place'.

The smiling owner answers the door and introduces herself as Jasmina. She shows me upstairs to the apartment which is huge and occupies the entire upper storey of the building. There are two double bedrooms. She apologises for the smell of cigarette smoke and says she has done everything she can to rid it from the rooms. I say it is no problem since I smoke. Jasmina places a hand over her heart and breathes a huge sigh of relief. We talk for a few minutes and, finding out I am a dog lover, she invites me to call in and visit Radoje, her dog, before I leave for the evening.

As I make coffee I receive a text from Vuja with his address. He tells me that, since Tomislav will no longer be joining us, he has arranged a translator. He also says to be there at 16:00 or before if I can. I check the route online, sketch a quick map onto a sheet of scrap paper and set out, but only after calling into Jasmina's apartment below and meeting her husband and Radoje. Miraculously, after a twenty-minute walk (most of which is uphill) I find the address, but unsure of the entrance to the two-storey corner building I loiter. At that moment a striking young woman, tall and slim with long blonde hair pulled back into a ponytail, dressed in jeans, boots and a black leather jacket steps out of a gateway a little further down the side-road. She walks towards me unleashing a smile which is evident even at 30 metres. 'Barry?' she says. 'I thought it was you. You looked lost. Come this way. I am Andjela'. Still smiling she leads me into a yard where a man I recognise as Vuja is waiting. He is dressed in blue jeans and a black t-shirt with a yellow Serbian motorcycle club motif and a blue hoody. He has thick, wavy shoulder-length dark brown hair and a broad, mischievous, smile. If I did not know that he is nearly as old as me, I would have put him at perhaps thirty-five years of age. He motions me to sit down in a car seat placed next to the front door. A car seat? I am a little wary, talk of Vuja's reputation as a joker uppermost in my mind. We sit down under a balcony and Vuja says it must be time for a drink. He says he is keen to get the interview started. 'Do you want beer? Or rakija?' I say beer will be fine but Andjela brings both beer and rakija. 'These glasses are very special', says Vuja handing me a small glass flask. It is the shape of an elongated and flat-bottomed tear-drop, with a lip around the top of its narrow mouth. 'These are Serbian rakija glasses. We will see if you are a man. And how long it is before you fall over'. I can tell that this is going to be an eventful interview.

Within a few minutes, a broad-shouldered young man with long dark hair arrives. 'This is Miloš', says Vuja. 'His band will play for us. You like Motorhead?' We smile and shake hands. With Miloš is another equally striking young woman with long blonde hair. 'This is Ivana. She will be our translator'. In this company – two athletic, fresh-faced, long-haired, rock 'n' rollers and two Slavic Bond Girls with chiselled cheekbones, and lucent eyes – I am decidedly dull. Vuja says he is keen to get started and he hopes we can get the interview done in an hour. I take this to mean he has other, more pressing, engagements to attend later in the day and he would like to quickly dispatch me back to my apartment. I can understand, he is probably a busy man. As we begin the interview the wind suddenly whips up, scattering my interview notes and rolling an empty beer can along the street. The sky darkens ominously within seconds. And then the first large drop of rain splashes on the pale concrete. 'Maybe we should move inside', says Vuja.

We move inside to the ground floor of Vuja's house and take shelter from the storm. We sit in a control room adjoining the studio in which Miloš's band Motorcharge are playing a superb version of Motörhead's 'Ace of Spades'. Over the next hour, the interview is sound-tracked by an entire set of equally uncompromising, and flawlessly performed, songs damped down by the acoustic defences of the studio walls. The interview is translated by Ivana (except for occasional comments in English by Vuja, who I suspect knows more English than he is admitting to). Vuja begins by saying, 'I will speak in Serbish […] And Ivana will translate to Bulgarian'.

Ivana raises her eyebrows, smiles says, 'I think it's very hard to translate. His sense of humour is very specific!'

It will later become clear that Vuja wants to get the interview completed as promptly as possible because then – of course – the full Balkan hospitality will begin. It will involve copious amounts of rakija and compliments on my ability to metabolise it. There will also be much amusement that I am nevertheless impaired to the degree that I fail the test of attempting to refill the 'special' rakija flasks without spilling any. This will be supplemented by an endless supply of cold beers and an equally generous buffet table. Another biker friend of Vuja's appears – a Balkan Johnny Cash, in a motorbike jacket. He is warm and friendly and drops immediately into gentle mocking. There are many jokes about Serbs, the wars, Croats, the British, the EU, Americans, the Dutch, NATO and even the ICTY. At 1 a.m. Vuja walks me back to my apartment but it has been a 'long night' and he gets temporarily disoriented in the city in which he was born and lived his entire life. The cafés and bars are closing, the streets quiet except for the hardy few, the drunken stragglers and young couples kissing in the Balkan moonlight. What a day. What an evening. But that may have been the rakija talking.

VUJA (SAŠA VUJIĆ): Kragujevac

Vuja, Ivana, Miloš, Johnny Cash, Andjela. Kragujevac.

Vuja (Saša Vujić) is best known as the founder member, guitarist, frontman and songwriter of Kragujevac three-piece KBO! Formed in 1982 they were the first punk band in the city of Kragujevac and took their name, not from some obscure anarchist acronym but from the sound made by a cartoon frog. The band have survived and flourished for thirty-five years producing eleven albums and featuring on a further three compilations. They were playing a hometown anniversary gig the week before I visited. Vuja is an icon, hero and role model to many. Several of his best-known songs deal with issues close to the hearts of his audience – most candidly, perhaps, 'Kragujevac' and 'Forever Punk' – and stay close to home. Vuja is very much a man of his people.

Two nights previously the highly respected rock-journalist Petar Janjatović had spoken of his fondness for Vuja and told me an anecdote to explain why the man is dear to so many:

> When I was back in Kragujevac, I gave a lift to the guitar player from
> a post-punk band from Kragujevac, who is ten years younger than

In Search of Tito's Punks

> Vuja. He told me, 'You don't know how much Vuja did for us. He had a studio in a small room in his house and we could record there. We were kids. We had a problem because we didn't have drums and we didn't have amplifiers. So we went to ask him how much we would have to pay to rent those things and he said go and play, without money.'

One Saturday evening in May 2018, as I am editing the transcription of this interview, a live Facebook video stream from Vuja's partner Andjela pops up on my screen. It is the festival to celebrate 'City Day' in Kragujevac and this year is notable as the 200th anniversary of the city becoming the first capital of modern Serbia. On a huge outdoor stage, at the main civic square, a school orchestra is seated in front of a black and yellow backdrop which says simply 'KBO!' A suited conductor takes to his rostrum with his back to the crowd and raises his baton. Vuja and the band ready themselves. Vuja shouts something at the crowd, they respond and he smiles and raises both arms. The conductor looks across at him and smiles. The drummer hits the open hi-hat four times as a count-in and the band and orchestra launch into a stirring version of 'Samoća'. By this time, having met Vuja and his family and friends, this all makes perfect sense. He is in his element, here in his home city. An unassuming and unorthodox inspiration to young (and not-so-young) people. And he is on stage doing what he does best. He is the undisputed figurehead of Kragujevac punk.

* * *

I was born in this town. I was raised in this house from day one. Of course, I was born in [a] hospital. But I have been living in this house all of my life. My mother was a housewife and my father was supporting us. He died fifteen years ago. He was working as a tailor.

We were all in high school, and in one class we decided to form a band because we were so bored with listening to the same hard-rock bands in Kragujevac. So it happened that we formed KBO! All of the bands in Kragujevac looked alike, their music was basically the same. There were a lot of concerts, but they were all the same and they all sounded the same. This was 1981 and it was very hard to get hold of the music that we wanted to listen to. But in 1982 we were listening to X-Ray Spex, Sex Pistols, the Clash, the Vibrators and stuff like that. Some friends from Slovenia sent us cassette tapes of these bands in the mail. We were listening to some Yugoslavian bands – Paraf, Pankrti, Kaos from Rijeka,[1] Termiti, Proces from

---

1. Kaos were a female-fronted punk and post-punk band. A cassette *Kaos: Kuca Na Vrata* ('Kaos: Knocking at the Doors') was released in 1982 and, much later, two compilation albums *KAOS*

Subotica.[2] I don't know why Yugoslavia had such a big punk scene. We had eastern and western influences, but the main reason probably was that it was very open-minded and liberal. Germany was mainly under American influences and basically did a 'copy and paste' of whatever the US was producing; Serbia and Yugoslavia was not. Maybe that's the main reason.

It may be that many of the Yugoslavian punks were from 'good' or 'wealthy' families and were rebelling against their parents more than the system. But in my case it is completely different. In our case we were not in conflict with our parents as the others were. We were actually fighting the system. In 1981 and 1982 there was the huge 'Nazi Punk Affair' in Yugoslavia and it was breaking news then. A lot of people were judging the punks and saying that they were the worst thing that had ever happened in Yugoslavia. The person who said, 'Punks are not fighting against the system but against the anomalies in the system', said that to defend them. The 'Nazi Punk Affair' was not very serious. They all got drunk and they knew that it was the wrong thing to shout. It was basically a joke and they just wanted to provoke; they were not serious. That was the most forbidden thing in Yugoslavia. You could not do that, and they specifically wanted to do it because it was forbidden. So it was a rebellion.

We actually wanted to fix the system, more than fight against it. Because we considered that being a punk was a good thing, and nobody else seemed to look at it that way. They basically looked at us as though we were outsiders. And we wanted to fight against that and to be who we are – no matter what our clothing looked like. Our dress style was extreme but we still did well at school and were well-behaved as people. We wanted to show that our way of life is not wrong and is not bad.

A lot of people bullied us because of our style. They tried to kick us out of the radio station just because of how we were dressed, not because we were being mean to anyone. This was the fight, and what we were fighting for. We had acts of violence against us in the early days. Our first concert was in February

---

1979–1984 (2010) came out on the Croatian Label Kaos Produkcija Rijeka and *Betonska Djeca* ('Concrete Children') on the Swedish label Ne! Records (2013).

2. The 2006 documentary *Nevidljiva nacija* ('Invisible Nation') by Darko Kovačević chronicles the growth of the punk scene in Subotica from the early days until the time of filming. Proces themselves were formed in 1979 and active in the embryonic Subotica punk scene but were yet another ex-Yugoslavian band whose potential was interrupted by successive spells in the Army for respective band-members. They released a 7" split EP on a Norwegian label in 1985 but had further enforced line-up changes (due to Army service). They broke up sometime around 1987 only to reform in 2007 and have periodically reformed with line-up changes since then.

1982 – so it was very cold outside here – and everyone who was in the audience threw something at us. So we threw it back from the stage! And now everyone sees it – to all of the bands from Kragujevac KBO! was a big influence and we are finally accepted.

I have two other bands. Trula Koalicija[3] ('Rotten Coalition') was formed in 1986 and I formed the band with my friend from Gornji Milanovac – a town very close to Kragujevac. The other is Zvoncekova Bilježnica[4] ('Zvoncek's Notebook') but the name is very difficult to explain. Zvoncek was formed in 1987 and I joined in 1989, so I wasn't in the first line-up of the band. The frontman of Zvoncekova Bilježnica is from Aranđelovac – 60 kilometres north of Kragujevac – and he is the main guy in the band. Both bands are still active. When it comes to Zvoncekova Bilježnica, I create the music and the frontman 'Toza' (Svetislav Todorović) creates the lyrics. There is also a fourth band called Dismissed and it's a bit extreme – influenced by the Exploited, Napalm Death and Discharge. I did not have any specific intentions to have that many bands! Dismissed have never played live; we have recorded one album and soon there will be another album. We're not really interested in playing live – it's just a way of listening to our ideas.

Kragujevac is currently the best rock and punk scene in Serbia when you compare the number of residents in the city. Belgrade has around two million people living there and Kragujevac has many fewer,[5] so in comparison with the size of the population, the scene is much stronger here in Kragujevac. Every kind of music – for instance hard rock, heavy metal, punk – is better in Kragujevac than in Belgrade and the whole of Serbia; Kragujevac is the best. Belgrade is a huge scene but the lifespan of those bands is relatively short. The bands in Kragujevac have a longer lifespan. Bands in Kragujevac respect each other and collaborate with each other, they are friends. The situation is not always like that in the rest of Serbia – that's why we love our town. Other bands elsewhere – probably in your case and in Britain – see each other as competition. In Kragujevac bands do not look at each other as competitors. We share our knowledge about everything – the sounds, instruments and everything like that. Whenever there is a concert somewhere the bands from Kragujevac sound the best because they share their

---

3. Trula Koalicija have released six studio albums and one live album. *Alkoholičarka*, perhaps the best known track by this 'side-project', has over two million views on YouTube.
4. Zvoncekova Bilježnica have recorded five albums and are renowned for a series of cover versions of iconic Yugoslavian new wave tracks and Devo's 'Mongoloid'.
5. Kragujevac has a population of approximately 180,000.

knowledge and their experiences of how to sound better. I think that it's much easier for bands in Europe and the UK because doors are open for them. And doors for us were not open because we could not even leave Serbia. So it was very hard for us to share experiences outside.

In 1992 our record label organised a European tour for us to go to Italy, France and other countries. But we couldn't go, just because we were from Serbia. We could not even send a letter, could not mail a letter – just because we were from Serbia. That year we released a CD and it was very popular. The entire world was interested in that CD and if we could have gone on that tour who knows where we would have been today? We were isolated for three or four years and it's very hard to get back on your feet when no one really knows about you anymore and no one can listen. Everybody forgot us. At those times we did play frequently in Serbia but that wasn't our goal, that wasn't the audience we were aiming for. We have played in Austria, Greece, Netherlands, Belgium, etc. We were on a tour in Belgium and Netherlands when the war in Slovenia broke out. And that's why we got two additional concerts because we were from Serbia as 'real stars'! 'Who is that fucking Serb band?' At that time we could have stayed there and been the real immigrants. We would have been protected like Polar bears are today! The first Yugoslavian refugees! We could have stayed. We were made offers to stay there. People from the Netherlands offered us the chance and said we would have money, protection, everything. But we came back and that was the end. The border closed up and … 'goodbye'.

We have just had our thirty-fifth anniversary. There wasn't a period in our entire career when we weren't producing music or playing. So, basically, we were constantly working. We didn't have any pauses or breaks. There have been some changes in the band line-up but our 'wish' kept us together and that wish still lasts. Before I went to the Army, I had an interview in the press and they asked me, 'Will you be the same person you are now when you come back?' And I said, 'If I stay the same person, my band will last'. And that's how it was. The army basically shapes your mind and changes you as a person. It changes people either to good or bad. Some people change for good and some people change for bad. And the Army may influence, also, your view on music and your musical tastes and things like that.

I earn my living from the bands who practise here and also by recording their music. I communicate a lot with all the bands. And when there is a concert in Kragujevac I work as a sound engineer. We released a new album recently – last week – and we also want to do a re-release of our previous album. We want to re-release every album that we issued so that people can get a copy for their collections. We wanted to do a cover album of songs which don't have anything to do with punk – they are just great songs. We just wanted to make them sound punk and they would be good songs played in a punk style. For the next thirty-five years? KBO! does not have any exact plans for what we will do from now. We will just do what we feel we should do.

TWENTY-ONE
Return to Belgrade: The House of Flowers
DAY THIRTEEN

A Bloody Fairy Tale, a Random Act of Kindness and Goodbye Yugoslavia

I wake at a reasonable time on Monday morning, but it is not the 8 a.m. start I was hoping for. In light of the night before it is nevertheless a decent effort. I pack and check out. It is another beautiful morning. Last night's storm has cleared the air and now we have blue skies and sunshine with just the odd cloud. My aim is to navigate my way to Šumarice and the 'October in Kragujevac Memorial Park' which commemorates the massacres of 19, 20 and 21 October 1941.

On 16 October, between the villages of Bare and Ljuljaci on the road between Kragujevac and the town of Gornji Milanovac, Partisans and Chetniks jointly attacked a German convoy. Ten soldiers were killed and twenty-six injured. Incensed, the Wehrmacht High Command triggered its preordained retribution; the summary deaths of 100 civilians for every German killed, and 50 civilians for every German injured. Initially, the Germans swept through the villages in the surrounding areas since they considered these to be strongholds of communists and resistance groups. The men and boys they seized were marched towards Kragujevac and then diverted to a meadow with a low hill. This was Šumarice.

Dragoljub Jovanović was seventeen years old at the time and was picked up in the first sweep. Dragoljub did not think for a moment that the Germans were going to shoot them. But they did. They opened fire with machine guns and mowed down the unarmed civilians. Dragoljub pushed his head into the ground, surrounded by the bodies of his friends and neighbours as twelve bullets smashed into his legs. He lay still and feigned death. When the shooting stopped and the Germans left, he lifted his head to see his mother standing just metres away. He later said that the expression on her face caused him greater pain than the bullets. She told him that he was alive but that he had no legs. She held his head and told him she would buy him some wooden legs. Over 430 were dead. This was only the beginning.

On the evening of 19 October, the Germans concluded that they were struggling to find enough civilians to meet their quota. So they ordered a further round-up. Roads were blocked, houses searched and every man between sixteen years and sixty years was taken. Still short of their desired tally they waived the

223

self-imposed age threshold and targeted the local high school from where teachers and children were seized. At some point during 20 October, they summarily executed those Jews and Communists they were holding. A few fortunate individuals were released if their professions were of particular value to the occupiers, or perhaps when local collaborators intervened on their behalf.

On the morning of 21 October, the Germans went about completing this miserable harvest. Their captives were taken to a field at Šumarice and the executions began again. In groups of up to 120, they were shot with heavy machine guns. Some reports say the shootings went on for seven hours. Some say that German soldiers were exhausted and broken. One, Josef Schulz, was said to have been executed for refusing to shoot the Serbs. In his memory a monument was erected in Kragujevac, with the German Ambassador as the guest of honour. The 'Schulz Affair' would invariably be discussed when Serbian and German politicians had diplomatic encounters. A film was made and the story became part of the school syllabus. Unfortunately, it was just that – a story. In 2011, after years of meticulous research, German journalist and author Michael Martens published *Hero Search: The Story of the Soldier Who Did Not Want to Kill* in which he laid the myth to rest. Schulz had actually been killed in a battle the day before the massacre began.

The massacre itself was only too real though. Afterwards, the Germans detained 600 unharmed prisoners to bury the bodies; a grotesque labour which lasted four days. Others were held hostage against future attacks.

Today there is some agreement that the total figure killed from 19 to 21 October was a fraction short of 3000 – the Germans took careful administrative records. At the museum in the Šumarice Memorial Park you can hear of the high school headteacher who insisted on being with 'his boys' to the end. There are the stories, perhaps apocryphal but nonetheless powerful in context, of the boys chanting 'We are Serbian children. Shoot'. The historian and former curator of the Memorial Museum, Staniša Brkić, calculated that 261 high school students – including forty boys aged eleven to fifteen years – were butchered during the 'retribution'. The entire district of Šumarice has been given over to create the park which memorialises the events. The grounds are said to contain 30 mass graves. Half a century later the memorial park itself was damaged when Kragujevac was targeted during the 1999 NATO bombing.

As I learned in Novi Sad, Kragujevac's Second World War story is a familiar one in ex-Yugoslavia. Throughout ex-Yugoslavia, between 600,000 and 1.4 million died as a result of military activity and crimes against humanity during the Second World War. This was amongst the highest casualty rate in the world. Whereas for the United Kingdom and its colonies, total deaths as a proportion of the 1939 population was (significant

224

but) less than 1 per cent and the United States just 0.3 per cent, the figure for Yugoslavia was between 6 and 11 per cent. It is, though, the Kragujevac Massacre which for Serbs somehow symbolises their suffering. In Serbia, 21 October is a public holiday and the national 'Day of Remembrance of the Serbian Victims of World War II'. The event is now immortalised in Desanka Maksimović's poem *The Bloody Fairytale*:

> They were all born the same year,
> they all went to school on the same days,
> they all attended the same ceremonies,
> they were all vaccinated for the same diseases,
> and together they all died on the same day.

Predictably, I take several wrong turns and the fifteen-minute walk to Šumarice takes forty-five minutes. This severely reduces my time to explore the 350-hectare site with its many memorials. The centrepiece is the 8 by 16 metres, brutalist three-dimensional concrete V of the 'Interrupted Flight' or 'Broken Wing' – symbolising truncated youth and premature death. Approaching it, the spectral figures of children emerge from its facade like ghosts from the mist, their faces staring out from the stone, forever young. I make a promise to myself that I will return at the first opportunity.

From Šumarice it is a steady downhill to the city centre. Today, the coffee shops and café bars are open and busy with shoppers and office workers. The bus leaves on time and we make our way back out onto the bypass and leave Kragujevac behind. The journey back to Belgrade is pleasant but largely uneventful featuring more hawks, tractors and trailers, old men sawing wood, and old Yugos parked on the verges.

After nearly two hours we finally begin the climb which marks the end of the plain. We crest the ridge and Belgrade is below and to our left. We stop momentarily on the long, shallow, descent; a handful of passengers disappear into a 1950s concrete residential suburb and are soon lost amongst the bored and the busy shoppers. Signs say, 'BELGRADE WATERFRONT 1.2 km'. We crawl through the streets immediately adjacent to the bus station, the shops and businesses are familiar to bus terminus users around the world – 'Slots', 'Sexy Shop', 'Betting', 'Hostel'.

I get off the bus and immediately it seems that the seasons have changed overnight. It is still sunny and the sky is predominantly blue. But it is considerably cooler than on previous days. If the raised coat collars and fake-fur-lined hoods are an indication, the people of Belgrade seem to feel it more than I do. I decide to walk back to the apartment. I make my way up the broad, tree-lined, Nemanjina Street – one of central Belgrade's main arteries. Busy with traffic and pedestrians, lined on both sides by solid and stoical civic buildings, compact urban parks and neat decorative trees, it is the definition of a central European boulevard.

At the intersection with Kneza Miloša is a dramatic and unsettling sight; here in the heart of the central business district is the husk of a wrecked office block. The entire middle section of this sizeable building is missing, completely destroyed. The tower on the right-hand side is ten storeys and the one on the left is eight storeys but the section which once linked the two is no longer there. The stumps of the steel reinforcing rods stick out at each floor level. Internal walls are missing from the two surviving towers, revealing the weathered contents of whole rooms. The shredded remains of a carpet spill over the lip and hang down the face of the building. Cupboards and light fittings are smashed, ducting and girders are exposed and mangled. At closer quarters, the absent middle section looks to have been cleared in a controlled demolition. I take some photographs with my phone and then see an armed policeman walking purposefully towards me, angrily motioning me to stop. I put the camera away and continue quickly on my way before he reaches me.

These are the preserved ruins of the Yugoslav Ministry of Defence Building 'A', bombed in the NATO 'humanitarian' raids of late Spring 1999. The Chinese Embassy was also hit – a case of mistaken identity when the CIA employed outdated and inadequate maps and an untested methodology in an opportunistic attempt to destroy a Serbian (and formerly Yugoslavian) arms agency – a longstanding irritant, and a minor impediment to their ambitions in the region.[1] Three Chinese journalists were killed and a further 27 people injured. Tensions escalated rapidly and for a few days geo-political commentators seriously debated the risk of an epochal conflict between the superpowers. Across Nemanjina are the remains of the other half of the building, Building 'B'. It had been designed to resemble a canyon on the Sutjeska River, the site of a famous Second World War battle. Nemanjina Street represented the river and the whole edifice symbolised a gateway; built to commemorate a war, reduced to a shell and now a memorial, by another war.

Within thirty minutes I am back at my apartment. I check out the route to the 'House of Flowers'. I am loathe to waste the last twenty hours of my trip – and Tito's Mausoleum (the House of Flowers) has long been on my list of 'must-do' sights. I set out, conscious that in an hour or two at most, the sun will dip below the skyline. I leave the building and turn right on Internacionalnih Brigada. After heading directly west for 750 metres, I emerge onto a main road, the other side of

---

1. This 'accidental bombing' explanation was disputed. In 1999, *The Guardian* – *The Observer* in the UK claimed to have evidence that the Americans had deliberately targeted the Embassy without the knowledge of their NATO partners.

which is an urban park. Much of the park is closed off with temporary fencing – another construction site. My route blocked, I turn and head up the hill. To my right is the iconic, white-walled and multi-domed Church of St Sava, one of the world's biggest Orthodox Churches; to my left is Karađorđev Park, named after the man credited with leading Serbia to its independence from the Ottoman Empire in the early nineteenth century.

Rebecca West admired Karađorđe ('Karadjordje') Petrović for his bravery and military acumen but considered him to be 'of definitely unstable temperament' and subject to 'gusts of violence'. An illiterate pig-herder from a village in rural Šumadija, his dynasty ruled the Kingdom of Yugoslavia until driven out by the Nazis in 1941. Tito applied the coup-de-grace by abolishing the Yugoslav monarchy in 1945. Today the Karađorđe family are once again in residence at the Royal Palace in Belgrade and there is significant momentum to restore them at the head of a constitutional monarchy – and significant resistance.

As I look up at the statue of Karađorđe silhouetted against the eastern sky, the light is fast fading. A three-quarter moon rises over his left shoulder. It is certainly time for me to move on if I am to find Tito's resting place. Following my map, I cross another small park and find the street I am looking for – Dr Subotića starijeg. It is not as I imagined. I pass through a large gateway and I am in the grounds of a sprawling hospital complex. On each side of the road are numerous fin-de-siècle buildings of four and five storeys, some external walls are stained by decades of air pollution. The way is lined with silver birch and fir trees and irregular grassed areas. Hospital visitors, administration staff, nurses and orderlies file out of buildings in ones, twos and threes and make their way towards the site exits. One large building has metal security grilles on every window. At one time this site must have been a model facility. In the sunshine it is probably pleasant enough. But now, in the late October gloaming, the overall ambience is a little sinister to an outsider. The horror movie potential is heightened when something draws my attention to an upper floor. It is the sunken, walnut face of a man, his deep wrinkles visible even from ground level. Like a Van Gogh, lit by the weak streetlights and framed by the open window he sits, staring dead-eyed into the creeping dusk and the harsh outlines of half-bare trees.

After 500 metres, I come to the end of the road and the boundary of the site. But the prospect ahead of me does not obviously correspond with the map I can now barely see in the gathering darkness. I am utterly lost. Everyone around me seems to be rushing.

At that moment I hear shouting and look up from the map. Across the other side of the street is a young man wearing jeans, a modern parka and a beanie hat. He is in his twenties and looks as though he may have some Eurasian or perhaps

Mongolian ancestry. I look directly at him and he is looking straight back at me. He shouts again. He is clearly shouting at me, in Serbian.

> I'm sorry, I don't understand.
> OK. Wait.

He crosses the road.

> Mister, where are you looking for? They have changed all the names and all of the roads.

I tell him that I am looking for the House of Flowers and he looks genuinely surprised.

> OK! You see where the white car goes?

He points to a single-track road which descends the steep hill.

> They should not go there. It is only for people walking. You walk down to the bottom of the hill. There is a blue bridge across the highway. A very busy highway. You go over the bridge. In front of you is a steep, steep, steep, steep, steep hill. You go to the top of the steep hill and on the left is my football club, Partisan.

He stops. I look at him expectantly …

> And Tito's tomb is in front of the big tower blocks.

Partisan is clearly a much bigger deal than Tito's tomb for this Samaritan.

> Thanks, you've been a great help. I was lost.

He points at my t-shirt, 'KBO! is the oldest punk band in Kragujevac. The first!' I tell him that I know. That the previous night I had been in Kragujevac with Vuja.

'Oh Saša! The last time I saw him I was so-high', he holds his hand palm-down next to his thigh, indicating a small child. 'He has a studio in Kragujevac you know? Vuja is a true punk. He has a true punk heart. You know that, right?'

> Yes, he is. And he certainly has a big heart.
> He is forever young,
> Forever punk,
> Yes! Forever punk!

I thank the young man again and we part with a handshake. I am increasingly conscious that time is against me if I am to get to the House of Flowers. I follow his directions and twenty minutes later I come to the Museum of Yugoslav

History where lights are being turned off and people are bidding goodnight at the main entrance. Just beyond the museum I find the House of Flowers. It is in darkness. Closed. But unlike the museum, it is utterly deserted and not a single light burns here. I later find out that the House of Flowers is closed, all day, on every Monday.

Defeated I turn back. I stop on the side of the steep, steep hill. From here the city is magical. I light a cigarette and take a few minutes to absorb the view. On the next ridge, across the valley, the main dome of St Sava Church stands above all. The floodlit white walls shine out against a blueberry night sky. It is not Athens or New York or Sydney but it has an alien-ness, a uniquely Balkan exoticism, which is equally intoxicating.

That night by the open window, lit only by the streetlights out on Internacionalnih Brigada, I listen to Kuzle, KBO! and KUD Idijoti. I find some online footage of *Adijo Ljubljana* from the 'Pankrti 40' concert. I unpack the travel speaker once again, plug it in and click 'play'. The sound is muddy and there is a lot of extraneous crowd noise but it does not detract. For a few, magical, minutes I am back in the Stožice Arena. Tomislav and I have our arms around each other's shoulders, we are singing at the top of our voices, grinning like teenagers with our whole lives ahead of us.

As a schoolboy, delusional though it may now seem, I dreamed of a 'career' playing punk rock. I did not ask for, nor expect, much; an undefined but nevertheless relatively comfortable way of life for which I would exchange my rebel gifts with an appreciative congregation. Real-life proved to be resistant. My musical 'career' simply delayed me getting a 'proper job' until I was of an age when many of my friends were beginning to picture being mortgage-free. Whilst they calculated pension pots, I hid from bailiffs, not fans or paparazzi.

More recently, I came to realise that music has rewarded me in ways far richer than I ever imagined. Little could I have known when we recorded 'No Room For You' that it would be the catalyst for this journey – where people would embrace me with an uncommon warmth and invite me into their homes the very first time we met. They would feed me generously and maintain a steady stream of beer, wine and rakija. I could not have conceived that a punk rock song might initiate new friendships which have already lasted several years and which I confidently anticipate surviving to the grave. Nor could I have realised the value of all of this. I travelled in hope and a fair degree of ignorance. Like Rebecca West, some of what I have learned serves only to heighten my anxieties. But I will leave rewarded many times over, and wise enough now to understand how little I knew.

My horizons have been tilted. Yugoslavia has changed me. I promise myself that I will return.

Adio Ljubljana, adio Kodeljevo,
adio prjatli zdej čas je za slovo ...

Goodbye Ljubljana, goodbye Kodeljevo,
Goodbye my friends ...
Goodbye Yugoslavia.
 ... Closed Groove

SLEEVE NOTES: Standing at the Gates of the West
Hitsville Yugo

Given the knowledge and expertise of many who were actually there – several of whom tell their stories in this book – it would be pretentious and unnecessary to even attempt an exhaustive synthesis of punk rock in the former Yugoslavia. However, given the dearth of material available in the English language and the need to satisfy my own ego, here are some of my own reflections. This is very much an outsider's view, pieced together from conversations and interviews, asides and anecdotes, documentaries and the hundreds of recommendations for music I should listen to. It is not an encyclopaedia nor a thesis; think of it more as a collage, or better, a mural.

In December 1976 punk exploded into the UK public consciousness with the Sex Pistols' scandalous TV interview and the ensuing 'The Filth and the Fury' newspaper headlines. By the summer of 1977 barely a day seemed to pass without television news, or newspapers, screaming hysterically about the threat to the nation's youth. Reports of pitched battles between the young punks and the Teddy Boys, illustrated with swastikas, anarchy symbols and the Queen's image punctured with safety pins, sought to justify another small-town, hitherto-unheard-of, local council banning a performance by some spotty teenagers. In late 1977 punk began to emerge, a little less uproariously, from the rehearsal spaces and bedrooms of Yugoslavia. The Slovenian pop singer Tomaž Domicelj had brought the first Sex Pistols, Damned and Vibrators singles to Yugoslavia in late 1976 and they were broadcast on Ljubljana's Radio Študent around Christmas time. Isolated punk bands existed in cities such as Ljubljana and Rijeka, but most commentators agree that 1978 was the year when punk and new wave achieved traction and lift-off in Yugoslavia.

During this time Tito's federation was still readily identifiable as the leader of the Non-Aligned Movement, squeezed between the Soviet Iron Curtain and the western consumerist bazaar; the Warsaw Pact and NATO. From the late 1970s to the mid 1980s, the country suffered economic turmoil catalysed by the oil crises and high foreign debt, yet this was a relatively stable period – socially and culturally. Yugoslavs could still travel freely if they had money. Foreigners visited on a large scale. By the late 1980s Yugoslavia hosted around eight million foreign tourists annually. They came primarily from West Germany, Austria and Italy, but also from Britain, Czechoslovakia and France. Punk bands formed and rehearsed with their imported East German and Czechoslovakian, or home-made instruments. They recorded and released records. Throughout the 1970s and into the 1980s, Yugoslav bands were extremely popular in Eastern Europe and many – amongst them Pankrti, Šarlo

Akrobata and Električni Orgazam – toured. Some cultural commentators suggest that Yugoslavia's openness to, and reinterpretation of, western culture imbued their artists with a certain rock 'n' roll exoticism and sleazy authenticity unavailable behind the Iron Curtain.[1] However, overseas tours were typically confined to the European mainland – few got as far as the United Kingdom or the United States.

Foreign bands were welcomed to Yugoslavia, a tradition which can be traced back at least as far as the summer of 1965 when Blackpool's Rockin' Vickers – featuring Lemmy Kilmister – famously interrupted their tour to join Tito for dinner. Records and magazines were still published as youth culture evolved under the double-edged sword of state support and state monopoly. The 'barriers' which existed appear to have been chiefly economic rather than ideological. As such they were extremely permeable. In this pre-MTV[2] and pre-internet era, access to music over the airwaves was limited to national – often student – radio stations in each of the republics. Radio Luxembourg was within range for some, but it did not have a particularly strong roster of punk and new wave DJs.

Imported UK music papers such as *New Musical Express* and *Melody Maker* were available, if in limited locations and quantities. The young Yugo-punks travelled to Italy or Austria, or even London, to get the latest releases. Most of these records would appear on general sale in Yugoslavia, but only once they had been licensed to the state companies such as PGP–RTB, Jugoton or Suzy, and pressed up domestically. This entailed a time lag, a delay between release in the United Kingdom or the United States and the licenced releases hitting the shops of Zagreb, Ljubljana or Belgrade. And which self-respecting young punk wanted to wait until the Clash album worked its way through the state bureaucracy? This, and the desire for 'originals', spawned an unlikely bond between an independent record shop in the small, Welsh-speaking, coastal town of Porthmadog, Gwynedd, North Wales (2011 population: 4185) and the punk rock youth of Yugoslavia.

Remarkably, Cob Records is still trading as a record shop, so I contacted them on the slim chance that someone there would remember sending records to Tito's Yugoslavia. Within hours I received a reply:

> It is really great to hear that we are still remembered there. Unfortunately, the gentleman who started it all off here, Bill, passed away last year. He was the one that started the mail order business from it being a café to

---

1. A point made to me in interviews with serious music journalists and musicians who had toured in the Soviet Union, in Croatia, Serbia and Slovenia.
2. MTV Europe did not launch until August 1987 and was not readily available everywhere even then.

what it is now. His son has taken over the running of the business but he is too young to remember those days to help you.

In its heyday, Cob's mail order customer base numbered 25,000 who purchased a total of up to 7500 albums per week.

> We were probably very fortunate in establishing the mail-order business – especially the export side – at the right time, when we could supply LPs to most countries weeks and sometimes months before they were released abroad; nowadays there is a near enough universal release date. The prices, quality and availability of U.K. product was also an advantage – today, this is not all necessarily the case […] We also lost a great deal of business in the former Yugoslavia, where we had some 5,000 customers, with the events leading up to the conflict and the conflict itself.

One-fifth of their mail order customers were in Yugoslavia; almost all were lost. A second crucial punk rock supply line developed between the United Kingdom and Yugoslavia's 'pankers'; Joly MacFie, the founder of Better Badges, sold the company decades ago and is now living in New York, but he well remembers the days of trading with Tito's young punks. Joly – who is still making punk badges – told me,

> Yes I used to take fistfuls of dinars to the bank on a weekly basis. For some reason Cockney Rejects were a big hit there. We made Yugoslav bands too […] Before I left BB in '82 I sold a press to one Antun Baric, who went into production in a big way in his own right.

In 1980 Belgrade police arrested a young punk called Djordje Obradović and questioned him for several hours about his collection of punk paraphernalia which included '41 Better Badges' of various punk bands. Why he was singled out is not clear but amongst the fanzines, posters, English music papers and Clash t-shirt, the 'police Evidence Sheet' also lists the name of my Novi Sad interviewee Stevan Gojkov. Stevan sent me a cutting from a 2007 Belgrade newspaper which describes the incident as a forgotten part of the nation's cultural heritage. No charges were brought but Djordje's belongings were never returned. The article offers a snapshot (in hindsight) of the atmosphere after the death of Tito:

> We must first go back to the 1980s, October […] Tito just died, politicians are nervous […] kids behave in completely new and

> unknown ways. Rokenrol, which the official faces have been accustomed to, is now quite different, and there is no conceptual leadership or party line about it.

Historians can debate, eternally, the degree to which Tito's reign was authoritarian. Tito and his close adviser Edvard Kardelj are said to have personally discussed policy with regards to 'rokenrol' – and agreed that the repressive attitude of Iron Curtain regimes was a path they did not want to tread. The punks were, in truth, a very long way down any list of credible threats to society. The result was, generally, a mutually beneficial relationship; the State would be tolerant, to the extent of occasionally offering state patronage, as long as the punks remained within the relatively broad parameters which defined Yugoslav socialism. Of course, there is little doubt where the power lay in this relationship. There was the so-called 'trash tax' (*'porez na šund'*) by which a record with lyrics not approved by the authorities effectively paid a surcharge. So records were not banned as such, but there was a financial incentive to amend the lyrics to something more palatable in the eyes of party officials. Implemented by regional committees and inherently inconsistent, even this relatively benign device lost its power to intimidate in the face of the young punks and the changing social and political atmosphere.

By the time of Tito's death there was a certain cachet attached to any punk release which carried the 'Trash Committee' sticker and penalty. As Branko Rosić says in the Pankrti documentary, 'Bands without that sticker were simply not good enough'. In the early 1980s a Slovenian ska punk band from Idrija actually took the name Šund in open defiance. Perhaps illustrating the uncertainty of officialdom, Pankrti's debut album *Dolgcajt* – released in 1980 – was subject to the šund tax and yet the following year earned them a place as one of the laureates of the prestigious award of the Seven Secretaries of the Communist Youth of Yugoslavia. All of this is not to say that the relationship between the state and the punks was entirely benign – far from it. In a 2017 newspaper interview, the professor of sociology and Pankrti co-songwriter and manager, Dr Gregor Tomc said, 'In 1977, we wanted to establish a parallel world in which we would live beyond the state and parents, which we tried to do primarily with music'.

The most notorious 'culture-clash' between the state and the free-spirited young punks has gone down in history as the 'Nazi Punk Affair'. In 1981, a Nazi sympathising skinhead band emerged in Ljubljana. As with the West, the first wave of punk in Yugoslavia was staunchly anti-fascist. Several of the most eminent bands, including Pankrti and KUD Idijoti, have recorded versions of anti-fascist Partisan and communist songs such as 'Bella Ciao' and 'Bandiera Rossa'. However, punk was becoming increasingly popular in Ljubljana at this time and punks were now visible on the streets – even illegally rebranding a central Ljubljana public square as 'Johnny

Rotten Square'. The authorities were already wary of punk's rebellious image, and any association with Nazism was seized upon both as proof that the punks were a threat to decent society and an excuse to instigate a clampdown. They launched what the local punk promoter, journalist, DJ and producer, Igor Vidmar, calls a 'witch hunt' and a 'media show trial'. Punks were taken off the streets and from their homes by police and questioned for hours on end, often repeatedly. Some were arrested and thrown into prison for wearing Dead Kennedys 'Nazi Punks Fuck Off' badges which incorporated a crossed-out swastika. Ironically, Vidmar had steadfastly refused to work with the Ljubljana Nazi-skinhead band precisely because of their beliefs.

> They had stupid racist lyrics and couldn't play, and I told them quite clearly, promising them they would never play publicly, as far as I and Radio Študent was concerned, due to the stupid bigotry of their lyrics and their musical ineptness.

In the mining town of Trbovlje, 50 kilometres east of Ljubljana, the band destined to become probably Yugoslavia's most famous punk/art/rock export was at this time preparing to drop its own unique cultural bomb onto the immediate post-Tito landscape. Using images appropriated from the Nazi-era and military smoke-bombs instead of dry ice, wearing military uniforms and singing in German, Laibach even took their name from the historic German title for Ljubljana – a provocative nod to the Fascist occupation of 1941. Calculated to shock and to challenge, within eighteen months they were effectively banned in Yugoslavia after screening pornographic movies as a backdrop, and simultaneously projecting images of Tito and a penis.

When the Slovene delegation at the 1982 National Congress of the Yugoslavian Communist Youth League challenged some of the negative stereotyping of punks by saying that they were not against the system but against the anomalies in the system, one young army officer snapped back, claiming to speak 'in the name of the coal miners' children, who do not have time to eat because they dig coal for our new wavers, punkers and other idlers to keep warm'.[3]

The Call Up ('I'm so bored with the JNA')

The spectre of the Jugoslav National Army hung heavy over punk during this pre-war period since all males were expected to serve between eleven and fifteen months

---

3. In *The Last Yugoslav Generation: The Rethinking of Youth Politics and Cultures in Late Socialism* by Ljubica Spaskovska.

of national service. Conscripts were usually sent to areas of the country hundreds of kilometres from their hometowns. Very few bands were left unscathed from the 'Call Up' but the better connected you were, the greater the chance that it could be postponed, delayed, minimised or avoided completely.

Kuzle ('Bitches') were unequivocally from the provinces – perhaps that was their undoing with regard to their failure to evade conscription. Idrija – a small-town (pop. 5800) in western Slovenia – lies midway between Ljubljana and the Italian border, isolated and encircled by wooded mountains. But through Andrej Šifrer's show, *Rock 'n' Roll To Every Village*, and trips to hang out at the record store over the Italian border in Gorica, punk penetrated the consciousness of the four teenagers. Dule Dule – whose punk pseudonym was inspired by Dee Dee Ramone – described the revelation: 'Then the Ramones came. I remember swapping three Bob Dylan records for one Ramones LP.' Also keen to find a way to impress the 200 schoolgirls recently relocated to the local school, the boys formed Kuzle in 1979. Initially, they encountered the more mundane challenges faced by small-town bands everywhere – getting hold of equipment and then finding rehearsal spaces and recording studios. Kuzle's first public performance was opening for the hugely influential proto-punk, shock-rock, Zappaesque, Slovenian band Buldožer; Kuzle's singer Bojan was just fifteen years old at the time of their debut. Their approach to music soon evolved away from the primitive punk and mirrored the eclecticism and political edge of the Clash. In the eponymous 2010 documentary, the band describe the landscape of their youth in the provincial Slovenian mercury-mining town:

> I remember how Idrija looked […] when we first started playing shows. It was a grey city. The mines were just starting to close down […] The hills were still bare, without vegetation. You could see the miners in their suits walk through the city from one shaft to the other.

In another country, there is a strong likelihood that Kuzle would have been one of the most successful exponents of the new wave. They had good melodies, sharp lyrics, compelling live performances and not a little youthful charisma. However, this hugely promising beginning was truncated, never to be adequately fulfilled, as the Jugoslav National Army summoned two members almost consecutively. Few teenage bands anywhere would survive what was effectively more than two years of enforced separation. As a consequence, during their initial life span, Kuzle made very few studio recordings and released no records of their own. They were, however, featured on the 1982 Slovenian punk compilation *Lepo je* ('It's nice') LP. In 2012 a Swedish record company curated and released a collection of Kuzle's home, live and studio recordings from those teenage years. Former members of the band also reformed in 2009 and recorded a studio album of those early songs, 'Do You Remember Kuzle Comrades?' which was released in 2010. Igor Vidmar has called Kuzle, 'One of the most important bands of the first post-punk wave'.

Guns on the roof

With wars came the sealing of borders inside the disintegrating Yugoslavia. For many, the external borders and communication channels with the outside world are slammed shut. Those who did not leave in time were now isolated, trapped. Punk rock in Yugoslavia was entering a new existential phase. Some lived in very real fear of shelling, snipers and murderous lawless militias. Where bands had previously toured and built followings throughout Yugoslavia – irrespective of their ethnicity or hometown – they were now confined to their own country, and for some their own city. It was as if the Clash or the Sex Pistols were prevented from venturing to Manchester, or even out of London. Some bands were ruptured when a member returned to their home country, to their family, and became trapped there. The Yugoslavian 'scene' had been atomised – reduced to several isolated, and sealed, inward-facing city scenes. And yet, within these restricted horizons, in cities away from the frontline such as Zagreb, Belgrade, Pula and Rijeka, these mini scenes flourished and many fine bands were formed and/or perfected their craft during these years.

However, Yugoslavia's isolation almost completely shut down access to international touring bands. There were, though, rare exceptions. In 1991 Ante Čikara and Sale Dragaš booked the ascendant Carter the Unstoppable Sex Machine to play the 'Jabuka' ('Apple') Club in the centre of Zagreb. It was part of a three-date tour which also took in Banja Luka (Bosnia) and Maribor (Slovenia) and as Jim Bob Morrison recalled in his band biography *Goodnight Jim Bob: On the Road with Carter The Unstoppable Sex Machine*:

> When we arrived in the Bosnian town of Banja Luka it was still in Yugoslavia. Mega City 4 had been caught up in rioting the week before in the Serb capital Belgrade and tensions right across the Balkans were high.

Jim Bob also confirms Ante's story of the Zagreb soundcheck upsetting President Tudjman's war cabinet meeting, adding that armed troops were dispatched to the venue and two were posted at the side of the stage for the entire gig, rifles over their shoulders. Carter returned to Zagreb during the wars – in 1994 – by which time they had become a huge global success. This time they played to 4000 adoring fans at the Doma Sportova and were fêted from start to finish of the visit. An announcement welcoming them by their full name, including to their embarrassment 'The Unstoppable Sex Machine' was made on board their Croatian Airlines flight. The Croatian tourist industry exploited the band's presence, launching a campaign to reverse the remorseless bad publicity arising from the war:

> [T]he build up to the gig had been more like something you'd expect for the Pope or the Beatles. There'd been previews and reports on Croatian TV weeks ahead of our arrival and the ball boys in the Croat equivalent of the F.A. Cup Final had worn Carter shirts.
>
> I got the impression that the crowd who'd had to fork out three days wages to get a ticket for the gig just wanted to get on with their lives, listen to some music, show off their home-made Carter shirts, shout, 'you fat bastard' in an exotic accent and dance.

That same year Nirvana also played a now legendary gig in ex-Yugoslavia; their Ljubljana date turned out to be their second last ever and the city has become something of a pilgrimage for some of the dedicated legions of their fans.[4] The band had also wanted to play in Croatia – bassist Krist Novoselić is from a Croatian family – but the country was still at war. Less well known is that their first attempt to play in Yugoslavia was also thwarted by war, not that such a minor hurdle prevented resourceful Yugoslav punks and post-punks from seeing them. Petar Janajatović directed me towards a tale which then took some unexpected turns:

> October or November of '91 – so the war in Croatia is heavy; Vukovar is burned down. Nirvana are about to play Ljubljana and their Managers, or somebody decided this was too close to the warzone, so they changed at a few days' notice and went to play some village near Trieste. And the audience was full with people from Slovenia and Croatia, and on the internet I found the audio. So you hear the audience and Wow! They are up on the stage and Krist Novoselić says in Croatian 'Dobro veče, mi smo Bijelo dugme!' And people started to laugh. Because Krist Novoselic, his

---

4. Nirvana played Ljubljana Tivoli Hall on 27 February 1994, and then Munich on 1 March – after which Cobain was taken ill and the remaining tour dates cancelled. Cobain committed suicide one month later.

background is from Croatia, so he made a joke: 'Good evening, we're Bijelo Dugme.' I love that!

The concert took place in the small Italian coastal town of Muggia (pop. 13,000), the only port in the Italian part of Istria. Three Slovenian gigs had been arranged (by fax) in late March 1991. But three months later the 'Republic of Ten Days' war began, pre-empting the much deadlier Yugoslav wars and break-up of the federation. In mid July, the Slovenian promoters sent a fax to Nirvana's Tour Manager saying, 'Since the situation in the Balkans is highly unstable, I think you have lost all hope of getting the band here'.

There was still a commitment to a single Ljubljana date but it appears that the band, and those around them, had concerns about the safety of fans travelling from Croatia to Slovenia, so chose the Trieste region as a compromise. A venue in Trieste was selected and posters printed. But the band and their management discovered the Trieste venue had seating which could not be removed and refused to play there. So the gig was hurriedly rearranged for 'G. Verdi Theatre' in Muggia. According to local press reports, the theatre was owned by the 'cultural arm' of the local PCI (Communist Party of Italy), the president of which was the famous Second World War Italian Partisan Giorgio Marzi. The promoters had to rely on the Communists agreeing to take out the seating and prepare the venue in order for the gig to take place. Marzi and the Communist Party were true to their word. Laura Marzi, the teenage daughter of Giorgi, was one of the 400–500 strong crowd. Also present was Marin Rosić who travelled from Ljubljana. Marin sent me a photograph of his original ticket for the gig, No. 0028, and said he estimated that 90 per cent of the audience had travelled from Croatia and Slovenia. Today Laura Marzi is the current Mayor of Muggia having been elected on a centre-left platform in 2016.

Laura told me,

> [i]n 1981 my father was president of the 'Luigi Frausin' Cultural Circle, which managed the building including the Verdi Theater, where the Nirvana concert took place. At the time the group was not so famous in Italy, because the fame came with the distribution in our country of the album 'Nevermind' [...] I was present at the concert, intrigued by the interest aroused in the many who already knew Nirvana. Kurt Cobain was not yet the star that he would become after a few months, even if he had the same shy and shady attitudes that probably in later years were read as a super-star attitude. There were so many people, the theater was full, and it was a good concert, certainly unusual for what were the

musical offerings that Muggia was used to. I must say that personally I was incredulous, years later, in realizing that I had witnessed an event that is written in the history of music of our territory!

During the wars some bands remained neutral, some nailed their colours to the mast of their country and some used music to actively campaign against war, against Milošević and Tuđman, and against nationalism. Front and centre amongst the anti-nationalist and anti-war activists was Rimtutituki. As described by Petar Janjatović who was part of this movement, members of Ekaterina Velika, Partibrejkers, Električni Orgazam came together to form a 'punk supergroup', which released only one single, *Slušaj vamo* ('Listen here'). Perhaps their most notable legacy is the six glorious minutes of footage from their anti-war protest in Belgrade's Republic Square on 8 March 1992. From a stage crowded with multiple backing vocalists and percussionists, Partibrejkers singer Zoran Kostić 'Cane' leads the crowd of 50,000 in the singing of *Slušaj vamo* with its refrain of '*Mir brate mir*' ('Peace Brother Peace'). It is powerful and joyous stuff. Defiant, and punk as fuck.

Lost in the supermarket

The post-war period saw Yugoslavia irredeemably fractured. Whilst Slovenia's 'Ten-Day War' was over in 1991 and conspicuous hostilities had ceased in Croatia and Bosnia in 1995, for Serbia and Kosovo the conflicts continued until the millennium was in sight. Thus the new nation-states embarked on reconstruction and transition to 'free-market economies' (or 'crony capitalism' if you prefer) at different times. Re-entry into the 'international community' was also staggered. Some cities had been besieged for years and deprived of electricity, whilst much of the neighbouring world was migrating to the new networking phenomenon, the internet, and learning a whole new vocabulary. Bands which had survived, and honed their art in, those lean years emerged from the long quarantine. International bands once more began to venture to the region. Emerging technologies facilitated better communications and the world shrank again. Meanwhile, all that was required to connect a provincial ex-Yugoslavian band, then little known outside of aficionados of the underground scene, and one of the most famous bands in rock history was Sale Dragaš, alcohol and serendipity:

> That was a funny story. I read *Flipside* magazine in 1998 and I was a little bit drunk. I read it before going to sleep and I thought 'Wow, REM will take a surf-rock band on their US Tour, as the support act!' I'd got it wrong, but I didn't know that I'd got it wrong because I was drunk. As I

knew the Manager from REM and the guys as well, I sent a fax message to REM Headquarters, 'As you are having a surf-rock act in the USA as a support act, could you be so kind to take – at least for a Slovenian show – Bambi Molesters, surf rock band from Croatia?' And I sent a text message and then sent recordings. The promoter from Croatia who was doing the Slovenian show with REM called me and said, 'We received a strange fax message from REM Headquarters,' and I asked what kind of message because I'd forgotten what I'd said to them. 'They've insisted that they have Bambi Molesters as the support act in Slovenia.' OK, nice. Good. I brought Bambi Molesters to Slovenia and they played before REM and the guys from REM watched them, listened to them and clapped them. And then Bambi Molesters came down and REM asked them if they could have a picture of them for the REM website. And Bambi Molesters said, 'Wait a minute, first we have to move our kit and then we'll have a photo.' After that, REM called them for three shows – in Germany, Austria and Switzerland, and Peter Buck and Scott McCaughey played for free on the album *Sonic Bullets: 13 from the Hip* by Bambi Molesters. So that was all because I got drunk! Of course that happened because Bambi Molesters are probably one of the best, not only surf-rock bands, but one of the best instrumental rock-bands ever.

Unsurprisingly, Sale Dragaš, Zdenko Franjić and Ante Čikara were all pivotal to the discovery and early advancement of the Bambi Molesters. Released in 2001, *Sonic Bullets: 13 From The Hip* is a masterpiece of instrumental surf-punk at least equal to anything produced since the days when Dick Dale and the Del Tones, the Chantays and Surfaris first rode the wave in Southern California in the early 1960s. Unlike their distinguished predecessors, the Bambi Molesters did not inhabit a world of barrels, blow-outs and double overheads. They came from Sisak – the home of Croatia's largest oil refinery, 60 kilometres southeast of Zagreb and more than 200 kilometres from the coast. My friend and Zagreb tour adviser, Dunja, is originally from Sisak. A few months after my trip Dunja came to visit and presented me with a copy of the album, beautifully signed by the whole band. 'They come from Sisak, so I know them. It's not a very big place', she said with a smile. The Bambi Molesters went on to become something of a global 'cult' band, forming a lasting professional relationship with Peter Buck and Scott McCaughey and contributing to several compilations including tributes to both R.E.M and the legendary US guitarist Link Wray. In July 2018, they announced that they were bringing the curtain down on an illustrious career.

Today the domestic punk scenes in the former Yugoslavia are primarily underground. Unlike for the first waves of Tito's punks, there is now little financial or logistical support from the state. There is no *Polet* magazine or YURM competition to break new bands. Today's punks are better connected than their predecessors; there is no longer the isolation from other musicians, nor the time lapse between music being released and being available to a global market. Where once the Yugoslav People's Army tore bands apart by despatching young musicians to the far-flung borders of Yugoslavia, today it is the promise of a brighter future in Canada, Australia, Germany, Austria or Ireland – fuelled by access to instant information.

Bands can once again gig in 'each other's countries', although bureaucracy in the form of work permits and differing taxation regimes are now impediments. Once again too, bands drawn from different cities, ethnicities or nationalities are making music together – sometimes rehearsing by internet and file sharing, getting together only to perform or record. Some bands, among them Hladno Pivo and Psihomodo Pop, have broken through into the national mainstream, whilst Repetitor, driven by a fearsome female rhythm section, is threatening to put ex-Yugoslavia – and specifically Belgrade – on the global map. Renowned UK punk guru, critic and singer/songwriter Jon Robb said of them, 'They make you fall in love with guitar rock all over again and are arguably the best guitar band on the planet right now. They are the 21st-century Nirvana who have come to save rock'.

So what is the story of Yugoslavian punk? Well, there is not one. There are, of course, many. Whilst Yugoslavian punk went through several waves which are instantly recognisable to aficionados worldwide – punk, new wave, new romantics, ska, industrial, second wave, post-punk, goth, Oi! streetpunk, old-school-retro 1977, etc. – it is also fair to say that punk (Yugoslav society as a whole) was played out against a backdrop of events which differentiate it from the other countries where punk rock was a phenomenon.

Defining the history of ex-Yugo punk by bookending a decade of wars would be lazy stereotyping and gives the risk of creating a false impression. As Petar Janjatović and Ante Čikara (one in Belgrade and the other in Zagreb) said, in historical terms the wars came quickly and unexpectedly. Yugoslavs had not lived their lives under constant threat of imminent conflict. And even during wartime – away from the frontlines – rock, punk rock, folk music, theatre, fanzines, etc. continued unreported by the flak-jacketed war correspondents, and the rolling newsreels and ticker-text of the twenty-four-hour news channels.

Overwhelmingly, the interviews in this book are characterised by a rejection of nationalism and a certain sense of sadness for the passing of the Socialist Federal Republic of Yugoslavia. Amongst the punk veterans there is a feeling that, whilst not perfect, times were better before the dissolution. Hand-in-hand with this is a prevailing conviction that, since the wars, the region has fallen victim to the worst kind of robber-barons and kleptocrats – or what more than one person described as 'Balkan turbo-capitalism'. Unsurprisingly – amongst a generation who predominantly define themselves as somewhere on the left of centre – the relatively benign socialism of the period from the 1960s to the break-up is considered markedly preferable. After all, the punks of Yugoslavia generally agree that they wielded their 'punk rock-electric-guitars' and flew their home-made banners 'not against the system but against the anomalies in the system'.

Amongst the younger torch-bearers for punk there is less unanimity with regards to the Republic which, after all, some are too young to remember well – if at all. For some, it would seem infinitely preferable to have grown up in the pre-war era; rather than the economic-flatlining, the dearth of opportunities and the mass emigration of the young and educated, which has been their post-war experience. Of course, some grew up during wartime and these feelings are even more acute. But who would not be fatigued of hearing about the 'golden days' and would wish to cut free from the harness of 'Yugonostalgia'? However, across the piece, the young punks are politically aware and often politically active, e.g. in campaigns against corruption and police brutality, or in support of animal rights and welfare, environmental issues, the homeless or workers involved in labour disputes.

Perhaps it is through the similarities that we can better feel the kinship with our peers. After all, only one record was 'banned' by both Tito and the BBC – the Sex Pistols', 'God Save The Queen'. Released to coincide with the Silver Jubilee of Queen Elizabeth II, it was re-released for her Golden Jubilee, released again for her Diamond Jubilee and, in 2022, one final time for her Platinum Jubilee. The monarchy has, however, endured her demise. A new king is already installed in the Palace. Meanwhile, the Sex Pistols saga is a costume-drama series on Disney TV.

The Queen was fifty-one years old in 1977, a decade younger than we original punks are today. Seemingly immune to the catastrophic power of Johnny Rotten's corrosive lyrics and Jamie Reid's iconoclastic images, the same Queen had continued to reign over us, her British 'subjects', for another forty-five years. It seems barely credible that she should also have outlived Yugoslavia by more than a quarter of a century, and yet, utterly predictable.

Remind me how it goes again?
No future, no future, no future for you.
No future, no future, no future for me.

TIMELINE: Yugoslavian Punk from 1975 Until Break-Up
Vinko Barić

Vinko Barić is the author of *Croatian Punk and New Wave 1976–87* and the *Complete Illustrated ex-Yu punk and New Wave Discography 1978–87*.

> 1975 – Art rockers BULDOŽER were formed in Ljubljana, Slovenia. Precursors to punk and new wave and an important influence on numerous bands which followed, BULDOŽER issued an eponymous debut album the same year.

> 1976 – The first punk singles were played on Ljubljana's Radio Študent. In Rijeka, Croatia's first punk group was formed; PARAF ('Initials') and they held their first gig on New Year's Eve (31 December 1976) in Rijeka. In Bosnia, the hard rock group LEPTIR ('Butterfly') from Sanski Most (arguably) made the first punk rock recording in Yugoslavia – a demo of '*Šipak*'. They then switched to a mixture of punk and hard rock.

> 1977 – In July, PARAF held an illegal gig at Nikola Host city park in Rijeka. During the summer a Yugoslav rock critic 'invented' the first domestic 'punk' groups. In truth, these were hard rockers Atomsko Sklonište and pub rockers Tetka Ana and were never really considered to be punks. Meanwhile, in Ljubljana in August 1977 some authentic punks were forming the band which would become perhaps the biggest Yugoslav punk band, PANKRTI ('the Bastards'). They held their first gig in Ljubljana on 18 October 1977; it was broadcast live by Radio Študent. Pankrti then got some press interest and organized the first Yugoslavian punk tour, the Anarchy in Yugoslavia tour 1977 which visited Ljubljana, Celje, Zagreb and Beograd, bringing punk to the rest of the country. The fake punk bands failed to sound 'punk' at the 1977 Boom festival, which in 1978 would be truly infiltrated by punk rock.

PANKRTI's Anarchy in Yugoslavia tour 1977 gig in the Zagreb Student Centre included AZRA, who would become the next big new wave name in years to come. This was the gig which brought punk to Zagreb. By that time two more punk groups were formed in Zagreb – LOŠ ZVUK ('Bad Sound') and PRLJAVO KAZALIŠTE ('Dirty Theatre'). LOŠ ZVUK had actually played the first punk gigs in Zagreb in 1977 but they were not recognised as punks at the time. In Rijeka, punk groups ZADNJI ('Last'), WHITE RIOT and BLANK GENERATION were also formed. In Serbia, ALEX PUNK COMPANY were formed in Niš, and they recorded one of the earliest punk demos.

> 1978 – PARAF held their first 'official' gig in Rijeka in February and gained some press coverage. In Slavonska Požega (a small town in eastern Croatia),

RUKOPOTEZNO POVLAČILO was formed in April and was notable for being – arguably – the first Yugoslavian new wave band to have a female vocalist (between 1978 and 1980). In Vinkovci (Croatia) POGREB X ('Funeral X') were playing their harder version of punk; their singer was the future Satan Panonski. In Zagreb, the Polet youth magazine organised a major all-day festival, which included PARAF, PRLJAVO KAZALIŠTE and AZRA. LOŠ ZVUK were also on the bill but dropped out. That historical punk gig, known as the 'Polet Rock Marathon', was held on 15 May 1978 on a playground near the Polytechnic, High School. One other gig that marked ground-zero for the future 'Punk Triangle' was in the Slovenian seaside resort of Koper, in May 1978. PANKRTI and BULDOŽER were the main attractions and there was a minor disturbance when the punk poet PETAR MLAKAR smashed a bottle onstage. Around this time, ALEX PUNK COMPANY changed into FLEKE ('Spots') and recorded some demos. On 29 May 1978 PRLJAVO KAZALIŠTE issued the first Yugoslavian punk record, a seven-inch EP containing three songs. In June 1978, the Stranglers and 999 became the first British punk groups to play Yugoslavia when they performed in Zagreb and Ljubljana on the Black & White Tour.

> By July 1978, the famous 'Punk Triangle' comprising Rijeka-Zagreb-Ljubljana was formed. The first concerts were organised in Ljubljana Menza Študent Centre, and in smaller places in Zagreb and Rijeka. The bands involved in this first generation of the punk triangle included PARAF and ZADNJI ('Rijeka'), PANKRTI and LJUBLJANA 78 ('Ljubljana'), PROBLEMI ('Pula'), PRLJAVO KAZALIŠTE, AZRA, LOŠ ZVUK and KLINSKA POMORA (a wordplay on Gas Chamber – Zagreb). In Serbia, in Novi Sad, PEKINŠKA PATKA ('Peking Duck') was formed in August of 1978. They began to play gigs almost immediately. There were several major events which featured punk during 1978, amongst them the 'Second Polet Rock Marathon' in Zagreb during September, and the 'Punk Rock Spectacle' in Rijeka in November, with almost 5000 attendees. In December 1978, the Boom Festival was held in Novi Sad and it hosted new punk groups PRLJAVO KAZALIŠTE, PARAF and PEKINŠKA PATKA. Finally, the public spotlight and the public attention were on domestic Yugoslavian punk. In November 1978, AZRA split into two groups, one retaining the name and the other being FILM who were to become another major new wave name as they embraced mod and ska sounds.

> By late 1978, PANKRTI issued their first single, independently for ŠKUC records. The record received good reviews in the *New Musical Express* (*NME*) and *Melody Maker*. In late 1978–early 1979, several new bands were formed – TERMITI ('Termite'), MRTVI KANAL ('Dead Channel') and KAOS were all from Rijeka, whilst in Ljubljana there were BULDOGI and GRUPA 92, and in Zagreb DIVIZIJA.

In Search of Tito's Punks

> In 1979, singles were issued by PARAF, PEKINŠKA PATKA, LEPTIR, LOŠ ZVUK, PRLJAVO KAZALIŠTE, PARNI VALJAK ('Steamroller – Zagreb') – all of which could be considered as punk or new wave. PRLJAVO KAZALIŠTE issued their eponymous first album in September 1979, widely acknowledged as the first punk album released in Eastern Europe.

> By early 1980, the 'Punk Triangle' scene had peaked, and the subsequent scene divided into Zagreb's power pop style, and a more orthodox punk style in Rijeka and Ljubljana. In 1980, AZRA, PEKINŠKA PATKA, PANKRTI and PARAF also issued their first albums. GRUPA 92 issued a single which received a positive review in the NME.

> Also in early 1980, in Trbovlje, Slovenia LAIBACH were formed, later to become the biggest name in Yugoslav avant-garde rock – perhaps in Yugoslav rock – to be recognised internationally. At around the same time, recording of the future iconic punk compilation began in Ljubljana; the *Novi Punk Val 78–80* LP, is an important document of, and ultimately a gravestone for, the 'Punk Triangle' scene. It was issued in January 1981.

> In 1981, the focus was mostly on the new wave scene as punk somehow sank from view, existing almost unseen in the local scenes of Rijeka, Ljubljana and Belgrade. The last major punk group active in Croatia in 1981 was the aforementioned POGREB X but their chances of surviving further were destroyed when Satan Panonski was jailed for committing murder that same year. In 1981, negotiations over TERMITI's first LP broke down and it would be 1992 before a cassette of their 1981 recordings was released and 1996 before an album saw the light of day.

The Belgrade punk scene was finally committed to vinyl in late 1981 on the *Artistička radna akcija – ARA* ('Artistic Work Action') compilation LP containing 20 songs from 10 bands. Most of the bands from that compilation had evaporated by 1982–83 although some had evolved into bands which would endure. Nevertheless, it is a great record.

> 1982 saw the release of the *Lepo je . . .* ('It's nice . . .') compilation showcasing second-generation punks from Slovenia – BULDOGI, KUZLE ('Bitches'), ŠUND ('Trash'), INDUST BAG, LUBLANSKI PSI ('Ljubljana Dogs') – in which the seeds of the Slovenian hardcore punk scene were very evident. Indeed, by late 1982, the first generation of Yugoslav hardcore punk groups was formed: NIET and UBR in Ljubljana, SOLIDARNOST in Knin and DISTRESS in Belgrade. It was in Ljubljana where, during 1983, the first local hardcore punk scene became visible and from this emerged the *Kaj je Alternativa* ('What's the alternative?') compilation cassette

album. By 1984, Yugoslavian hardcore was at its peak with bands such as UBR and NIET but also now STRES DA, ODPADKI CIVILIZACIJE ('Civilisation Waste'), DEPRESIJA ('Depression'), HERPES DISTRESS, SOLUNSKI FRONT, SKOL, KRIVO SRASTANJE ('Wrongly Growing'), PROCES, GUZ and THT. At the same time, a more melodic side of punk started to blossom in Pula with 1977 style punk bands such as KUD IDIJOTI, 77, BESPOSLIČARI ('Truant'), GOLA JAJA ('Naked Bollocks') and NAFTA ('Oil').

> In 1983, the first known Yugoslav Oi! band DVA MINUTA MRŽNJE ('Two Minutes of Hate') was formed in Novi Sad. They disbanded in 1985. Oi! was not big in Yugoslavia during the 1980s but there was a small Oi! scene in Belgrade during 1985–86.

After the initial 'explosion' and interest of 1980–81 no single punk group received as much press coverage as the earlier days, and very few punk bands released LPs. Punk on vinyl would appear again in the late 1980s. There were a few exceptions such as the 1984 UBR EP, PROCESS split EP and TOŽIBABE EP from 1986. Everything else was limited to being issued on low-budget cassette releases.

During the 1980s, a circuit of clubs was founded which paved the way for the scene to develop. This pan-Yugoslavian scene was destroyed by the outbreak of war in 1991 which shattered the single scene into six separate – and obviously much smaller – scenes; one in each of the individual, newly 'independent' countries.

Author's note: In addition to the bands whose members are interviewed, or mentioned elsewhere in this book, an eclectic selection of 'new wave' bands from the 'Tito's Yugoslavia' period worthy of further investigation include ABORTUS, BOA, ELVIS J. KURTOVIĆ & HIS METEORS (at the vanguard of the influential Sarajevo based, 'New Primitivism' movement) FOL JAZIK (the first Macedonian punk band), ŽENEVSKI DEKRET ('Geneva Decree', an enduringly popular, melodic hardcore group from Mostar, Bosnia and Herzegovina), LINDJA (from Priština, Kosovo, probably the only Albanian language punk band of the era), NARODNO BLAGO ('National Treasure'), OTROCI SOCIJALIZMA ('Children of Socialism'), PAUK ('Spider'), PREPOROD ('Revival'), RADNIČKA KONTROLA ('Workers Control'), RITAM NEREDA ('Rhythm Disorder'), ZABRANJENO PUŠENJE ('No Smoking') and ZMIJSKI UGRIZ MLADOG LAVA ('The Snakebite of the Young Lion – ZMUL'). There are many more – sincere apologies to anyone omitted.

SELECTED DISCOGRAPHY

Atheist Rap, 'Blu Trabant' from the album *Maori i Crni Gonzales* (Take It Or Leave It Records, 1993), CD album, cassette.
Atheist Rap, 'Pritilend' from the album *Osveta Crnog Gonzalesa* (Multimedia Records, 2005), CD album.
Azra, 'Jablan' from the album *Azra* (Jugoton, 1980), vinyl album (multiple reissues – various formats).
Bambi Molesters, 'Theme From Slaying Beauty' from the album *Sonic Bullets: 13 From the Hip* (Dancing Bear, 2001), vinyl album, CD, cassette (multiple reissues – various formats).
Boye, *78* (Search & Enjoy, 1990), vinyl album.
Buldožer, 'Slovinjak Punk' from the album *Izlog jeftinih slatkiša* (Helidon, 1980), vinyl album, repress.
Carina, 'Lublanca Sava' from the album *Od Lublance do Save* (Nika Records, 2005), CD album.
Darko Rundek, *Apokalipso* (Jabukaton, 1996), CD, cassette (multiple reissues).
Demob, 'No Room For You' (Round Ear, 1981), 7 inch single (reissued on multiple compilation albums).
Disciplina Kičme, 'Uživaj' from the album *Sviđa mi se da ti ne bude prijatno* (Helidon, 1983), vinyl album (multiple reissues – various formats).
Električni Orgazam, 'Zlatni papagaj' from the album *Električni Orgazam* (Jugoton, 1981), vinyl album, cassette (multiple reissues – various formats).
Elvis J. Kurtovich & His Meteors, 'Mala glupača' from the album *Mitovi i legende o kralju elvisu* (ZKP RTVL, 1984), vinyl album, cassette.
Haustor, 'Noć U Gradu' from the album *Haustor* (Jugoton, 1981), vinyl album (multiple reissues – various formats).
Idoli, 'Rusija' from the album *Одбрана И Последњи Дани* (Jugoton 1982), vinyl album (multiple reissues – various formats).
KBO!, 'Samoča' from the album *Pozovi 93* (Start Today Records, 1990), vinyl album.
KUD Idijoti, *Kad sunce opet zađe – live at Uljanik Club 1992* (Regional Express, 1992), official video, YouTube.
KUD Idijoti, 'To nije mjesto za nas' from the album *Glupost je neuništiva* (Helidon, 1992), vinyl album (multiple reissues – various formats).
Kuzle, 'Smej se' from the album *Še pomnite Kuzle tovariši?* (Dallas Records, 2010), vinyl album, limited edition.
Laibach, 'My Favourite Things' from the album *The Sound of Music* (Mute, 2018), vinyl album, CD.

Selected Discography

Lutajući Dj Zdena (Zdenko Franjić), 'A kaj da delam' bw 'Šetnja noću' (Balkan Veliki, 2016), MP3.

Majke, 'Loš život' from the album *Majke* (Slušaj Najglasnije! 1988), cassette album (multiple reissues – various formats).

Obojeni Program, 'Štipaljka' from the album *Najvažnije je biti zdrav* (Search & Enjoy, 1990), vinyl album.

Overflow, 'Wasted' from the album *"Live" at ... parties* (Anubis Records, 2006), CD album.

Pankrti, 'Adijo Ljubljana' from the album *Sexpok* (Jugoton, 1987), vinyl album.

Pankrti, 'Bandiera Rossa' from the album *Rdeči Album* (ZKP RTVL, 1984), vinyl album (multiple reissues – various formats).

Pankrti & Glen Matlock, 'Pretty Vacant' – Live from 40 let Stožice (RTV Slovenia, 2017), official video, YouTube.

Pankrti, 'Lublana je bulana' bw 'Lepi in prazni' (ŠKUC, 1978), 7 inch single (multiple reissues – various formats).

Pankrti, 'Osmi Dan' from the album *Pesmi sprave* (ZKP RTVL, 1985), vinyl album.

Paraf, 'Narodna pjesma' from the album *A dan je tako lijepo počeo* (RTV Ljubljana, 1980), vinyl album.

Partibrejkers, 'Hoću da znam' from the album *Kiselo i slatko* (B92, 1994), vinyl album, CD, cassette.

Pekinška, 'Patka Biti ruzan, pametan i mlad' (Jugoton, 1979), 7 inch single.

Pekinska Patka, 'Biti ruzan pametan i mlad' from the album *Plitka poezija* (Jugoton, 1980), vinyl album (multiple reissues).

Pogonbgd, *Vagoni* (2017), official video, YouTube.

Problemi, 'Sranje' from the compilation *Novi Punk Val Vol. 78–80* (ŠKUC and ZKP RTVL, 1981), vinyl album compilation (vinyl and cassette reissues).

Protektori, 'Ekstremno' from the album *Kretenov let* (Slušaj najglasnije! 2013), CD album.

Prljavo Kazalište, 'Sretno Dijete' from the album *Prljavo Kazalište* (Suzy Records 1979), vinyl album (multiple reissues – various formats).

Psihomodo Pop, 'I'm In Love With Gobac' from the album *Sexy magazin* (Jugoton, 1990), vinyl album, cassette, CD.

Radnička Kontrola, 'Dosada' from the album *Artistička radna akcija* (Jugoton, 1981), vinyl album compilation (multiple reissues – various formats).

Repetitor, 'Suženi snovi' from the album *Gde ćeš* (Moonlee Records 2016), vinyl album.

Rimtutituki, *Slušaj vamo/Mir brate mir NE RACUNAJTE NA NAS (Live)* (1992), official Električni orgazam video, YouTube.

Šarlo Akrobata, 'Oko moje glave' from the album *Paket aranžman* (Jugoton, 1981), vinyl album compilation, cassette (multiple reissues – various formats).
Saša 21, 'Kratko i konkretno' from the album *VD-i1* (PDV 2014), vinyl album, limited edition.
Satan Panonski, 'Čaj od maka' from the album *Satan Panonski* (Rest in Punk, 2016), vinyl album.
Termiti, 'Vjeran pas' from the compilation album *Novi Punk Val 78-80* (ŠKUC and ZKP RTVL, 1981), vinyl album (vinyl and cassette reissues).
Tožibabe, *Dežuje EP* (FV Založba, 1986), 7 inch EP.
Trnje, *Mile Bereta* (2018), official video, YouTube.
Trotakt projekt, 'Zaplešimo' (Jugoton, 1984), 7 inch single.
Trula Koalicija, 'Alkoholičarka' from the album *Plakao sam kad je pala sekuritatea* (Not on label 1992), cassette album.
Urbana Gerila, 'Proces' from the album *Artistička radna akcija* (Jugoton, 1981), vinyl album.
Various, *Bosanske narodne pjesme i plesovi* (Jugoton, 1956), 10 inch vinyl album.
Various, *Novi Punk Val 78-80* (ŠKUC and ZKP RTVL, 1981), vinyl album compilation (vinyl and cassette reissues).
Various, *Yugoslavian Folk Music Of Macedonia* (Olympic Records, 1976), vinyl album compilation.
Various, *Za Tebe – A Tribute To Kud Idijoti* (WTF Records, 2021), CD album.
Ženevski Dekret, *Neću da budem dio jebene mase* (Ne! Records, 2007), 7 inch EP.
Zvoncekova Bilježnica feat. Pera Janjatović, *Samo pravo* (2014), official video, YouTube.

Index

999 49, 4n160, 245

A
Albania 1n36, 82, 181, 247
Amsterdam 1, 4, 22, 28, 34, 48–58, 67, 97, 137, 157, 161, 171
Anti-Nowhere League (band) 86
Aranđelovac 4, 220
Arsenijević, Vladimir 170, 172
Artistička radna akcija/ARA (compilation album) 115, 158, 2n158, 6n162, 246
Au Pairs (band) 84–85
Azra (band) 18, 22, 33, 37, 63, 92, 157, 160, 244–47

B
Bambi Molesters (band) 17, 30, 241
Banja Luka 15, 148, 237
Beatles, the (band) 21, 73, 202, 203, 238
Belgrade 4, 18, 19, 20, 31, 34, 51, 57, 58, 63, 64, 71, 72, 78, 93, 101, 131, 132, 134, 135, 147–51, 154, 156–64, 166–69, 170–77, 178–84, 185, 186, 195, 199, 206, 208, 209, 212–13, 220, 225–30, 232–33, 237, 240, 242, 246, 247
  Belgrade Waterfront 149, 181–82, 212, 225
Berliner Strasse (band) 170, 173
Better Badges (Joly MacFie) 198, 202, 233
Bijelo Dugme (band) 19, 1n19, 63, 92, 132, 159, 2n176, 198, 238–39
Black Lamb and Grey Falcon: A Journey through Yugoslavia (West) 13, 24, 25 *see also* Rebecca West
Bombardiranje New Yorka (compilation album) 31, 52
Bosnia and Herzegovina 15, 27, 31, 32, 33, 35, 39, 44–45, 58, 72, 77, 79, 82, 100, 106, 126, 148, 161, 162, 164, 2n176, 179, 213, 214, 237, 240, 244, 247
Bowie, David 30, 83, 84, 85, 88, 144, 145
Boye (band) 17, 20, 52
Brotherhood and Unity Highway 38–39, 147–49, 212–13
Brutalism 13, 149, 212, 225
Buldogi (band) 73, 245, 246
Buldožer (band) 31, 63–64, 73, 236, 244–45
Bulgaria 20, 72, 131, 180, 203, 213, 216

C
Cabaret Voltaire (band) 83
Carina (band) 69, 73
Carter USM (Unstoppable Sex Machine) (band) 17, 49, 52–53, 55, 237–38
Chetniks 188, 223
Čikara, Ante 1, 17, 48–58, 237, 241, 242
Clash, the (band) 2, 22, 3n22, 23, 36, 37, 49, 63, 84, 119, 121, 171, 197, 201, 218, 232, 233, 236, 237
Cob Records 20, 50, 198, 232–33
Cobain, Kurt 4n238, 239
Cockney Rejects (band) 71, 74, 171, 180, 233
Cramps, the (band) 18, 22, 50, 1n142
Crass (band) 18, 136, 172, 205
Crkveni pacovi (band) 197
Črnac, Branko 'Tusta' 125–27, 133, 163
Cure, the (band) 30, 124, 1n142
Czechoslovakia/Czechia 20, 22, 2n39
Czechoslovakian guitars 204, 231

D
Danube (Magris) 13 *see also* Claudio Magris
Dead Kennedys (band) 70, 74, 200, 203, 204, 235
Deep Purple (band) 49, 159, 203
Demob (band) 1–6, 80, 126, 134, 142–46
depopulation 15, 58, 106, 114, 180, 243
Discharge (band) 3, 133, 200, 220
Disciplina Kičme (band) 58, 125, 6n162
Dragaš, Aleksandar 'Sale' 15, 17–23, 49, 51, 63, 237, 240, 241

251

Drakulić, Slavenka 115, 117
Dubioza kolektiv (band) 206
Dylan, Bob 96, 236
Džuboks (magazine) 18, 51, 64, 93, 199, 209

E
East German guitars 204, 231
East Germany 131, 133, 4n205
Električni Orgazam (band) 93, 121, 158, 1n158, 164, 9n164, 168, 180, 232, 240
European Union (EU) 15, 21, 25, 1n30, 113, 114, 179, 180, 195
EXIT Festival 189
Exploited, the (band) 3, 171, 220

F
fanzines 17–18, 31, 51, 72, 120, 133, 144, 172, 173–74, 188, 197, 203, 233, 242
Film (band) 93, 160, 245
Flipside (magazine) 18, 240
folk music (Yugoslavian) 1n19, 33, 96, 98, 131, 132, 157, 164, 204, 209, 242
Klapa (Croatian folk) 132, 135
Macedonian rhythms 98
Sevdah (Bosnian folk) 33
Tamburitza/Tambura (Slavonian folk) 96, 208
football (in the Balkans) 40, 61, 74, 159, 176–77, 180–81, 206, 228
FK Partizan Belgrade 176, 3n177, 181, 228

OFK Belgrade 176
racism in Balkan football 177, 181
Red Star Belgrade 176, 181
foreign tourists (in the Tito era) 39, 202, 231
Franjić, Zdenko 27–28, 29–35, 52, 79, 112, 241

G
Gang of Four (band) 85, 98, 159
gastarbeiter/gastarbajteri 39, 2n39, 55, 76
glam rock (influence of) 30, 73, 85, 171
Glavan, Darko 79, 93
Gojkov, Stevan 188, 192–93, 195, 197–209, 233
Goldman, Vivien 171
Goli Otok (island prison camp) 5n32, 118
Good Vibrations: The Movie 14–15, 20, 183
Goribor (band) 32, 34
Gorizia/Gorica 30, 70, 74, 236
Goths/'Darkeri' 30, 74, 121
Gracia (band) 81, 89
Greece 5, 35, 38, 55, 107, 147, 157, 213, 221

H
Haustor (band) 92–93, 98–100, 160
hitchhiking/interrailing (by young punks) 56, 97, 157, 171
Hladno Pivo (band) 12, 106, 125, 242

homosexuality (attitudes to) 67, 75, 121
House of Flowers (Tito's mausoleum) 226–29
Human League (band) 5, 83, 85
Hungary/Hungarians 6, 20, 22, 55–56, 128, 194–95, 202

I
Idoli (band) 93, 98, 158, 1n158, 160, 175
Idrija 73, 234, 236
Ilić, Mirko 119, 4n119
In Europe: Travels through the Twentieth Century (Mak) 13 *see also* Geert Mak
International Brigades 152–53
International Criminal Tribunal for Yugoslavia (ICTY) 5, 7–10, 43–47, 49, 102–04, 167, 193, 216
Iron Curtain/Warsaw Pact (geopolitical) 2, 65, 99, 122, 131, 142, 180, 202, 231, 232, 234
Istria 22, 60, 79, 98, 105–12, 125–29, 130–33, 162, 208, 239

J
Jabuka (club) 19, 52, 237
Jam, the (band) 3, 143, 4n143
Janjatović, Petar 153–55, 156–64, 168, 217, 240, 242
Jeger, Rujana 115–24, 2n158

Index

Jews (Second World War, persecution) 26, 187, 193–96, 224
Jones, Mick 22, 138 *see also* the Clash
Joy Division (band) 15, 20, 30, 50, 72, 84, 88, 116, 173

K

Kaos (band) 107, 121, 218, 245
Kardelj, Edvard 234
Karlovac 4, 36, 105–06, 110
KBO! (band) 163, 210, 217–22, 228, 229
Koprivnica 33, 52
Kosovo 25, 72, 104, 167, 179, 186, 191, 240, 247
Kostić, Goran 'Kosta' 54
Kostić, Zoran 'Cane' 11n164, 170, 240
Kraftwerk (band) 22, 84
Kragujevac 1, 4, 163, 166, 179, 195, 210, 211, 213–16, 217–22, 228
    massacre of 1941 223–25
Krautrock 83, 84, 88, 208
KUD Idijoti (band) 2, 80, 106, 125–27, 130–36, 161–63, 178, 189, 208, 229, 234, 247
Kuzle (band) 72–73, 229, 236–37, 246

L

Labin/Labin Art Express 110
Laibach (band) 21, 73, 86, 129, 173–74, 235, 246
Leb i sol (band) 63, 168

Lepo Je (compilation album) 72, 236, 246
Ljubljana 4, 18, 19, 20, 21, 27, 30, 34, 36–42, 53, 59–62, 62–65, 66–68, 69–76, 77, 85, 95, 134, 135, 160, 173, 199, 231, 232, 234–35, 236, 238–39, 4n238, 244–46
London (Yugoslav punks in) 19, 22, 23, 33, 34, 37, 56–57, 82, 84, 93, 100, 119, 120, 156, 157, 161, 171, 198, 201, 203, 232
Loš Zvuk (band) 30, 244–46
Lovšin, Peter 'Pero' 4, 21, 41–42, 59–62, 62–65

M

Macedonia 35, 1n36, 38, 82, 96, 98, 162, 168, 203, 208, 213, 214, 247
Magris, Claudio 13, 185
Majke (band) 17, 32, 52
Mak, Geert 13, 185, 186, 191–92
Maksimović, Desanka 225
Marx, Karl 122, 207
Matlock, Glen 36, 41 *see also* Sex Pistols
Mega City Four (band) 17, 52, 56
Melody Maker 18, 143, 193, 199
Metelkova 34, 67, 71, 74
Metković 81–90, 112
Mijatović, Cvijetin (President) 161, 162, 6n162, 7n162
Mijatović, Mira and Maja 161, 162, 6n162

Milosević, Slobodan (President) 54, 3n54, 160, 164, 167, 175, 189, 191, 205, 206, 208, 240
Mirković, Igor 91–93, 4n119
Mladić, Ratko 43–46
Montenegro 35, 51, 77, 101, 3n114, 179
Monty Python's Flying Circus 76
Morrissey 173, 175, 189
Moste High School 62, 66
Muja/Muggia 73–74, 239, 240
Music Is the Art of Time (film) 36, 37, 62, 69

N

National Service/conscription in Yugoslav Army 30, 51, 64, 72, 77, 89, 133, 159, 173, 174, 203–04, 208–09, 2n219, 221, 235, 236, 242
NATO 43, 167, 186, 190–92, 195, 213–14, 216, 224, 226, 1n226, 231
'Nazi Punk Affair' 21, 219, 234, 235
New Musical Express (NME) 18, 20, 171, 193, 198–99, 232, 245, 246
New Romantics 30, 201, 242
Nirvana (band) 18, 73, 238–39, 4n238, 242
Niš 34, 54, 244
Non-Aligned Movement/non-alignment 37, 65, 97, 128, 202, 5n208, 231
Novi Punk Val (compilation album) 72, 246

253

Novi Sad 4, 20, 34, 149, 153, 166, 179, 185–89, 190–96, 197–209, 212, 224, 233, 245, 247
massacre of Jews in 1942 194–95

O
Obojeni Program (band) 1, 17, 20, 52, 189
Only Fools and Horses 30, 76, 183
Overflow (band) 32, 52

P
Paket aranžman (compilation album) 158
Pankrti (band) 4, 19, 21, 22, 33, 36–37, 40–42, 59, 61, 62–65, 66–67, 69–71, 73, 92, 106, 120, 121, 125, 157, 172, 173, 180, 198, 218, 229, 231, 234, 244–46
Paraf (band) 71, 87, 92, 107, 120, 121, 173, 199, 200, 218, 244–46
Parni Valjak (band) 19, 92, 246
Partibrejkers (band) 125, 164, 9n164, 11n164, 168, 170, 172, 189, 240
Partisans 22, 39, 50, 91, 117, 1n128, 153, 194, 223, 234, 239
Peel, John 2, 18, 62, 70
Pekinška Patka (band) 93, 121, 173, 189, 193, 197–205, 245–46
Petrovaradin 186–89
Petrović, Karađorđe 227

Pogonbgd (band) 166, 168, 169, 178–84
Polet (magazine) 18, 51, 71, 84, 85, 1n85, 86, 91, 92, 97, 242, 245
Pop Group (band) 30, 1n142, 173
Pop, Iggy (and the Stooges) 22, 30, 41, 54, 120, 121, 168, 2n176, 189
Popović, Jure 78–79, 81–90, 93, 112
Praljak, Slobodan 43, 47
Prljavo Kazalište (band) 91–93, 199, 244–46
Problemi (band) 33, 125, 133, 245
Profa, Lou 30, 33–34
Psihomodo Pop (band) 106, 125, 242
Public Image Ltd (band) 23, 49, 198
Pula 4, 30, 33, 72, 80, 101, 105, 110–13, 115, 125–29, 130–36, 162, 163, 237, 245, 247

Q
Queen Elizabeth II 21, 91, 99, 128, 144, 231, 243

R
racism in Balkan football 177, 181
radio stations
  Radio B92 164, 9n164
  Radio Belgrade 157
  Radio Ljubljana 18
  Radio Luxembourg 132, 157, 232

Radio Študent (Ljubljana) 18, 30, 64, 70, 231, 235, 244
Radio Zagreb 18, 49
Radusinović, Vladimir 'Radule' 197–209
Ramones (band) 18, 22, 37, 71, 72, 119, 120, 121, 124, 132, 134, 236
Reading Festival 22, 51, 56
record labels
  Dancing Bear 34
  Good Vibrations (Terri Hooley) 14
  Jugoton 21, 31, 52, 88, 132, 158, 232
  PGP-RTB/S 52, 132, 9n164, 232
  Rough Trade 70, 173
  Slušaj Najglasnije! 29, 34
  Suzy Records 16, 49, 197, 232
Reed, Lou 22–23
religion 20, 26, 87, 88, 122, 176, 207
REM (band) 23, 241
Repetitor (band) 163, 242
Rijeka 20, 32, 33, 2n71, 74, 87, 107–10, 3n114, 115, 120, 129, 179, 200, 218, 1n219, 231, 237, 244–46
Rimtutituki (band) 164, 12n164, 168, 170, 240
Ritam (magazine) 51
Rockin' Vickers (band) 20, 232
Rolling Stones (band) 21, 73, 85, 144
Rosić, Branko 166–69, 170–77

254

Index

Rosić, Marin 36, 37, 59, 61, 66–68, 69–76, 239
Rotten, Johnny (John Lydon) 23, 234–35, 243
Rundek, Darko 92–94, 95–101, 108, 189
Ruts, the (band) 3, 49, 71, 1n142, 159–60

S

Saints, the (band) 49, 84, 198
Šangaj 186, 190–92
Šarlo Akrobata (band) 98, 121, 158, 1n158, 180, 231–32
Satan Panonski (Ivica Čuljak) 32–33, 34, 245, 246
Savić, Sava 193, 197–209
Scheveningen 7–10, 43–47, 48, 102–03
Sex Pistols (band) 4, 21, 36, 37, 41, 62, 63, 91, 99, 119, 132, 133, 159, 171, 176, 189, 203, 218, 231, 237, 243
sexism and sexuality (punk as a liberating factor) 120–21
Sheffield 4, 13, 20, 82, 83, 84, 88, 152
Šifrer, Andrej 236
Skinheads 3, 203, 208, 234, 235
Slade (band) 73, 144, 145, 171
Smith, Patti 64, 121, 189
Smith, Robert 'Miff' 2–4, 137–39, 141–46
Smiths, the (band) 124, 173, 176

Socialist Youth League/Organisation/Tito's Pioneers 88, 91, 118, 133, 2n133, 235
Sounds (music paper) 199
Specials, the (band) 19, 139, 1n142
Sremska Kamenica 186, 190–91
Sretno Dijete (film) 63, 91–93, 4n119
Stalin 74, 118, 5n208
Stiff Little Fingers (SLF) (band) 3, 133, 171, 200
Stranglers, the (band) 19, 49, 71, 138, 160, 4n160, 171, 245
Strossmayer, Josip Juraj (Bishop) 26, 192
Studentski List (magazine) 51, 97, 99
Štulić, Branimir 'Johnny' 33, 63, 92, 157, 158
Subotica 34, 93, 218, 2n219
Šumarice (Memorial Park) 223–25
Šund (band) 72–73, 234, 246
Sweet (band) 30, 73, 171, 203

T

T Rex (and Marc Bolan) (band) 30, 85
Talking Heads (band) 51, 54, 98, 160
Termiti (band) 33, 107, 120, 121, 218, 245, 246
The Sound of Music (film) 129
Tisma, Aleksandar 185, 193, 194, 196

Tito, Josep Broz (Marshal) 13, 14, 20, 22, 25, 1n30, 37, 38, 39, 2n39, 50, 65, 1n65, 71, 74, 77, 88, 90, 91, 97, 118, 122, 126, 128, 1n128, 153, 157, 160, 161, 162, 175, 186, 206, 208, 5n208, 226–29, 231–35, 243, 247
 death of 19, 20, 25, 40, 78, 92–93, 149, 157, 159, 160, 161, 173, 233, 234
 see also House of Flowers
Tomc, Gregor 37, 62–64, 234
Top of the Pops (UK TV show) 3, 56, 144
trash tax (šund) 234
Trbovlje (town in Slovenia) 235, 246
Trieste (Italy) 20, 1n30, 70, 71, 73, 3n114, 131, 209, 238, 239
Trotakt Projekt (band) 78–79, 81–90
Trula Koalicija (band) 220
Tuđman, Franjo (President) 12, 52–53, 162, 237, 240
typewriters (antique, exhibition of) 187–88

U

UK Subs (band) 71, 74, 1n142, 171
Uljanik (shipyard and rock club) 111, 125, 126, 127, 128–29, 130, 163
Undertones, the (band) 2, 3, 64, 4n143
United Nations (UN) 43, 44

United Nations Detention
 Unit (UNDU) 10, 43,
 102–04
Urbana Gerila (band)
 2n158, 11n164, 170,
 172–73, 175
Uskoks (bandits) 109–10

V
Vermeer in Bosnia
 (Weschler) 45–46
Veruda, Sale (Sasa
 Milanović) 80, 110–12,
 130–36, 162
Vidmar, Igor 18, 19, 60, 70,
 235, 237
Vojvodina 35, 185–87, 190–96
von Trapp, Georg (von
 Trapp family) 129
Vučić, Aleksandar
 (President) 164, 182
Vuica, Matija 78–79, 81–90,
 112
Vujić, Saša (Vuja of KBO!)
 163, 210, 215–16,
 217–22, 228

W
Warsaw Pact/Eastern Bloc
 (geopolitical) 131, 171,
 180, 202, 208, 231
Weschler, Lawrence 45–46
West, Rebecca 13, 24–26,
 108, 184, 185, 227, 229
Westwood, Vivienne (and
 'Sex' boutique) 81, 176

Y
YU Grupa (band) 63, 159
Yugos (cars) 191, 213–14,
 225
Yugoslav monarchy 24,
 227
Yugoslavian cinema 4n32,
 33, 63, 77, 101, 1n128,
 5n161, 9n164
 Generation '68 101, 119
 Ko to tamo peva? 77–78,
 9n164
 Outsider 63
 Skupljači perja 63
 Tko pjeva zlo ne misli 32,
 4n32

YURM (music contest)
 85–86, 242

Z
Zagreb 1, 4, 12–16, 17–23,
 24–28, 29–35, 37,
 38, 49–58, 63, 71, 72,
 77–80, 81–90, 91–94,
 95–101, 105, 106,
 112–14, 115–24, 132,
 147, 148, 159, 160, 161,
 5n161, 199, 213,
 232, 237, 241, 242,
 244–46
Zappa, Frank 56, 236
Zastava/Fiat (factory)
 213–14
Zebić, Tomislav
 'Tompa' (backstory)
 113–14
Zvoncekova Bilježnica
 (band) 220